"We Cannot Escape History"

"We Cannot Escape History"

LINCOLN AND THE
LAST BEST HOPE OF EARTH

EDITED BY

James M. McPherson

University of Illinois Press
Urbana and Chicago

This book is printed on acid-free paper.

Library of Congress Cataloging-in-Publication Data

We cannot escape history : Lincoln and the last best hope of Earth /
edited by James M. McPherson.
    p.   cm.
   ISBN 0-252-02190-8
   1. Lincoln, Abraham, 1809–1865. 2. United States—Politics and
government—1849–1861. 3. United States—Politics and government—
Civil War, 1861–1865. I. McPherson, James M.
   E457.8.W38 1995
   973.7'092— dc20   95-2279
                                                        CIP

Contents

PART 3: LINCOLN'S LEGACY

Preface

The essays in this volume originated as papers delivered at the Huntington Library in San Marino, California, on October 15 and 16, 1993. This two-day symposium marked the opening of the Huntington Library's exhibit "The Last Best Hope of Earth: Abraham Lincoln and the Promise of America." The largest exhibition of original Lincoln materials ever mounted, "The Last Best Hope of Earth" remained open to the public for thirteen months and attracted nearly a half-million viewers. Several hundred of them attended the symposium and participated in spirited exchanges of ideas during the question period after each paper and during the luncheon breaks. One participant, a veteran of perhaps four score and seven symposia and conferences, said that this one was the first in which the papers held his attention every minute, with no straying of the mind into paths of reverie.

The introduction and the nine essays focus on the themes of Lincoln's vision of America as the "last best hope of earth" for the advancement of liberty and democracy, his efforts as president to make that vision a reality during the rending trauma of war, and the meaning of Lincoln's legacy not solely for Americans but for all people everywhere. Written by leading Lincoln scholars, these essays offer new perspectives on questions both old and new: slavery, nationalism, democracy, equality, war, peace, the power of ideas, and the means of communicating them.

Thanks are due to many people for making this book possible. Robert A. Skotheim, president of the Huntington, the late William A. Moffett, director of the library, and Robert C. Ritchie, director of research, made the marvelous facilities of the Huntington Library available for the symposium and performed as perfect hosts. The Lincoln materials in the exhibit that provided a stimulating setting for the symposium were from the collections of the Huntington, of the Illinois State Historical Library, and of Louise and Barry Taper. To the Tapers, to John Rhodehamel, curator of American history at the Huntington, and to Thomas F. Schwartz, curator of the Lincoln Collecation at the Illinois State Historical Library, we are indebted not only for the inspiration provided by this extraordinary exhibit but also for their support of the symposium. Last but far from least in this list of vital aiders and abettors is Richard L. Wentworth, director of the University of Illinois Press, who has manifested his usual wisdom and patience in bringing this book into the world.

Introduction:
Last Best Hope for What?

JAMES M. MCPHERSON

Abraham Lincoln is the quintessential American icon. Born in a log cabin on the frontier, he rose to become president in a time of the nation's greatest crisis. Overcoming apparently insurmountable odds against the survival of the *United* States, he led the Union to victory and ended the institution that had mocked American professions of liberty, only to be struck down at the moment of triumph by the fell hand of an assassin. This martyrdom produced an apotheosis of Lincoln that is enshrined in marble and bronze at hundreds of places in America and around the world and in thousands of books, articles, poems, and other writings that make Lincoln the most written about American by a wide margin. The Gettysburg Address has immortalized the best ideals of what Americans want their country to stand for in the world.

Lincoln is therefore our most cherished historical possession. Most of the essays in this volume explore the meaning of Lincoln for the destiny of the United States. The final essay, by Merrill D. Peterson, analyzes the image of Lincoln abroad during the Great War that shattered Europe's world a half-century after the American Civil War re-United the States. This Introduction bookends Peterson's essay by analyzing the international impact of Lincoln and of America's internecine conflict during the 1860s. The Civil War shaped the destiny not only of America but also, as Lincoln put it, of "the whole family of man."

On December 1, 1862, Lincoln delivered his second annual message to Congress. Today we would call it the State of the Union Address. The state of the Union in December 1862 was perilous in the extreme. The Confederate States of America stood proud and defiant as an independent nation whose existence flouted the pretense of Union. Most European statesmen assumed that it was merely a matter of time until Lincoln recognized the inevitable truth that the Union had ceased to exist and gave up his bloody, quixotic effort to cobble it together again by force. At home, political opposition menaced Lincoln's ability to continue the war. That opposition focused particularly on the Emancipation Proclamation announced the preceding September and scheduled to go into effect on January 1, 1863. Lincoln had embraced emancipation both as a way to weaken the Confederacy by depriving it of slave labor and as a sweeping expansion of Union war aims. Many in the North did not approve this expansion. Nevertheless, Lincoln forged ahead. No longer would the North fight only for restoration of the old Union—a Union with slavery. Now the North would fight to give that Union a "new birth of freedom," as Lincoln put it a year later at Gettysburg.

By that time the prospects of Union victory appeared brighter than they had a year earlier. Even so, Lincoln's eloquence in December 1862 anticipated the Gettysburg Address. "Fellow-citizens, *we* cannot escape history," he told Congress—and the American people. "The fiery trial through which we pass, will light us down, in honor or dishonor, to the latest generation. . . . In *giving* freedom to the *slave*, we *assure* freedom to the free." For America, Lincoln insisted, this was the crossroads of history; this was where "we shall nobly save, or meanly lose, the last best, hope of earth."[1]

What did Lincoln mean? Why did he consider the Union to be the last best hope of earth? The last best hope for what?

Like other political leaders of his generation, Lincoln was painfully aware of the fate of most republics through history. Some Americans alive in 1861 had seen two French republics rise and fall. Republican governments in Latin America seemed to come and go with bewildering frequency. The hopes of 1848 for the triumph of popular governments in Europe had been crushed by the counterrevolutions that brought a conservative reaction in the Old World. The brave experiment launched in Philadelphia four score and seven years before Lincoln spoke at Gettysburg seemed fragile indeed in this world bestrode by kings, emperors, czars, dictators, theories of aristocracy, and inequality. Would the American experiment also succumb to the fate of most republics and collapse into tyranny or fall to pieces?

Not if Lincoln could help it. The central vision that guided him was preservation of the United States as a republic governed by popular suffrage, majority rule, and the Constitution. If the Confederate rebellion succeeded in its effort to sever the United States, popular government would be swept into the dustbin of history. The next time a disaffected minority lost a presidential election, as Southern Rights Democrats had lost in 1860, that minority might invoke the Confederate precedent to proclaim its own secession. The dis-United States would fragment into a dozen petty, squabbling fiefdoms. "The central idea pervading this struggle," said Lincoln in 1861, "is the necessity that is upon us, of proving that popular government is not an absurdity. We must settle this question now, whether in a free government the minority have the right to break up the government whenever they choose. If we fail it will go far to prove the incapability of the people to govern themselves." Nor was this struggle "altogether for today," Lincoln told Congress in 1861. "It is for a vast future also." It "embraces more than the fate of these United States. It presents to the whole family of man, the question, whether a constitutional republic, or a democracy . . . can, or cannot maintain its territorial integrity." If it could not, the forces of reaction in Europe would smile in smug satisfaction at this proof of their contention that the upstart republic launched in 1776 could never survive—that government of, by, and for the people had indeed perished from the earth.[2]

Most northern people in 1861 shared Lincoln's conviction that the fate of democratic government hung on the outcome of the Civil War. That passion sustained them through four years of the bloodiest war in the Western world between 1815 and 1914. "We must fight," insisted the *Indianapolis Daily Journal* on April 27, 1861, two weeks after the firing on Fort Sumter, "because we *must*. The National Government has been assailed. The Nation has been defied. If either can be done with impunity neither Nation nor Government is worth a cent. . . . War is self preservation, if our form of Government is worth preserving. If monarchy would be better, it might be wise to quit fighting, admit that a Republic is too weak to take care of itself, and invite some deposed Duke or Prince of Europe to come over here and rule us. But otherwise, *we must fight.*"

None felt this sense of democratic mission more strongly than Union soldiers, who imperiled their lives for it. "I do feel that the liberty of the world is placed in our hands to defend," wrote a Massachusetts private to his wife in 1862, "and if we are overcome then farewell to freedom." In 1863, on the second anniversary of his enlistment, an Ohio private wrote in his diary that he had not expected the war to last so long, but no matter how much longer it took it must be carried on "for the great principles of liberty and self government at stake, for should we fail, the onward march of Liberty in the Old World will be retarded at least a century, and Monarchs, Kings, and Aristocrats will be more powerful against their subjects than ever."[3]

Some foreign-born soldiers expressed such convictions with even greater intensity. In 1863 an Irish-born carpenter, a private in the 28th Massachusetts Infantry of the famous Irish Brigade, rebuked both his wife in Boston and his father-in-law in Ireland for questioning his judgment in risking his life for the Lincoln administration's war aims. "This is the first test of a modern free government in the act of sustaining itself against internal enemys," he wrote almost in echo of Lincoln. "If it fail then the hopes of milions fall and the designs and wishes of all tyrants will succeed the old cry will be sent forth from the aristocrats of europe that such is the common lot of all republics. . . . Irishmen and their descendants have . . . a stake in [this] nation. . . . America is Irlands refuge Irlands last hope destroy this republic and her hopes are blasted." In 1864 a forty-year-old Ohio corporal who had immigrated from England wrote to his wife to explain his decision to reenlist for a second three-year hitch: "If I do get hurt I want you to remember that it will be not only for my Country and my Children but for Liberty all over the World that I risked my life, for if Liberty should be crushed here, what hope would there be for the cause of Human Progress anywhere else?" Later that summer, in the Atlanta campaign, he gave his life for these convictions.[4]

It is not surprising that Americans both native and adopted felt this way. They had never hidden their self-proclaimed beacon light of freedom under a bushel. But did people of other lands share the belief in America's mission to show them the path upward from autocracy and oppression? For liberals, reformers, radicals, and revolutionaries of all stripes, the answer is yes. During the first century of its history as a nation, the United States did serve as a model for the European and Latin American "Left" that sought to reform or overthrow the ancien régimes in their own countries. In the Preface to the twelfth edition of his monumental *Democracy in America*, written during the heady days of the 1848 uprisings in Europe, Alexis de Tocqueville urged the leaders of France's newly created Second Republic to study American institutions as a guide to "the approaching irresistible and universal spread of democracy throughout the world." When instead of democracy France got the Second Empire under Napoleon III, the liberal opposition to his regime looked to the United States for inspiration. Napoleon's interior minister noted sourly that "one would almost be tempted to think that there was a fixed determination or combination to offer the United States always as an example for everything."[5]

Anti-Americanism was the hobby of the European Right in those years, particularly in England. As a British radical newspaper expressed it in 1856, "to the oppressors of Europe, especially those of England, the [United States] is a constant terror, and an everlasting menace" because it stood as "a practical and triumphant refutation of the lying and servile sophists who maintain that without kings and aristocrats, civilized communities cannot exist."[6] This rhetoric may have overstated the case. But the sentiments it described certainly existed among high tories—and some not so high. Many of them expressed delight, at least in private, at the "immortal smash" of the dis-United States in 1861, which demonstrated "the failure of republican institutions in time of pressure." The Earl of Shrewsbury looked upon "the trial of Democracy and its failure" with pleasure. "I believe that the dissolution of the Union is inevitable, and that men before me will live to see an aristocracy established in America." The voice of the British Establishment, the *Times* of London, considered the downfall of "the American colossus" a good "riddance of a nightmare. . . . Excepting a few gentlemen of republican tendencies, we all expect, we nearly all wish, success to the Confederate cause."[7]

We must not overgeneralize from such examples. A simple dichotomy between British liberals who admired American democracy and supported the Union, and conservatives who detested both, simplifies a complex pattern and ignores many exceptions. Nevertheless, most members of that minority of Englishmen who owned enough property to vote—and who were therefore represented in Parliament—probably would have welcomed the dissolution of the American republic. The foremost British champion of the Union, John Bright, explained to an American friend that "Our Govt is made up of men drawn from the aristocratic families . . . and from a natural instinct, it must be hostile to your greatness & to the permanence of your institutions." Bright's pro-Union colleague, Richard Cobden, may have exaggerated only slightly when he wrote in December 1861, at the height of the furor over the Union navy's seizure of Confederate envoys James Mason and John Slidell from the British ship *Trent,* that "three fourths of the House [of Commons] will be glad to find an excuse for voting for the dismemberment of the Great Republic." When Sir John Ramsden, a Tory member of the House, expressed satisfaction that "the great republican bubble had burst," loud cheers broke forth from the back benches.[8]

We know less about conservative attitudes toward the Civil War in other countries. What we do know, however, finds conservatives outside Britain also expressing satisfaction with the failure of democracy. In 1862 a royalist Spanish journal, the *Pansiemento Espanol,* found it scarcely surprising that Americans were butchering each other, for that nation "was populated by the dregs of all the nations of the world. . . . Such is the real history of the one and only state in the world which has succeeded in constituting itself according to the flaming theories of democracy. The example is too horrible to stir any desire for emulation."[9] In Paris, *La Patrie,* semiofficial spokesman for Emperor Napoleon III, stated with ill-concealed relish in August 1861 that "the work of George Washington has come to an end." Napoleon's foreign policy was the most pro-Confederate of any European power. If the emperor had been able to persuade Britain or Russia to go along, France would have offered mediation and diplomatic recognition of the Confederacy. The French liberal Edgar Quinet exaggerated only slightly when he wrote from exile in Switzerland in 1862 that Napoleon's purpose was "to weaken or destroy Democracy in the United States . . . because in order for Napoleonic ideas to succeed, it is absolutely indispensable that this vast republic disappear from the face of the earth."[10]

Whether or not Napoleon thought he could destroy republicanism in the United States, he undertook to do so in Mexico. That unhappy country experienced its own civil war in the 1860s between a reactionary alliance of Church and large landowners against followers of the republican liberal Benito Juárez. Under the pretext of collecting debts owed to French citizens, Napoleon sent an army of thirty-five thousand men to Mexico to overthrow Juárez. Napoleon's main motive was to reestablish the French presence in the New World yielded by his uncle sixty years earlier when he had sold Louisiana to the United States. Napoleon was also quite willing to go along with his fellow emperor, Franz Joseph of Austria, whose younger brother Ferdinand Maximilian was at loose ends. Why not set him up as emperor of Mexico, thereby reclaiming at least part of the vast Spanish domain once ruled by the Hapsburgs? King Leopold of Belgium, Maximilian's father-in-law, had an additional purpose in mind. Describing the Lincoln administration as being characterized by "the most rank Radicalism," Leopold feared that if the North won the war, "America, in collaboration with Europe's revolutionaries, might undermine the very basis of the traditional social order of Europe." Therefore, he strongly supported the installation of Maximilian as emperor of Mexico in 1864 "to raise a barrier against the United States and provide a support for the monarchical-aristocratic principle in the Southern states."[11]

While these emperors were fishing in troubled New World waters, the most autocratic of them all, Czar Nicholas of Russia, proved to be the Union's most steadfast friend. This friendship did not result from reasons of sentiment or ideology. Quite the contrary; no two regimes could have been farther apart in political philosophy and cultural values. Russo-American relations during the Civil War were a marriage of convenience founded on the self-interest of both parties: the Russian interest in a strong United States as a counterweight to Britain, Russia's enemy in the Crimean War a half-dozen years earlier, and American dependence on Russia as a counterweight to French and British flirtation with recognition of the Confederacy. In 1863 the Russian fleet visited American ports, staying for months, ostensibly as a good-will gesture but in reality to prevent the British navy from bottling up Russian ships in their home ports during a period of tension over Russian suppression of an uprising of Polish nationalists.

Although ideology did not inhibit the strange-bedfellow entente between Russia and the United States, that does not mean ideology was absent from Russian perceptions of the war's meaning for democracy. The confidential dispatches of the Russian minister to the United States, Edouard de Stoeckl, to the Russian foreign minister Prince Alexander Gortchakov provide a fascinating glimpse of the crosscurrents and contradictions of realpolitik and ideology. Stoeckl had lived in the United States for twenty years before the war. He liked Americans and married one in 1856. But he fancied himself an aristocrat and enjoyed being addressed as "Baron," although he had no title of nobility. He supported the Union cause but considered it hopeless until almost the end of the war. He detested democracy and regarded the Civil War as proof of its failure. "The republican form of government, so much talked about by the Europeans and so much praised by the Americans, is breaking down," he wrote to Prince Gortchakov in December 1863. "What can be expected from a country where men of humble origin are elevated to the highest positions?" He meant Lincoln, whose abilities Stoeckl held in low regard. "This is democracy in practice, the democracy that European theorists rave about," continued Stoeckl. "If they could only see it at work they would cease their agitation and thank God for the government which they are enjoying."[12]

Those theorists at whom Stoeckl sneered—that is, European liberals and radicals—initially viewed the American Civil War with alarm. Perhaps the reactionaries were right after all and the downfall of Lincoln's last best hope of earth would prove the absurdity of everything they believed in. French liberals, wrote one of them in 1861, "feel somehow humbled and certainly very distressed by this deplorable Civil War" because "it may very well bring about the failure of a society" held up by liberals as the "defenders of right and humanity."[13]

In England, John Bright, the great spokesman for expanded democracy, described America as "that free country and that free government [which] has had a prodigious influence upon freedom in Europe and in England" and was now fighting with backs to the wall as the "advocates and defenders of freedom and civilization." The famous economist and political philosopher John Stuart Mill, who fervently favored the Union cause, believed that Confederate success "would be a victory for the powers of evil which would give courage to the enemies of progress and damp the spirits of its friends all over the civilized world. . . . [The American war] is destined to be a turning point, for good and evil, of the course of human affairs."[14]

Slavery was a sticking point for both Union and Confederacy in their quest for European sympathy and support. Having abolished the institution in their colonies, European countries now prided themselves on their antislavery stance. Even autocratic Russia had ended serfdom in 1861. Britain regarded itself as the world's policeman against the slave trade.

Confederate envoys in Britain seeking diplomatic recognition in 1861 acknowledged ruefully that "the public mind here is entirely opposed to the Government of the Confederate States of America on the question of slavery. . . . The sincerity and universality of this feeling embarrass the Government in dealing with the question of our recognition." Lincoln recognized this truth when he said privately in January 1862, "I cannot imagine that any European power would dare to recognize and aid the Southern Confederacy if it became clear that the Confederacy stands for slavery and the Union for freedom."[15]

The problem was that in the first seventeen months of the war the Union did not stand for freedom. This fact perplexed and even embittered some Europeans who failed to understand the constitutional and political constraints that hindered Lincoln from turning the war for Union into a war against slavery. Since "the North does not proclaim abolition and never pretended to fight for anti-slavery," asked perturbed Englishmen in September 1861, how "can we be fairly called upon to sympathize so warmly with the Federal cause?"[16]

This attitude helps explain the ambivalent attitude of British workingmen toward the American war. On the one hand, most of them sympathized with the Union as the great symbol of progressivism and equal rights—the last best hope of earth for democracy—even though the livelihood of workers in Britain's largest industry depended on slave-grown cotton. By 1862 workers in the textile industry were suffering grievous unemployment and hardships because of the blockade of southern ports. Some of their spokesmen, therefore, urged recognition of the Confederacy and British intervention to break the Union blockade and get cotton. So long as the North fought merely for restoration of the Union—a Union with slavery—many labor leaders saw little moral difference between North and South. In a typical editorial a British labor newspaper declared in October 1861: "Now that it is clear that the Northerners in America are not fighting for the emancipation of the slaves, we are relieved from any moral consideration in their favor, and as the Southerners are not worse than they are, why should we not get cotton? . . . If the North, in blockading the Southern ports, had had emancipation in view, we might have seen the sacred cause of free labour was on their side." Since that was not the case, "Why should we starve any longer?"[17]

Lincoln recognized the force of this question. Years earlier he had noted that "the monstrous injustice of slavery . . . deprives our republican example of its just influence in the world—enables the enemies of free institutions, with plausibility, to taunt us as hypocrites." In September 1862 Lincoln agreed with a delegation of antislavery clergymen that "emancipation would help us in Europe, and convince them that we are incited by something more than ambition." When he said this, Lincoln had already decided to issue an emancipation proclamation and was only awaiting a Union military victory to announce it.[18]

That victory came a few days later, at Antietam. But to Lincoln's disappointment, the Emancipation Proclamation did not immediately transform critical European opinion. The preliminary nature of the edict that Lincoln issued on September 22, 1862, to go into effect the following January 1, the exemption of Unionist areas from its application, and the justification of the proclamation on grounds of military necessity, not morality and justice, gave European cynics a field day. Many regarded it as a Yankee trick to encourage slave insurrections, undertaken not from moral conviction but as a desperate measure to destroy the Confederacy from within because Union armies could not defeat it from without. The British chargé d'affaires in Washington branded the proclamation as "cold, vindictive, and entirely political." Foreign Secretary Lord John Russell, who had previously withheld sympathy from the Union because it did not act against slavery, now perversely pronounced the Emancipation Proclamation a vile encouragement to "acts of plunder, of incendiarism, and of revenge."[19] Choosing not to understand why Lincoln, under the Constitution, had to exempt the loyal border states and Union-occupied portions of the Confederacy, the London *Spectator* sneered that "the principle asserted is not that a human being cannot own another, but that he cannot own him unless he is loyal to the United States." Even the most radical British labor newspaper lamented that "Lincoln offers freedom to the negroes over whom he has no control, and keeps in slavery those other negroes within his power. Thus he associates his Government with slavery by making slaveholding the reward to the planters of rejoining the old Union."[20]

But in the end all of this sound and fury signified little. Most British liberals understood the great portent of the Emancipation Proclamation. A friendly London newspaper pronounced it "a gigantic stride in the paths of Christian and civilized progress—the turning point in the history of the American commonwealth—an act only second in courage and probably results to the Declaration of Independence." When Lincoln, contrary to the prediction of European cynics, followed through with the final Emancipation Proclamation on January 1, 1863, many former skeptics became believers. Implicitly responding to criticisms of the preliminary proclamation, Lincoln this time pronounced emancipation to be "an act of justice" as well as of military necessity and enjoined freed slaves to refrain from violence.[21]

Even though the final proclamation exempted one-quarter of the slaves, Lincoln had nevertheless announced a new war aim. Thenceforth the Union army became officially an army of liberation. If the North won the war, slavery would exist no more. As recognition of this truth began to dawn across the Atlantic, a powerful pro-Union reaction set in, especially in England. Huge meetings roared their approval of emancipation and endorsement of the Union cause. Many of these meetings were organized by workingmen. The speech of a worker at a rally in Manchester on February 24, 1863, offered a typical sentiment. The people of the North, he said in the paraphrased words of a reporter, were "not merely contending for themselves, but for the rights of the unenfranchised of this and every other country. If the North succeed, liberty [will] be stimulated and encouraged in every country on the face of the earth; if they fail, despotism, like a great pall, [will] envelop all our political and social institutions."[22]

The Emancipation Proclamation quenched any lingering chance that existed for British recognition of the Confederacy. Richard Cobden reported in February 1863 that one of the largest of the pro-Union mass meetings, at Exeter Hall in London, "has had a powerful effect on our newspapers and politicians. It has closed the mouths of those who have been advocating the side of the South. Recognition of the South, by England, whilst it bases itself on Negro slavery, is an impossibility." In France a year later, at a time when Napoleon was toying with the idea of recognizing the Confederacy in return for Confederate recognition of his puppet Maximilian in Mexico, twelve prominent French citizens of Tours addressed a public letter to Confederate envoy John Slidell, telling him bluntly: "It is useless to make any appeal to the people of France. It may be to our interest to support you. There may be strong material and political reasons for a close alliance between us, but as long as you maintain and are maintained by slavery, we cannot offer you our alliance. On the contrary, we believe and expect you will fail!"[23]

The Confederacy did fail. The last best hope of earth for democracy did not perish from the earth, but experienced a new birth of freedom whose impact was felt abroad with telling effect. From Spanish republicans in 1865 came congratulations to "a people democratically governed" who have "carried to its close the greatest enterprise in history." The Italian patriot and revolutionary Guiseppe Mazzini blessed the Northern people who "have done more for us in four years than fifty years of teaching, preaching and writing from all your European brothers have been able to do." None other than Karl Marx declared that "as in the eighteenth century the American War of Independence sounded the tocsin for the European middle class, so in the nineteenth century, the American Civil War sounded it for the working class."[24]

It is scarcely surprising that European liberals and radicals expressed relief and delight at the news of Union victory. Perhaps even more illustrative of the impact of that victory were the responses of conservatives. A

British Tory in the House of Commons, a critic of American culture and democracy, remarked sourly to an American acquaintance that he considered Union success a misfortune. "I had indulged the hope that your country might break up into two or perhaps more fragments. I regard the United States as a menace to the whole civilized world." A Tory colleague spelled out the menace as "the beginning of an Americanizing process in England. The new Democratic ideas are gradually to find embodiment."[25]

Most remarkable of all was the reaction of Edouard de Stoeckl, the Russian minister who disliked democracy, had considered the Civil War proof of its failure, and had predicted Confederate victory until almost the eve of Appomattox. When the outcome proved him wrong, he ate humble pie in a dispatch to Russian Foreign Minister Prince Gortchakov. By "an irresistible strength of the nation at large," wrote Stoeckl, "this exceptional people has given the lie to all predictions and calculations. . . . They have passed through one of the greatest revolutions of a century . . . and they have come out of it with their resources unexhausted, their energy renewed . . . and the prestige of their power greater than ever."[26]

The consequences of this triumph of democracy were more than symbolic. It encouraged liberals in Britain who wanted to expand voting rights there. For almost four years they had endured the taunts and jibes of Tories. "Our opponents told us that Republicanism was on trial," recalled Edward Beesly, a liberal professor of political economy at University College, London, in 1865. "They insisted on our watching what they called its breakdown. They told us that it was for ever discredited in England. Well, we accepted the challenge. We staked our hopes boldly on the result. . . . Under a strain such as no aristocracy, no monarchy, no empire could have supported, Republican institutions have stood firm. It is we, now, who call upon the privileged classes to mark the result. . . . A vast impetus has been given to Republican sentiments in England."[27]

A two-year debate in Parliament, in which the American example figured prominently, led to enactment of the Reform Bill of 1867, which nearly doubled the eligible electorate and enfranchised a large part of the British working class for the first time. With this act the world's most powerful nation took a long stride toward democracy. It would be an oversimplification to attribute this achievement mainly to Union victory in the Civil War. But perhaps it is no exaggeration to say that had the North lost the war, thereby confirming Tory opinions of democracy and confounding the liberals, the Reform Bill would have been delayed for years.[28]

If the triumph of democracy in Britain was an indirect result of the American Civil War, the triumph of Benito Juárez and republicanism in Mexico was in part a direct result. The United States sent fifty thousand veteran troops to Texas after Appomattox, while Secretary of State Seward pressed the French to pull their troops out of Mexico. Napoleon did so in 1866, whereupon the republican forces under Juárez regained control of the country, captured Maximilian, and executed him in 1867. Three years after the fall of Maximilian, Napoleon himself lost his throne, an event attributed by the historian of his liberal opposition in part to the example of triumphant republicanism in the United States five years earlier.[29]

This is pushing things too far; the birth of France's Third Republic was a consequence of French defeat in the Franco-Prussian War, not of Union victory in the American Civil War. But perhaps it was more than coincidence that within five years of that Union victory the forces of liberalism had expanded the suffrage in Britain and toppled emperors in Mexico and France. And it was also more than coincidence that after the abolition of slavery in the United States the abolitionist forces in the two remaining Western Hemisphere slave societies, Brazil and Cuba, stepped up their campaigns for emancipation, which culminated in success two decades later. If he had lived, Lincoln would have been gratified by the statement of a Brazilian intellectual in 1871, referring to his government's commitment to emancipation, that he rejoiced "to see Brazil receive so quickly the moral of the Civil War in the United States."[30]

Lincoln would have applauded even more the essay written in 1993 by a seventeen-year-old girl from Texas in a contest sponsored by the Huntington Library in connection with its exhibit on Lincoln. This girl, whose forebears had immigrated from India thirty years earlier, wrote that "if the United States was not in existence today, I would not have the opportunity to excel in life and education. The Union was preserved, not only for the people yesterday, but also for the lives of today."[31]

If many people living in the last best hope of earth today seem to have lost hope, let them read and ponder the essays in this volume. They show how Lincoln led the country through the worst of times to a triumph that left America stronger, more free, and more democratic. And that offers a lesson not only for Americans but also for "the whole family of man."

Notes

1. Roy P. Basler, ed., Marion Dolores Pratt, and Lloyd A. Dunlap, asst. eds., *The Collected Works of Abraham Lincoln*, 9 vols. (New Brunswick: Rutgers University Press, 1953–55), 5:537 (hereafter cited as *Collected Works*).

2. Tyler Dennett, ed., *Lincoln and the Civil War in the Diaries and Letters of John Hay* (New York: Dodd, Mead, 1939), 19–20; *Collected Works*, 5:53, 4:426.

3. Josiah Perry to Phebe Perry, Oct. 3, 1862, Josiah Perry Papers, Illinois State Historical Library, Springfield; Robert T. McMahan Diary, entry of Sept. 3, 1863, State Historical Society of Missouri, Columbia.

4. Peter Welsh to Mary Welsh, Feb. 3, 1863, Peter Welsh to Patrick Prendergast, June 1, 1863, in *Irish Green and Union Blue: The Civil War Letters of Peter Welsh*, ed. Laurence Frederick Kohl and Margaret Cosse Richard (New York: Fordham University Press, 1986), 65, 66, 102; George H. Cadman to Esther Cadman, March 6, 1864, Cadman Papers, Southern Historical Collection, University of North Carolina, Chapel Hill.

5. Tocqueville, *Democracy in America*, 12th ed., trans. George Lawrence, ed. J. P. Mayer (New York: Doubleday Anchor Books, 1969), xiii; Serge Gavronsky, *The French Liberal Opposition and the American Civil War* (New York: Humanities Press, 1968), 12.

6. Quoted in G. D. Lillbridge, *Beacon of Freedom: The Impact of American Democracy upon Great Britain 1830–1870* (Philadelphia: University of Pennsylvania Press, 1955), 80.

7. William H. Russell to John Bigelow, April 14, 1861, in John Bigelow, *Retrospections of an Active Life*, 2 vols. (New York: Baker and Taylor, 1909), 1:347; the Earl of Shrewsbury quoted in Ephraim D. Adams, *Great Britain and the American Civil War*, 2 vols. (New York: Russell and Russell, 1925), 2:282; *Times* quoted in Frank L. Owsley, *King Cotton Diplomacy: Foreign Relations of the Confederate States of America*, 2d ed., rev. Harriet C. Owsley (Chicago: University of Chicago Press, 1959), 186.

8. John Bright to John Bigelow, Jan. 3, 1862, in *Europe Looks at the Civil War*, ed. Belle Becker Sideman and Lillian Friedman (New York: Orion Press, 1960), 129; Cobden to "Mr. Paulton," Dec. 1861, ibid., 91; Ramsden quoted in Jay Monaghan, *Diplomat in Carpet Slippers: Abraham Lincoln Deals with Foreign Affairs* (Indianapolis: Bobbs-Merrill, 1945), 116. See also Donald Bellows, "A Study of British Conservative Reaction to the American Civil War," *Journal of Southern History* 51 (1985): 505–26, and Sheldon Vanauken, *The Glittering Illusion: English Sympathy for the Southern Confederacy* (Worthing, England: Churchman Publishing, 1988).

9. Quoted in Sideman and Friedman, eds., *Europe Looks at the Civil War*, 173–74.

10. *La Patrie* and Quinet quoted in Gavronsky, *The French Liberal Opposition*, 58, 167.

11. King Leopold to Queen Victoria, Oct. 17, 1861, in Sideman and Friedman, eds., *Europe Looks at the Civil War*, 98; Leopold also quoted in A. R. Tyrner-Tyrnauer, *Lincoln and the Emperors* (New York: Harcourt, Brace and World, 1962), 69, 109.

12. Quoted in Albert A. Woldman, *Lincoln and the Russians* (Cleveland: World Publishing, 1952), 216–17.

13. *Revue des deux mondes*, Aug. 15, 1861, quoted in Sideman and Friedman, eds., *Europe Looks at the Civil War*, 81.

14. Bright quoted in H. C. Allen, "Civil War, Reconstruction, and Great Britain," in *Heard Round the World: The Impact Abroad of the Civil War*, ed. Harold M. Hyman (New York: Knopf, 1969), 96, 75; Mill quoted in Sideman and Friedman, eds., *Europe Looks at the Civil War*, 117–18.

15. William L. Yancey and A. Dudley Mann to Robert Toombs, May 21, 1861,

in *A Compilation of the Messages and Papers of the Confederacy*, comp. James D. Richardson, 2 vols. (Nashville: U. S. Publishing, 1906), 2:37; Lincoln quoted in *The Reminiscences of Carl Schurz*, 3 vols. (New York: McClure, 1907–8), 2:309.

16. *Saturday Review*, Sept. 14, 1861, quoted in Ephraim D. Adams, *Great Britain and the American Civil War*, 2 vols. (New York: Russell and Russell, 1925), 1:181; *Economist*, Sept. 1861, quoted in Karl Marx and Friedrich Engels, *The Civil War in the United States*, ed. Richard Enmale (New York: Citadel Press, 1937), 12.

17. *The Working Man*, Oct. 5, 1861, quoted in Philip S. Foner, *British Labor and the American Civil War* (New York: Holmes and Meier Publishers, 1981), 27–28.

18. *Collected Works*, 2:255, 5:423.

19. Chargé d'affaires quoted in Brian Jenkins, *Britain and the War for the Union*, 2 vols. (Montreal: McGill-Queen's University Press, 1974–80), 2:141; Russell quoted in Howard Jones, *Union in Peril: The Crisis over British Intervention in the Civil War* (Chapel Hill: University of North Carolina Press, 1992), 187.

20. *Spectator*, Oct. 11, 1862, quoted in Jenkins, *Britain and the War for the Union*, 2:153; *Bee-Hive*, Oct. 11, 1862, quoted in Foner, *British Labor and the American Civil War*, 29.

21. *Morning Star*, Oct. 6, 1862, quoted in Allan Nevins, *The War for the Union*, 4 vols., vol. 2: *War Becomes Revolution* (New York: Charles Scribner's Sons, 1960), 270; *Collected Works*, 6:30.

22. Quoted in Foner, *British Labor and the American Civil War*, 52.

23. Cobden to Charles Sumner, Feb. 13, 1863, in Sideman and Friedman, eds., *Europe Looks at the Civil War*, 222 (citizens of Tours quoted on 261–62).

24. For quotations of Spanish republicans and Mazzini, see ibid., 274, 282; Marx quoted in R. Laurence Moore, *European Socialists and the American Promised Land* (New York: Oxford University Press, 1970), 7.

25. Sir Edward Bulwer-Lytton to John Bigelow, April 1865, quoted in Sideman and Friedman, eds., *Europe Looks at the Civil War*, 282; Hyman, ed., *Heard Round the World*, xi.

26. Stoeckl to Gortchakov, April 14, 1865, in Woldman, *Lincoln and the Russians*, 256–59.

27. Quoted in H. C. Allen, "Civil War, Reconstruction, and Great Britain," in Hyman, ed., *Heard Round the World*, 73.

28. Ibid., 49–83.

29. Gavronsky, *The French Liberal Opposition*, 13.

30. Quoted in Harry Bernstein, "The Civil War and Latin America," in Hyman, ed., *Heard Round the World*, 323.

31. Reena Mathew, "One Set of Footprints," essay in my possession.

Part One

LINCOLN'S AMERICA

Chapter One

Lincoln's History

KENNETH M. STAMPP

Nearly all twentieth-century presidents have turned to history, especially to the records of their predecessors, to find justification for the policies they have wished to pursue. As Richard N. Current put it, they have been "fond of quoting or misquoting the statements and recalling with more or less relevance and accuracy the actions of presidents who have gone before."[1] During the 1992 presidential campaign, George Bush put on the ill-fitting mantle of "give 'em hell" Harry Truman, while Bill Clinton sometimes spoke and gestured like a latter-day John F. Kennedy. In short, for one purpose or another, presidents have managed to uncover or, sometimes, to invent a usable past.

George Washington, Thomas Jefferson, Andrew Jackson, and Abraham Lincoln have been the authorities most frequently enlisted in twentieth-century presidential causes. Among them, Lincoln, a brilliant politician whose historical reputation nevertheless transcends partisan politics, has been the favorite of Democrats and Republicans alike. Theodore Roosevelt, William Howard Taft, Dwight D. Eisenhower, and Richard M. Nixon all invoked his name to justify policies of their own. On the other hand, both Woodrow Wilson and Franklin D. Roosevelt accused Republicans of repudiating everything Lincoln stood for and claimed him for the Democrats. Harry Truman, during the Korean War, compared the trouble that General Douglas MacArthur caused him with the trouble that General George B. McClellan caused Lincoln. Lyndon Johnson affirmed that as Lincoln had abolished slavery he, in like manner, would abolish poverty. Herbert Hoover once impatiently reminded Democrats that Lincoln, after all, had been a Republican.[2]

As twentieth-century presidents have used Lincoln to justify their policies, Lincoln himself found politicians of the past whose acts or ideas were sometimes useful to him. He admired Thomas Jefferson, called him "the most distinguished politician of our history," and claimed that the Republicans of the 1850s, rather than the Democrats, were his ideological heirs. Although in the 1830s Lincoln the Whig partisan had few kind words for Andrew Jackson, in later years Lincoln the Republican nationalist praised him for his firm Unionism. Above all, he identified with Henry Clay, his "beau ideal of a statesman," whom he "revered as a teacher and leader."[3] Accordingly, Lincoln can be studied not only as a historical figure but also, as I propose to attempt here, as a student of history who had a particular view of the American past.

Lincoln's understanding of his country's history stemmed from a belief, shared by many of his contemporaries, that the fathers of the Republic had undertaken at its birth a special mission to humanity. Garry Wills views his Gettysburg Address, celebrating a "new nation" dedicated to the principles of the Declaration of Independence, as "the most profound statement of this belief in a special American fate."[4] Thanks to the Revolutionary fathers, Lincoln said on an earlier occasion, Americans found themselves "in the peaceful possession, of the fairest portion of the earth," living under a government more protective of civil and religious liberty than any other system of political institutions in history. The task of his generation, he believed, was to defend the country from invaders and its tradition of liberty and equal rights from usurpers, transmitting both unblemished to future generations.[5]

In 1838, in an address delivered before the Young Men's Lyceum of Springfield, Illinois, Lincoln explained how this duty could be fulfilled. He did not fear an invasion by "some transatlantic military giant," he said. Rather, whatever danger arose would come from a domestic source. "If destruction be our lot, we must ourselves be its author. . . . As a nation of freemen, we must live through all time, or die by suicide." He pointed to one tendency posing an immediate danger: "the increasing disregard for law" that pervaded the country; the disposition to substitute "the wild and furious passions" of "worse than savage mobs" for the sober judgment of courts of law. If mobs were permitted to burn, loot, and murder with impunity, he warned, "depend on it, this government cannot last." These were the historical circumstances that reared tyrants—men who would subvert liberty in the name of law and order. The remedy was to instill in every child, in the home and in the schools, reverence for the laws—respect even for bad laws until they were repealed. "As the patriots of seventy-six did to the support of the Declaration of Independence," Lincoln urged, "so to the support of the Constitution and Laws, let every American pledge his life, his property, and his sacred honor."[6]

In the same address Lincoln spoke at length of a second historic danger to liberty. The fathers of the Revolution, he said, had launched a political experiment the success of which had long been considered at best uncertain, "namely, *the capability of a people to govern themselves.*" Their experiment was successful, and they had "won their deathless names in making it so." That struggle was over, and the glory of it belonged to the heroes of that generation. But, Lincoln warned, history tells us that other ambitious men will emerge, seeking fame as others had done in the past. Some will be content to hold a seat in Congress, or a governorship, or the presidency. Such men, however, *"belong not to the family of the lion, or the tribe of the eagle."* An Alexander, or a Caesar, or a Bonaparte aspires to more. He "thirsts and burns for distinction," and he will win it, "whether at the expense of emancipating slaves, or enslaving freemen." Was it unreasonable, Lincoln asked, to expect that such a man "possessed of the loftiest genius, coupled with ambition . . . will at some time spring up among us?"[7]

Lincoln's rhetoric, uncharacteristically flamboyant, was no doubt designed to impress his young Springfield friends, but several psychoanalytic historians have found in it a deeper meaning. The Lyceum Address, they argue, was more than a straightforward warning of danger based on historical insight. Rather, it defined *Lincoln* for much of his career. In their view *he* was the jealous son, resentful of the Revolutionary fathers, burning for distinction, and the role of "towering genius" of which he spoke was one he dreamed of playing himself. This argument has not stood up well against a barrage of critical analysis. Some critics have suggested that the tyrant Lincoln may have had in mind was Emperor Napoleon who, not long ago, had destroyed the First Republic, or, perhaps, Andrew Jackson, whom his fellow Whigs had considered a tyrant and had designated "King Andrew I."[8] In any case, Lincoln's description of the "tribe of the eagle" was far too negative to be considered a plausible self-image. In later years he repeated his warning against tyrants many times. On one occasion, for example, he claimed that the assertion in the Declaration of Independence that "all men are created equal" was put there as "a rebuke and a stumbling block to the very harbingers of re-appearing tyranny and oppression."[9]

Lincoln admonished his countrymen to frustrate the designs of any ambitious tyrant by uniting in defense of and reverence for the Constitution and laws. Beyond that he hoped that the deeds and ideals of the Revolutionary fathers would never be forgotten, that in history they would be "read of and recounted, so long as the bible shall be read." Lincoln supported public education, he once said, to enable everyone "to read the histories of his own and other countries, by which he may duly appreciate the value of our free institutions."[10]

Lincoln's response to political events of the 1850s—the passage of the Kansas-Nebraska Act, the violent conflict over slavery in Kansas Territory, and the Supreme Court's decision in the Dred Scott case—brought him into national prominence as a leader of the young Republican party. His protracted dispute with his Illinois rival, Democratic Senator Stephen A. Douglas, culminating in their famous debates of 1858, largely involved conflicting interpretations of the early political history of the Republic. Specifically, they disagreed about the ideas and goals of the authors and signers of the Declaration of Independence and about the intentions of the men who framed the federal Constitution. In the main, Lincoln's history was better than Douglas's, but each was a resourceful mythmaker when it served his purpose.

The Kansas-Nebraska Act, introduced by Douglas and adopted by Congress in 1854, substituted the principle of popular sovereignty for the provision of the Missouri Compromise of 1820 that had excluded slavery from these new territories. Popular sovereignty permitted territorial settlers to introduce or prohibit slavery as they pleased. Douglas argued that his policy conformed with the democratic principle of self-government and was neither proslavery nor antislavery. It was a historic principle, he said, that long ago had brought about the abolition of slavery in the older northern states and subsequently had made a free state of Illinois.[11]

Lincoln responded with an attack on Douglas's posture of moral indifference to the possible expansion of slavery into western territories. The spirit of the Revolutionary fathers and the spirit of the Kansas-Nebraska Act, he avowed, were "utter antagonisms." In Lincoln's history the fathers had merely tolerated an institution that they had inherited, and they "cast blame upon the British King for having permitted its introduction." In the Constitution "they forbore to so much as mention the word 'slave' or 'slavery,'" hiding it instead "as an afflicted man hides away a wen or a cancer." The reason for their "covert language," Lincoln said, was that after slavery had been abolished "there should be nothing on the face of the great charter of liberty suggesting that such a thing as negro slavery had ever existed among us."

He credited Jefferson, although a slaveholder, with the idea of preventing slavery from invading the territory north of the Ohio River, an idea embodied in the Ordinance of 1787. Thus, said Lincoln, "in the pure fresh, free breath of the revolution" Congress put into practice the policy of excluding slavery from areas where it did not already exist. "Thenceforward, ... until in 1848, the last scrap of this territory came into the Union as the State of Wisconsin, all parties acted in quiet obedience to this ordinance." The Northwest became "what Jefferson foresaw and intended— the happy home of teeming millions ... and no slave amongst them."[12]

Denying Douglas's claim that the principle of popular sovereignty had encouraged the abolition of slavery in the northern states, Lincoln asserted that it was "the principle of the REVOLUTION and not the principle of the Nebraska bill, that led to emancipation." Federal legislation, not popular sovereignty, had made Illinois a free state. To prove his point he compared the histories of Illinois and Missouri, between which there was little difference in soil or climate. In 1810 only a few slaves lived in each territory; a decade later, when the territories were ready for statehood, the number of slaves in Illinois had decreased, whereas in Missouri the number had grown to ten thousand. Illinois entered the Union as a free state, Missouri as a slave state. The reason, Lincoln argued, was that in Missouri no federal law kept slavery out, whereas the Northwest Ordinance prohibited it in Illinois. In fact, he noted, since 1800 federal legislation had prohibited slavery in every territory that subsequently entered the Union as a free state. Thus, Lincoln concluded, the history of the country proved that Douglas's principle of popular sovereignty had put freedom at a great disadvantage.[13]

A year after the passage of the Kansas-Nebraska Act, a pessimistic Lincoln feared that there was no prospect for a peaceful end to slavery in the United States. "On the question of liberty, as a principle," he wrote, "we are not what we have been. When we were the political slaves of King George, and wanted to be free, we called the maxim that 'all men are created equal' a self-evident truth; but now when we have grown fat, and have lost all dread of being slaves ourselves, we have become so greedy to be *masters* that we call the same maxim 'a self-evident lie.'. . . The Autocrat of all the Russias will resign his crown, and proclaim his subjects free republicans sooner than will our American masters voluntarily give up their slaves."[14]

In Lincoln's view, the Supreme Court's Dred Scott decision of March 6, 1857, like the Kansas-Nebraska Act, had interrupted a benign historical process that the fathers of the Republic had set in motion. By denying Congress the power to prohibit slavery in the territories, the Court's majority had ruled the Northwest Ordinance, the Missouri Compromise, and other restrictive territorial legislation unconstitutional. All territories were now open to slavery, for Chief Justice Roger B. Taney's opinion for the Court's majority held that even a territorial legislature could not prohibit it.

This, said Lincoln, was not what the founders of the Republic had intended. The Union had endured for more than eighty years because, until recently, the public mind had rested "in the belief that slavery was in course of ultimate extinction. . . . The adoption of the Constitution and its attendant history led the people to believe so; and such was the belief of the framers of the Constitution itself." Douglas, in response to Lincoln's House Divided speech of 1858, had asked, "Why can't this Union endure permanently, half slave and half free?" In reply, Lincoln asked, "Why can't we let it stand as our fathers placed it? I say when this government was first established it was the policy of its founders to prohibit the spread of slavery into the new Territories of the United States, where it had not existed." All he desired was that slavery be returned to its original status. It was this status that had led "all just and right-minded men to suppose that slavery was gradually coming to an end, and that they might be quiet about it, watching it as it expired." Give them that assurance again, Lincoln urged, and the country would enjoy the peace that Douglas and the Court had disrupted.[15]

The fathers of the Republic, especially those from the Deep South, had been less united in their desire to put slavery on the road to ultimate extinction than Lincoln claimed. However, he did offer good historical evidence that the framers of the Constitution had granted Congress the authority to exclude it from the territories. In 1789, he noted, the First Congress had reenacted the Northwest Ordinance without dissent. Among the members of that Congress, sixteen had been delegates to the Constitutional Convention, and Washington, its president, had signed the bill. Again, during the debates over the Missouri Compromise, twenty-one of the twenty-three congressmen who had been convention delegates indicated their belief, directly or indirectly, that the constitutional power given Congress to govern the territories included the power to prohibit slavery. Therefore, Lincoln concluded, those who endorsed Chief Justice Taney's Dred Scott decision were assuming that he and they understood the Constitution better than its authors.[16]

Lincoln also differed with Taney and Douglas over two historical questions concerning the status of African Americans at the time of the Revolution and Constitutional Convention. First, had they ever been, or could they ever be, recognized as citizens of the United States? Second, were they entitled to the "unalienable rights" of "all men" affirmed in the Declaration of Independence? In Taney's opinion, "they were not included, and were not intended to be included, under the word 'citizen' in the Constitution." Moreover, he added, at the time the Declaration of Independence was written, even free African Americans were not "acknowledged as a part of the people, nor intended to be included in the general words used in that memorable instrument." Rather, they were then considered "so far inferior, that they had no rights which the white man was bound to respect." Douglas fully endorsed Taney's racial views. "No one," he said, "can vindicate the character, motives and conduct of the signers of the Declaration of Independence, except upon the hypothesis that they referred to the white race alone." Similarly, the government under the Constitution "was formed on the white basis. It was made by the white man, for the benefit of the white man, to be administered by white men, in such manner as they should determine."[17]

Given the widespread racism in the northern electorate, Lincoln, like most Republican politicians, dealt cautiously with this part of Taney's Dred Scott decision and with Douglas's concurrence. Nevertheless, he asserted that the majority decision was based in part "on assumed historical facts which were not true." Citing the dissenting opinion of Associate Justice Benjamin R. Curtis, Lincoln noted that at the time of the Revolution five states recognized free African Americans as citizens. They were able to vote, and "in proportion to their numbers, had the same part in making the Constitution that the white people had." Nothing in the federal Constitution, Lincoln argued, had changed this, and each state still had the power, if it chose, to grant citizenship to African Americans.[18]

As for the Declaration of Independence, Lincoln accused Taney and Douglas of doing "violence to [its] plain unmistakable language." He believed that its authors intended to declare the equality of all men, but not necessarily their equality in all respects. Rather, he said, they "defined with tolerable distinctness, in what respects they did consider all men created equal—equal in 'certain inalienable rights, among which are life, liberty, and the pursuit of happiness.' This they said and this they meant." With these words, Lincoln claimed, they revealed "their lofty, and wise, and noble understanding of the justice of the Creator . . . to the whole great family of man." Conceding that the African American was "perhaps" not the equal of the white American in some respects, he insisted that "in the right to put into his mouth the bread that his own hands had earned, he is the equal of every other man, white or black."[19]

If we were to accept Taney's and Douglas's assertion that our historic Declaration was not intended to apply to African Americans, Lincoln wondered, where would such reasoning carry us? "If one man says it does not mean a negro, why not another say it does not mean some other man?" Recent immigrants—Germans, Irish, and Scandinavians—who were not direct descendants of the Revolutionary fathers might then be vulnerable. But if we apply the principles the fathers pronounced in 1776 to all men, they too would be able to claim to be "blood of the blood and flesh of the flesh of the men who wrote the Declaration, and so they are." Lincoln urged his countrymen to "discard all this quibbling about this man and the other man—this race and that race and the other race being inferior, and therefore they must be placed in an inferior position." Rather, "let us unite as one people . . . until we shall once more stand up declaring that all men are created equal."[20]

Lincoln was generous—probably too generous—in attributing motives to those who signed the Declaration of Independence. They knew, he said, that all men did not enjoy the equality they proclaimed, but they set equality as an ultimate goal toward which each generation must strive.

Their purpose was to establish "a standard maxim for free society, which should be familiar to all, and revered by all, constantly looked to, constantly labored for, . . . and thereby constantly spreading and deepening its influence, and augmenting the happiness and value of life to all people of all colors." Lincoln viewed the Declaration not as a manifesto written merely to justify the American Revolution but as a legacy to posterity, encouraging "the progressive improvement in the condition of all men everywhere." Through his humane historical interpretation he gave it meaning for all time.[21]

Douglas and other northern Democrats, as well as remnants of the conservative old Whigs, denounced Lincoln and other antislavery Republicans who, like Senator William H. Seward of New York, described the ideological differences between the slave and free states as an "irrepressible conflict between opposing and enduring forces." They denied that the conflict was irrepressible. Instead, they asserted, it was generated deliberately by irresponsible abolitionist fanatics and by reckless Republican politicians merely to gratify their ambition for political power. "Why should this slavery agitation be kept up?" Douglas asked during his 1858 campaign for reelection. "Does it benefit the white man or the slave? Who does it benefit except the Republican politicians, who use it as their hobby horse to ride into office." According to Edward Everett, a Massachusetts Whig, slavery would soon disappear if only "unprincipled agitation of the subject for electioneering purposes could be stopped."[22]

A group of twentieth-century Civil War historians, who called themselves "revisionists," agreed with the Douglases and Everetts of the 1850s. They argued that the sectional conflict would have been "repressible" if moderates such as Douglas had been heeded, and that the Civil War was a "needless war" brought on by a "blundering generation" of irresponsible politicians. "When nations stumble into war," wrote James G., Randall, "there is at some point a psychopathic case. Omit the element of abnormality, of bogus leadership, or inordinate ambition for conquest, and diagnosis fails." A second revisionist, Avery Craven, attributed responsibility for the sectional conflict to "a generation of well-meaning Americans" who "permitted their short-sighted politicians, their overzealous editors, and their pious reformers to emotionalize real and potential differences and to conjure up distorted impressions of those who dwelt in other parts of the nation." The genuine differences between the sections, Craven believed, "were but the materials with which passions worked. . . . The conflict was the work of politicians and pious cranks."[23]

Like Lincoln, most present-day historians find a good deal more substance in the antebellum sectional conflict than mere political opportunism. Accordingly, as Douglas made a historical case for the "revisionists," Lincoln made one for their critics. Was it true, he asked, "that all the difficulty and agitation we have in regard to this institution of slavery springs from office-seeking—from the mere ambition of politicians?" Reviewing the history of previous sectional crises, he claimed that, directly or indirectly, each involved a dispute over the morality of slavery or an effort to expand its domain. Moreover, "does *not* this question make a disturbance outside of political circles? . . . Is it not this same mighty, deep seated power that somehow operates on the minds of men, exciting and stirring them up in every avenue of society . . . in all the manifold relations of life? Is this the work of politicians? Is that irresistible power which for fifty years has shaken the government and agitated the people to be stilled and subdued by pretending that it is an exceedingly simple thing, and we ought not to talk about it?" That had been tried in the past, Lincoln said, but each time a new crisis, more violent than the last, soon developed. At bottom, he maintained, the issue was between "the property idea that slavery is right, and the idea that it is wrong." These ideas "come into collision, and do actually produce that irrepressible conflict which Mr. Seward has been so roundly abused for mentioning."[24]

In one of his debates with Douglas, Lincoln interpreted the American conflict as one episode in an eternal worldwide struggle between two principles "that have stood face to face from the beginning of time." One, he said, was "the common right of humanity and the other the divine right of kings. . . . It is the same spirit that says, 'You work and toil and earn bread, and I'll eat it.' No matter in what shape it comes, whether from the mouth of a king who seeks to bestride the people of his own nation and live by the fruit of their labor, or from one race of men as an apology for enslaving another race, it is the same tyrannical principle."[25] On numerous occasions during the ensuing Civil War, notably in his Gettysburg Address, Lincoln reiterated the essence of this historical interpretation.

Lincoln's victory in the presidential election of 1860 and the subsequent attempt of eleven southern states to secede brought to a climax still another historical debate over the intentions of the delegates to the Constitutional Convention of 1787. What sort of Union did they intend to create? A Union that could not be broken except by an extra-constitutional act of revolution? A Union from which each sovereign state could peacefully secede when the interests of its citizens seemed to make it desirable to do so? Unfortunately there is no explicit clause in the Constitution to settle this question. One delegate proposed the insertion of a declaration that "the Union shall be perpetual," but his proposal was never brought up for formal discussion. The debates in the state conventions elected to ratify the Constitution did little to clarify this ambiguity, nor did the famous *Federalist Papers* written by John Jay, James Madison, and Alexander Hamilton in support of ratification. Before the Civil War, no case directly testing the right of a state to secede was ever argued before the U.S. Supreme Court. As a result, this crucial question remained unresolved at the time of Lincoln's election.[26]

For several decades after the adoption of the Constitution the Union was widely perceived as an experiment whose future was at best uncertain. To be sure, nearly everyone seemed to hope that it would succeed. Few, Edmund Randolph wrote, could "read without emotion the future fate of the States if severed from each other." Yet, the fear of failure troubled President Washington when he delivered his Farewell Address. "Is there doubt whether a common government can embrace so large a sphere?" he asked. "Let experience solve it. . . . It is well worth a fair and full experiment."[27]

Almost from the start Unionists were apprehensive that one state or another, perhaps several, would become disaffected and claim the right to secede. At the Constitutional Convention one delegate speculated that the southern states might feel their interests threatened and say "do us justice or we will separate." Another believed that the country was too large to remain permanently united. Still another predicted that before long the states would become "distinct Governments perfectly independent of each other." Thomas Jefferson never doubted the right of a state to secede. He toyed with the idea of Virginia's secession in the late 1790s, and during his presidency he speculated that the eastern and western states might one day divide and form two nations. "God bless them both," he wrote, "and keep them in the union if it be for their good, but separate them if it be better." In fact, before 1860 disgruntled politicians in every region, including New England, had at one time or another threatened secession.[28]

Needless to say, secessionists found no provision in the Constitution listing the terms or explaining the procedures for a dissolution of the Union. They had to interpret history and read the Constitution in such a way as to *infer* the right they claimed. Their argument began with the assertion that the states were older than the Union—that they had in fact created the Union. However, in doing so the Articles of Confederation, adopted in 1781, assured the states that they retained their "sovereignty, freedom and independence." According to Jefferson, they did not surrender their sovereignty when they ratified the Constitution. Rather, he wrote in resolutions adopted by the Kentucky legislature in 1798, that document was a compact to which the states agreed, thereby creating a general government with certain specific powers but reserving to themselves the residuary mass of powers. If the federal government were to assume undelegated powers, its acts would be "unauthoritative, void, and of no force." Moreover, Jefferson asserted, each individual state, not the Supreme Court, would judge the constitutionality of federal acts and, in case of a violation, determine the proper "mode and measure of redress."[29] One proper measure, said South Carolina's John C. Calhoun three decades later, was nullification by a state convention; another, he and other defenders of "southern rights" said, was secession.

In December 1860, South Carolina secessionists led the way. In a "Declaration of the Causes of Secession" a state convention accused the northern states of denouncing "as sinful the institution of slavery," of permitting antislavery societies to assist slaves to escape, and of inciting slave rebellions. The new president, the convention charged, intended to exclude slavery from the territories and to wage war upon it until it was abolished in all the southern states, thus depriving them of their equal rights in the Union. Therefore, the convention solemnly declared, South Carolina had resumed "her position among the nations of the world, as a separate and independent State."[30]

On this issue Lincoln's history differed from Jefferson's as expounded in his Kentucky Resolutions. Lincoln professed to have first learned the history of the Revolutionary generation from another source. In his youth, he recalled, he had read "Parson" Mason L. Weems's eulogistic biography of George Washington. He remembered Weems's account of the "struggles for the liberty of our country.... I recollect thinking then ... that there must have been something more than common that those men struggled for; ... something even more than National Independence; ... something that held out a great promise to all the people of the world to all time to come." Lincoln was now "exceedingly anxious that this Union, the Constitution, and the liberties of the people shall be perpetuated in accordance with the original idea for which that struggle was made." This, he said, placed upon him a task "greater than that which [had] rested on Washington."[31]

Lincoln's interpretation of the Constitution and of its authors' intentions drew heavily on the speeches and writings of the nationalists of the 1820s and 1830s. They were the ones who had developed the first systematic argument supporting the idea of a perpetual Union. His debts were especially great to Daniel Webster and to President Andrew Jackson's Proclamation on Nullification of 1832. Contrary to the secessionists, in Webster's and Jackson's history, as in Lincoln's, the Union was older than the states. It was formed, Lincoln argued in his first inaugural address, by the Revolutionary Continental Congresses and confirmed by the Declaration of Independence, which proclaimed the freedom of the "united colonies" from British rule. The Union was further matured, he continued, "and the faith of all the then thirteen States expressly plighted and engaged that it should be perpetual, by the Articles of Confederation. And finally, in 1787, one of the declared objects for ordaining and establishing the Constitution, was 'to form a more perfect union.'" But if one or more states can lawfully destroy the Union, Lincoln asserted, "the Union is *less* perfect than before the Constitution, having lost the vital element of perpetuity." At this point Lincoln's history becomes a bit problematic, because the Constitution says nothing explicitly about perpetuity. Still, if one accepts his assumption that perpetuity is an essential ingredient of perfection, his argument from the preamble is plausible enough.

Accordingly, Lincoln held "that in contemplation of universal law, and of the Constitution, the Union of these states is perpetual." Having reached that conclusion, he suddenly changed his argument and thereby almost conceded that the authors of the Constitution had failed to provide the words that he needed to place his historical interpretation beyond dispute. "Perpetuity," he now postulated, "is implied, if not expressed, in the fundamental law of all national governments. It is safe to assert that no government proper, ever had a provision in its organic law for its own termination." Therefore, he could contend quite accurately that secessionists could not destroy the Union "except by some action not provided for in the instrument."[32] That was perhaps his strongest historical argument, one that secessionists never attempted to refute. However, they could claim in turn that he could not stop them without some action of equally questionable constitutionality. In the end, neither Lincoln nor the secessionists could overcome these historical ambiguities. Thirty years earlier, John Quincy Adams had written sadly, "It is the odious nature of the question that it can be settled only at the cannon's mouth."[33] And so it was.

Southern secession and the resulting Civil War seemed to produce a significant change of emphasis in Lincoln's ideas about historical causation. During the sectional conflict of the 1850s he had balanced his moral feelings about slavery with a tolerant environmental determinism, which he believed controlled, or at least limited, the choices open to individuals. From this perspective, although determined to prevent slavery from entering new territories, he could not and did not hold the present generation of southerners morally responsible for the slavery that they had inherited. He would not interfere with slavery in the southern states, leaving to the future the manner of its ultimate extinction. "If we were situated as they are," he once said, "we should act and feel as they do; and if they were situated as we are, they should act and feel as we do." On another occasion he noted that "some southern men do free their slaves, go north, and become tip-top abolitionists; while some northern ones go south, and become most cruel slave-masters."[34] In short, it all depended on where one lived.

On the eve of his inauguration, however, Lincoln suggested that human affairs were affected not only by secular environmental restraints but also by an all-powerful deity whose intervention sometimes shaped the course of history. In a speech before the New Jersey legislature he declared that he would be "most happy indeed" to be "a humble instrument in the hands of the Almighty" for preserving the gains that humanity had won through the American Revolution. As the war progressed, his conviction of a divine purpose increased, but why the bloodshed must go on so long was beyond his understanding. In the summer of 1862, in a private memorandum, he wrote: "In the present civil war it is quite possible that God's purpose is something different from the purpose of either party. . . . I am almost ready to say this is probably true—that God wills this contest and wills that it shall not end yet. . . . He could give the final victory to either side any day. Yet the contest proceeds." The following year, in a proclamation appointing a day of national fasting, he asked, "may we not justly fear that the awful calamity of civil war, which now desolates the land, may be but [God's] punishment, inflicted upon us, for our presumptuous sins, to the needful end of our national reformation as a whole people?"[35]

Until the summer of 1863 Lincoln's reflections on the will of God as a force in history had not affected his determination to wage the war solely to preserve the Union and the ideals upon which it was founded. But in its third year his vision broadened and, shaken by the ever-mounting casualties, he began to perceive the war as a conflict not only to defeat the southern Confederacy but also to purge the land of slavery. Then he discovered a reason for the war's long duration. In a letter to a Kentuckian in April 1864 he observed, "Now, at the end of three years struggle the nation's condition is not what either party, or any man devised, or expected. God alone can claim it. Wither it is tending seems plain. If God now wills the removal of a great wrong, and wills also that we of the North as well as you of the South, shall pay fairly for our complicity in that wrong, impartial history will find therein new cause to attest and revere the justice and goodness of God."[36]

Lincoln's new vision was fully revealed in his memorable second inaugural address. Here, as he subordinated the struggle for the Union to the approaching end of slavery, he also abandoned his secular view of history and resigned himself to serving as an instrument in the hands of his God. "The Almighty has his own purposes," he confessed. "If we shall suppose that American Slavery is one of those offences which, in the providence of God, must needs come, but which, having continued through His appointed time, He now wills to remove, and that He gives to both North and South, this terrible war, as the woe due to those by whom the offence came, shall we discern therein any departure from those divine attributes which the believers in a Living God always ascribe to Him? Fondly do we hope—

fervently do we pray—that this mighty scourge of war may speedily pass away." Yet, Lincoln feared that it may be God's will "that it continue, until all the wealth piled by the bond-man's two hundred and fifty years of unrequited toil shall be sunk, and until every drop of blood drawn with the lash, shall be paid by another drawn with the sword."[37]

One final question must be raised about Lincoln's historical perspective. Did his environmental determinism of the 1850s and, during the war, his view of himself as a mere instrument implementing the will of his God leave any room for human choice and for the responsibility of individuals for what they do? He must have thought so, because he had praised the Revolutionary fathers not as instruments of the Almighty but as autonomous men whose achievements were the result of their own wisdom and courage. Perhaps Lincoln's wartime view of his historic role as God's instrument—always a dangerous and often a deadly illusion, we have learned—was more a solace to him in the time of his own urgent need than a more general explanation of historical causation.

In any case, in his second annual message to Congress, Lincoln spoke as one who believed that men and women did, after all, for good or ill, have a hand in choosing their destinies. "Fellow-citizens," he warned, "we cannot escape history. We of this Congress and this administration, will be remembered in spite of ourselves. No personal significance, or insignificance, can spare one or another of us. The fiery trial through which we pass, will light us down, in honor or dishonor, to the latest generation."[38] If one detects here a conflict in Lincoln's history between individual responsibility and historical determinism, dictated either by the secular environment or by the will of God, one must admit that it is a conflict that still troubles historians today.

Notes

1. Richard N. Current, *Speaking of Abraham Lincoln: The Man and His Meaning for Our Times* (Urbana: University of Illinois Press, 1983), 126.

2. Current, *Speaking of Abraham Lincoln*, 126–45; David McCullough, *Truman* (New York: Simon and Schuster, 1992), 837–38.

3. Roy P. Basler, ed., Marion Dolores Pratt and Lloyd P. Dunlap, asst. eds., *The Collected Works of Abraham Lincoln*, 9 vols. (New Brunswick: Rutgers University Press, 1953–55), 2:249 (hereafter cited as *Collected Works*); Current, *Speaking of Abraham Lincoln*, 138–39.

4. Garry Wills, *Inventing America: Jefferson's Declaration of Independence* (New York: Random House, 1978), xix.

5. *Collected Works*, 1:108.

6. Ibid., 1:109–13.

7. Ibid., 1:113–14.

8. For the psychoanalytic argument, see Edmund Wilson, *Patriotic Gore: Studies in the Literature of the American Civil War* (New York: Oxford University Press, 1962), 106–8; George B. Forgie, *Patricide in the House Divided: A Psychological Interpretation of Lincoln and His Age* (New York: W. W. Norton, 1979), passim; Dwight G. Anderson, *Abraham Lincoln: The Quest for Immortality* (New York: Knopf, 1982), 68–78; and Charles B. Strozier, *Lincoln's Quest for Union: Public and Private Meanings* (Urbana: University of Illinois Press, 1987), 56–61. For the critique, see Harry F. Jaffa, *Crisis of the House Divided* (New York: Doubleday, 1959), 182–232; Current, *Speaking of Abraham Lincoln,* 140; Don E. Fehrenbacher, *Lincoln in Text and Context* (Stanford: Stanford University Press, 1987), 282; and Garry Wills, *Lincoln at Gettysburg: The Words That Remade America* (New York: Simon and Schuster, 1993), 79–83. For a debate on the issue, see Gabor S. Borritt, ed., *The Historian's Lincoln: Pseudohistory, Psychohistory, and History* (Urbana: University of Illinois Press, 1988), 211–312.

9. *Collected Works,* 3:374–76.

10. Ibid., 1:8, 15.

11. Robert W. Johannsen, *Stephen A. Douglas* (New York: Oxford University Press, 1973), 401–34.

12. *Collected Works,* 2:240–42, 249–50, 274–75, 361, 3:307–8. Lincoln gave Jefferson a more consistent antislavery record than he deserved. For his position on both slavery and race, see John C. Miller, *The Wolf by the Ears: Thomas Jefferson and Slavery* (New York: Free Press, 1977); Winthrop D. Jordan, *White Over Black* (Chapel Hill: University of North Carolina Press, 1968), 429–81.

13. *Collected Works,* 2:278, 3:454–57, 467–68, 484–86.

14. Ibid., 2:318.

15. Ibid., 2:491–92, 3:18, 117, 407.

16. Ibid., 3:522–38.

17. Kenneth M. Stampp, *America in 1857: A Nation on the Brink* (New York: Oxford University Press, 1990), 93–95; Johannsen, *Douglas,* 570–72; Robert W. Johannsen, ed., *The Lincoln-Douglas Debates of 1858* (New York: Oxford University Press, 1965), 33. The best study of the Dred Scott case is Don E. Fehrenbacher, *The Dred Scott Case: Its Significance in American Law and Politics* (New York: Oxford University Press, 1978).

18. *Collected Works,* 2:404–5, 3:179.

19. Ibid., 2:405–6, 520, 546.

20. Ibid., 2:499–501.

21. Ibid., 2:406–7, 3:220, 302.

22. Stampp, *America in 1857,* 112–13; Kenneth M. Stampp, ed., *The Causes of the Civil War,* rev. ed. (New York: Simon and Schuster, 1991), 111.

23. James G. Randall, "A Blundering Generation," in *Lincoln the Liberal Statesman* (New York: Dodd, Mead, 1947), 36–64; Avery Craven, *The Coming of the Civil War* (New York: Scribner's, 1942), 2; Avery Craven, *The Repressible Conflict* (Baton Rouge: Louisiana State University Press, 1939), 5, 63–64. For a critique of Civil War revisionism, see Kenneth M. Stampp, *The Imperiled Union: Essays on the*

Background of the Civil War (New York: Oxford University Press, 1980), 191–245.

24. Collected Works, 3:87, 310–11, 4:14–30.

25. Ibid., 3:315.

26. Stampp, The Imperiled Union, 3–10. See also Paul C. Nagel, One Nation Indivisible: The Union in American Thought, 1776–1861 (New York: Oxford University Press, 1964), and Alpheus Thomas Mason, "The Nature of Our Federal Union Reconsidered," Political Science Quarterly 65 (Dec. 1950): 502–21.

27. Stampp, The Imperiled Union, 20–22; Nagel, One Nation Indivisible, 13–31.

28. Stampp, The Imperiled Union, 13–14, 22–24; Merrill D. Peterson, Thomas Jefferson and the New Nation: A Biography (New York: Oxford University Press, 1970), 610, 623–24, 772, 1003.

29. Peterson, Jefferson, 612–14.

30. Frank Moore, ed., The Rebellion Record, 12 vols. (New York: G. P. Putnam, D. Van Nostrand, 1861-68), 1:3–4.

31. Collected Works, 4:190, 204, 226, 235–36.

32. Ibid., 4:264–65, 432–36; Stampp, The Imperiled Union, 11–12.

33. Calvin Colton, ed., The Private Correspondence of Henry Clay (New York: A. S. Barnes, 1855), 313.

34. Collected Works, 2:230, 255.

35. Ibid., 4:236, 5:403–4, 518, 6:156.

36. Ibid., 7:282, 301.

37. Ibid., 8:333.

38. Ibid., 5:537.

Chapter Two

Lincoln's Narrative of American Exceptionalism

JEAN H. BAKER

Narrativity certainly in factual storytelling and probably in fictional storytelling as well, is intimately related to, if not a function of, the impulse to
moralize reality, that is to identify it with the social system that is the
source of any morality we can imagine ... this value attached to narrativity
as a representation of real events arises out of a desire to have real events
display the coherence, integrity, fullness and closure of an image of life
that is and can only be imaginary.[1]

In the late 1830s Abraham Lincoln began to write a historical narrative
that, like all good stories, had a plot, a central subject, villains and heroes,
a well-marked beginning, and a setting along with the necessary dynamic
metaphors and tropes that accompany any well-conceived tale. From its
beginning, Lincoln's depiction employed the traditional ingredients of
conflict, crisis and resolution, suspense, and enigma, although because
his political drama unfolded throughout his life and was not finished at
the time of his death, its ending was never certain. His point of view
shifted, over time, from that of the omniscient observer to the first-per-
son voice when he became the protagonist of his story. Ultimately, Lincoln came to see the Civil War as a narrative whose outcome God would
determine.

Lincoln did not develop the threads of his narrative systematically;
instead, they emerged spontaneously throughout his life in speeches, letters,
and public messages. To Lincoln, this tale of his nation was not manifest in
any more formal sense than premonitions and dreams, whose plots, increasingly in the last year of his life, he shared with his wife and secretaries.
Bernard Bailyn has provided a useful distinction between manifest and
latent history—the latter referring to the patterns later observers fathom

as they survey the landscape of a subject from a perspective unavailable to contemporary participants. Granted such an interpretation, Lincoln unconsciously put forth a descriptive narrative, but only in retrospect is his historical story, itself a part of the awakening of American nationalism, apparent.[2]

Unlike such professional novelists of his time as Nathaniel Hawthorne, Herman Melville, and Susan Bass Warner, who completed their novels and short stories and then moved on to something else, Lincoln pursued one grand narrative for more than a quarter of a century. Despite this difference, he shared many similarities with the novelists of the mid-nineteenth-century American Renaissance of letters, although he read little of theirs or any generation's fiction. He did not need to, for as Richard Hofstadter once wrote, "The first author of the Lincoln legend and the greatest of Lincoln dramatists was Lincoln himself."[3]

Besides his own imagination and his nation's history, Lincoln's dramatic sense was heightened by his reading of Shakespeare, especially by three of that playwright's tragedies with highly developed plots—*Hamlet, Richard III,* and *Macbeth.* And as a young man Lincoln had been impressed by John Bunyan's *Pilgrim's Progress,* the tale of a Christian hero who left behind his own people so that he might reach the Heavenly City. Apparently, Lincoln had also been entranced by literary adventures and romance. Once he told his cousin Dennis Hanks, who complained that the exotic tales of *Arabian Nights* and *Aesop's Fables* were "a pack of lies," that they were "mighty fine lies." But Lincoln was too much a public man to find his narrative in the sentimental fiction of his day or the unrealistic fantasies of the past. Instead, his understanding was shaped by the vision of his first party—the Whigs and its leader Henry Clay.[4]

Like Bunyan and Shakespeare and Clay, Lincoln wrote for a vast audience. In one form or another, most Americans know at least parts of a story that came to include the author as a principal agent of his plot. Most of Lincoln's tale was well-told in the chaste style that the critic Edmund Wilson once complimented as "more efficient . . . , terser and less pretentious" than other writers of his time.[5] Such spare prose separated him from nineteenth-century authors of lush expression. But he shared with the best of them a compelling subject, and, like some of them, Lincoln personified his theme, thereby attaining the power of human identification that has always marked good literature and made it more popular reading than the dry abstractions of politicians. Moreover, he understood the power of expression, once commenting that "he who moulds public sentiment is greater than he who makes statutes."[6]

Lincoln did not go so far, however, as the Baltimore author and Know-Nothing propagandist Anna Ella Carroll, who, in *The Great American Battle,* named her central character "America" and provided "him" with dialogue. (A forgettable sample has America saying to his mother, "Oh God! What a day was that day I took a stand in the front of nations.") But because Lincoln's text was no less than American exceptionalism—a nineteenth-century version of the trials and tribulations, tests and triumphs of the nation he called in his annual message to Congress in 1862 "the last best hope of earth"—his story relied on the fiction of a collective American identity, a form of the national character that came to fascinate social scientists in the twentieth century. In time, Lincoln's exposition became an instructive classic and an exhibit of nineteenth-century presentations of the doctrine of American exceptionalism.[7]

Lincoln began writing his historical drama in his much-remarked Lyceum Address delivered in Springfield in January of 1838. At the time, he was twenty-eight and had little reason to suspect, despite the distance he had already traveled from his hardscrabble days as a farm boy on the middle border, that he would become a central figure in his own story. The subject of Lincoln's speech was how and whether the extraordinary political institutions of the United States could be sustained in the face of challenges of a different sort to the next generation of Americans. As James Russell Lowell had written, "It is only first-rate events that call for and mould first-rate characters."[8]

What then was left for ambitious sons? Lincoln wondered. Could they sustain the exceptionalism of the new republic that, according to this prescient young Springfield lawyer, would never be overrun by "some transatlantic military giant . . . even with a Buonaparte for a commander," but which instead would face internal tests?[9]

Thus Lincoln began his story, as fiction writers are, or were, accustomed to doing, at the beginning, with the creation of the United States of America —a republic with noble institutions. He also assumed the novelist's prerogative of a dramatic opening, analogous to the traditional fictional framework of a central character's journey from birth into the world—a pilgrim's progress, or, in this case, the journey of a unique society from birth onward. "In the great journal of things happening under the sun," Lincoln wrote in the second sentence of his Lyceum Address, "we, the American People, find our account running." As with any hero embarking on a perilous life journey, the course of the Union contained classic possibilities for declination, deterioration, and corruption, especially because the system of government established at its birth should be the future for all humanity.[10] That exalted status of responsibility was what worried Lincoln, whose use of personification led him to humanize the nation into a person, subject to the stages of man from infancy to old age.

In Lincoln's rendering of these themes in the Lyceum speech, the sons of the Founders—his generation—were denied the opportunities for greatness afforded their sanctified fathers who fought the American Revolution and then wrote the Declaration of Independence and the Constitution. The heroic Founders had taken possession of the land and built "a political edifice of liberty and equal rights." They sought immortality through acts of creation. "If they succeeded, they were to be immortalized; their names were to be transferred to counties and cities, and rivers and mountains; and to be revered and sung and toasted through all time. . . . They succeeded."[11]

Unlike most Americans in the 1830s, Lincoln feared that the challenge to heroic America's survival loomed in lawlessness, which was demonstrated by lynchings and the disorder of Jacksonian mob rule in Mississippi, Missouri, and elsewhere. Like an adolescent tempted by evil, the nation faced the onslaughts of potential tyrants and the seductions of misplaced passion as well as a generation of ambitious demagogues raised not with republican virtue but with prosperity. Only by discipline and "reverence for the laws" could the unique goodness of America be maintained. Thus Lincoln located the heart of his subject in its self-governing institutions established by the people who, like parents, had created this marvelous offspring.[12]

Instead of placing his discussion of these civic questions within the more formal oratorical conventions of the day, which often rendered public issues impersonal even in an age that savored politics, Lincoln used the family metaphor so familiar to his generation. Domesticity had become the central topic of nineteenth-century authors of fiction, and so it was appropriate for Lincoln's narrative. Thus the central tension he developed in his first chapter is that of family tension occurring in the house of the Union—the ancient, Oedipal conflict of a virtuous father and possibly prodigal son. No wonder a generation of historians led by George Forgie and Charles Strozier have fixed their psychoanalytic gaze on this as Lincoln's symbolic personal patricide. But the trope is also part of a story that merged Abraham Lincoln's public and private understandings into a continuing political drama.[13]

Having established dramatic conflict, Lincoln continued his story in the 1850s. That is not to say that he did not think about the progress of America—and even add to a characterization of personified nationality—during the 1840s. On the contrary, by the end of that decade he had grafted onto his subject a devotion to Henry Clay's American System, with its internal improvements, banks, and implicit commitment to state-supported development. Now his central character—the exceptional Union—carried a new virtue to the world: economic opportunity in the land of the free, where all laborers could rise, improve their condition, and, as he told Kentucky's Cassius Clay in a possibly apochryphal tale, presume that the man who made the corn ate the corn.[14]

As Lincoln expressed this idea in the 1840s, "To [secure] to each labourer the whole product of his labor or as nearly as possible is a most worthy object of any good government."[15] In such a characterization, American exceptionalism was expanded beyond self-government to represent, in the cliché of the eighteenth century, "the best poor man's country in the world." As Lincoln later asserted, "Many independent men everywhere in these states, a few years back in their lives were hired laborers. The prudent, penniless beginner in the world, labors for wages awhile, saves a surplus with which to buy tools or land for himself; then labors on his own account another while, and at length hires another beginner to help him."[16]

In his 1852 eulogy, Lincoln praised Henry Clay as "burning with a zeal for its advancement, prosperity and glory, because he saw in such, the advancement, prosperity and glory, of human liberty, human right and human nature. He desired the prosperity of his countrymen because partly they were his countrymen, but chiefly to show to the world that freemen could be prosperous." Like Lincoln, Clay was an authentic American who had come to summarize the nation. In America's journey toward becoming a showplace for the rest of the world, prosperity became part of a national moral obligation.[17]

During a decade in which the author took his place in the Illinois state legislature and in the U.S. Congress, this view of American exceptionalism reflected his own story. Ambitiously, autobiography conflated with narrative exposition. In practical terms, Lincoln's fast-growing, right-to-rise America required various institutional supports and public props to prosper. In particular, Lincoln's Union needed to go to school, education being "the most important subject which we as a people can be engaged in."[18]

As the author moved beyond his personal parochialism, so his imagined nation abandoned the Illinois localism that had proved so harmful by exacting from promoters the direct benefits of a railroad terminus and a cash subsidy from every town on the line. Lincoln's America must be a national entity not, as his principal opponent Stephen Douglas insisted, a network of different localities. Thereafter what impaired the general welfare—whether slavery or secession—became an obstacle to exceptionalism.

By the 1850s, in the second part of his narrative of American exceptionalism, threatening external events earlier suspected—the background that plays such a critical role in all good dramas—engaged the American Launcelot. The drumbeat of sectional controversies and public policies designed to solve them—from the Compromise of 1850 to the Kansas-Nebraska Act of 1854 and the Dred Scott decision in 1857—had shattered the father-Founders' containment of slavery. Young America was now challenged by what Lincoln had introduced in his first chapter as "the approach of danger. . . . As a nation of freemen, we must live through all time, or die by suicide."[19] And the resolution of this struggle had implications beyond the boundaries of the United States, for in the agency of the Union was entrusted freedom and liberty for all humanity.

Again the author relied on a family metaphor from a family book full of stories—the Bible—to make his point. In the House Divided speech, delivered when he accepted the Republican nomination for the U.S. Senate in 1858, Lincoln described the dilemma of America as that of a divided personality. The nation could not survive half slave and half free, but must become all one thing or the other, a point not intended to support or predict abolitionism (as his political opponents charged), but rather built into Lincoln's view that the nation was perpetual—a living body, in his imagination, whose separation was as ridiculous as truncating a man at his waist. Maturing America would perhaps be subverted by the extension of domestic slavery (the inclusion of the adjective *domestic* suggested a family drama) from its opportunity to serve as an exemplar to the world to whom God had entrusted freedom. Or, the Union might live up to the expectations of its fathers and serve as a global messenger of republican liberty to the world.

In the debates with Stephen Douglas that followed the House Divided speech, Lincoln described the characteristics that made America exceptional. By this time, like most of his countrymen, he found the nation a unique expression of government, sanctioned by a beneficent God "who had shielded America against unfriendly designs from abroad."[20] Given his understanding of history as a story, Lincoln transformed cold theorems into the personal characteristics of human beings. In the process, he glorified America's ability to govern itself and argued that slavery, which he humanized into a cancer or wen, was intended for extinction by the Founders. (Surely Lincoln's impressive use of such metaphors derived from his understanding that American history is a narrative.) As he said in the debate. held in the canal town of Ottawa in the northern part of Illinois, "If we would arrest the spread of [slavery]—if we would place it where Washington, Jefferson and Madison placed it, it would be in the course of ultimate extinction, and the public mind would be at rest in the belief of its ultimate extinction."[21]

More than a homely medical image of reification, the cancer of slavery emerged, in Lincoln's vision, as a moral defect. Thereby Lincoln appropriated to the United States an ethical sensitivity lacking in other societies and separating youthful America from old, decadent Europe. "I hate this [indifference to slavery] because it deprives our republican example of its just influence in the world and enables the enemies of free institutions to taunt us as hypocrites."[22] And in 1860 he again personalized an abstract subject by characterizing the South's refusal to accept a Republican president as "a highway man [who] holds a pistol to my ear and mutters through his teeth, 'Stand and deliver, or I shall kill you, and then you will be a murderer!' "[23]

Although he accused Stephen Douglas of callousness on the issue of black slavery, Lincoln's America was nonetheless white. He explained this discrimination in his debate in Charleston, Illinois: "While [the two races] remain together there must be the position of superior and inferior, and I as much as any other man am in favor of having the superior position assigned to the white race."[24] Thus Lincoln's persistent notion of transplanting American Africans to various parts of the world was grounded in his belief that the nation's exceptionalism would be undermined in a biracial society. And only when Lincoln found a place in his narrative for black soldiers—"some black men who can remember that with silent tongue and clenched teeth and steady eyes and well-poised bayonet they have helped mankind"—did he drop his proposals for colonization.[25]

Moral, intelligent, hard-working, disciplined, on the rise, committed to freedom, and an exemplar for all humanity, Lincoln's protagonist was now threatened by a secret plot organized by villains calculating his destruction. Again Lincoln emphasized narrative exposition as a way to make sense of the events of his time. And, as was the case with most of Lincoln's ideas, he shared this concept of conspiracy with many Americans—North and South, Democrat and Republican—for the belief was a legacy of the Revolutionary fathers operating in the political culture of eighteenth-century republicanism. Thus while Stephen Douglas transformed Lincoln into an abolitionist plotting to disrupt the peace, Lincoln accused the incumbent senator of being part of a secret cabal to nationalize slavery. The charges of a slave power conspiracy were hardly new, although Lincoln's transformation of Douglas into a plotter was novel. It further displays Lincoln's tendency to transform public events into a story, thereby highlighting moral issues as narrative habitually does.[26]

In his House Divided speech and in the Ottawa debate, Lincoln personalized the conspiracy theme, telling the story of four men named Stephen (Douglas), Roger (Taney), Franklin (Pierce), and James (Buchanan) who were building a frame house that represented, in his parable, national slavery. If all the pieces fit together with one common missing piece, "We find it impossible to not believe that Stephen and Franklin and Roger and James, all understood one another from the beginning and all worked upon a common plan or draft drawn before the first lick was struck."[27] What Lincoln feared was the possibility of a judicial conspiracy, perhaps in the Court's ruling in the *Lemmon v. the People* case making its way through the system and that, given the preferences of the Taney Court, might apply the principles of Dred Scott more precisely to northern states.

Through his conspiracy story Lincoln resolved a central dilemma in his epic: the paradox of evil in a heroic society now headed for possible disintegration. Yet the nineteenth century was a romantic age that preferred happy endings, and the claim of a conspiracy identified a few evil agents intent on destroying the "last best hope of earth." Attributing disruption to a handful of subversives, Lincoln could absolve the people and adhere to his view that the Union was perpetual and indivisible. But this understanding required heroes to oppose evil, and thus a sense of dramatic opportunity accompanied Lincoln to the White House. Later, his policies of reconstruction for the liberated states of Tennessee and Louisiana also displayed this conviction that the sins of the Confederacy rested with a few conspirators, not the southern people.

In 1861 the great crisis of Lincoln's life-narrative arrived, and his final depiction of it appears in public documents written after his election to the presidency and the South's secession. Even before he was inaugurated, American exceptionalism had emerged as "the central idea, some basic belief or principle from which all minor thoughts radiate." Not by chance did his Gettysburg Address, along with the Second Inaugural the most compelling of his wartime statements, employ a narrative structure that began with Lincoln's effort to locate his story in time and place with the now immortal words "four score and seven years ago."

Earlier he had used an analogy familiar to a generation accustomed to conceptualizing nationhood as a ship of state. As he said in February, 1861, "I understand a ship to be made for the carrying and preservation of the cargo, and so long as the ship can be saved, with the cargo, it should never be abandoned. This Union should likewise never be abandoned unless it fails and the probability of its preservation shall cease to exist without throwing the passengers and cargo overboard."[28]

The nation's cargo represented, of course, those special characteristics of the United States—representative freedom for all, economic opportunity, an end to slavery, and constitutional liberty. Such baggage—perhaps, more accurately, such a compass—made the ship of state worth saving, as he explained in his famous letter to Horace Greeley. In turn, the protection of what made the United States different and better than the rest of the world underwrote any extension of presidential authority. Even his assumption of the power to organize for war emanated from the republican correction of a past when kings "had always been involving and impoverishing their people in wars." Meanwhile, "the free institutions we enjoy have developed powers and improved the condition of our people beyond any example in the world."[29]

The test of American exceptionalism continued throughout the Civil War. In time, Lincoln came to see the conflict as God's judgment on Americans and, through them, all humanity. But the judgment was beyond human agency to understand, much less dispose. In his first message to Congress on July 4, 1861, Lincoln described the political crisis as "embracing more than the fate of these United States. . . . It presents to the whole family of man the question, whether a constitutional republic, or a democracy— a government of the people, by the same people—can, or cannot, maintain its territorial integrity, against its own domestic foes."[30]

By 1864 even the secular activity of his reelection signified more than any personal or party triumph, and for "the most reliable indication of public purpose in this country" Lincoln gave thanks to "Almighty God for having directed my countrymen to a right conclusion."[31]

In the final resolution of the story, even though he might expect to lead the United States for a second term, Lincoln no longer saw himself as a protagonist. In narrative terms his voice changed as he became a mortal agency of the Almighty. The powerful statement of this new understanding came in his Second Inaugural Address, which contained language that was explicitly religious. By this time the president defined slavery as more than a blight on his nation's institutions. Now, slavery might be that offence for which Americans must suffer:

> The Almighty has His own purposes. . . . If we shall suppose that American Slavery is one of those offences which, in the providence of God, must needs come, but which, having continued through His appointed time, He now wills to remove and He gives to both North and South, this terrible war, as the woe due to those by whom the offence came, shall we discern therein any departure from those divine attributes which the believers in a Living God always ascribe to Him? Fondly do we hope—fervently do we pray—that this mighty scourge of war may speedily pass away. Yet if God wills that it continue until all the wealth piled by the bond-man's two hundred and fifty years of unrequited toil shall be sunk, and until every drop of blood drawn with the lash, shall be paid by another drawn with the sword . . . , so it must be said "the judgments of the Lord, are true and righteous altogether."[32]

It was the nation's virtuous uniqueness, a moral good dependent on its political order, and ultimately the providence of the Almighty that became the "electric chord" of Abraham Lincoln's historical narrative. Such a point of view was hardly original—however extraordinary its expression— but instead framed the political culture of his time. From the Democrats Lincoln gathered his idea of a white society, although his version was less aggressive and held out for blacks at least a restricted economic equality. He borrowed his sensitivity to an innocent young republic embarking on a political pilgrimmage from that party's Young Americans, of whom his political opponent Stephen Douglas was a charter member. But Lincoln's characterization of America's messianic role had no room, as Douglas's did, for exploits below the Texas border or in the Caribbean islands.

From the Know-Nothings, whom he could not join because of their exclusionism against "foreigners and catholics," Lincoln gathered his comparative framework, his linking of despotism to Europe, and his understanding of the personification of America.[33] From his own life history, he drew an understanding that what he had accomplished in the United States could not be duplicated in Greece or Russia or even in England—the latter a place for, as Disraeli once said, "the few, the very few."[34] From his mentors in Springfield, he absorbed the regnant nationalism of his time as leaders like Edward Baker—whose name his second son bore—inveighed for "shouts of Union as the perpetual author of hope and joy to be repeated by a thousand advancing generations."[35] From the providential legacy of Protestantism, Lincoln derived the conviction, as he told an audience in Trenton on his way to Washington in 1861, that the "United States was on its way to becoming God's almost Chosen People."[36] And during his presidency he came to see his role in this story of a nation that held out promise "to all people of the world for all time to come" as God's agent, "the representative man of the moment in the hands of the Almighty" who had become "a humble instrument" working God's unknowable will.[37]

Lincoln's narrative of exceptionalism remained comparative and unremittingly committed to the Union's superiority "as a means to inspire the hearts of men everywhere in the world."[38] Yet in an irony that might have disappointed Lincoln, after the hero's assassination, in an act some of his contemporaries read as their president's obligatory sacrifice for the perpetuation of the Union, the associated principles of American uniqueness and exceptionalism, and God's Providence deteriorated into arrogance in foreign policy. Lincoln was ambivalent about war, but war came to be a catalyst of national pride. America soon considered itself the best and by the end of the nineteenth century, and especially in the twentieth century, dubbed by Henry Luce as "the American Century," needed no measuring rod but itself. Lincoln's idea that America must be pure to be messianic disintegrated until the messenger was good simply because he was American.[39]

Notes

1. Hayden White, "The Value of Narrativity in the Representation of Reality," in On Narrative, ed. W. J. Mitchell (Chicago: University of Chicago Press, 1981), 14, 23.

2. Bernard Bailyn, "The Challenge of Modern Historiography," *American Historical Review* 87 (Feb. 1982): 1–24.

3. Richard Hofstadter, *The American Political Tradition and the Men Who Made It* (New York: Vintage Books, 1960), 94.

4. Keith Jennison, *The Humorous Mr. Lincoln* (New York: Crowell, 1965), 4.

5. Edmund Wilson, *Patriotic Gore: Studies in the Literature of the American Civil War* (New York: Oxford University Press, 1962), 639–40.

6. Harold Holzer, *The Lincoln-Douglas Debates* (New York: HarperCollins, 1993), 75.

7. Anna Ella Carroll, *The Great American Battle; or, The Contest between Christ and Political Romanism* (New York: Auburn, Miller, Orton, and Mulligan, 1856), 90. For a recent analysis of the historiography of the concept of American exceptionalism, see Michael Kammen's insightful "The Historiography of American Exceptionalism: A Reconsideration," *American Quarterly* 45 (March 1993): 1–43.

8. Quoted in George Forgie, *Patricide in the House Divided: A Psychological Interpretation of Lincoln and His Age* (New York: W. W. Norton, 1979), 63–64.

9. Roy P. Basler, ed., Marion Dolores Pratt and Lloyd P. Dunlap, asst. eds., *The Collected Works of Abraham Lincoln*, 9 vols. (New Brunswick: Rutgers University Press, 1953–55), 1:109 (hereafter cited as *Collected Works*).

10. *Collected Works*, 1:108.

11. Ibid., 1:108–15, quotation on 113. For an evocative discussion of the Lyceum Address, see Forgie, *Patricide in the House Divided*, 55–86.

12. *Collected Works*, 1:112.

13. Forgie, *Patricide in the House Divided*; Charles Strozier, *Lincoln's Quest for Union: Public and Private Meanings* (Urbana: University of Illinois Press, 1987).

14. Allen Thorndike Rice, ed., *Reminiscences of Abraham Lincoln by Distinguished Men of His Time* (New York: North American Publishing, 1886), 297.

15. *Collected Works*, 1:412.

16. Kammen, "The Problem of American Exceptionalism," 8; *Collected Works*, 5:52.

17. Fred Somkin, *Unquiet Eagle: Memory and Desire in the Idea of American Freedom 1815–1860* (Ithaca: Cornell University Press, 1967), 29; *Collected Works*, 2:126.

18. Gabor Boritt, *Lincoln and the Economics of the American Dream* (1978; rpt. Urbana: University of Illinois Press, 1994), 43; Gabor Boritt, "The Right to Rise," in *The Public and Private Lincoln*, ed. Cullom Davis et al. (Carbondale: Southern Illinois University Press, 1979), 57, 69.

19. *Collected Works*, 1:109.

20. Ibid., 8:55.

21. Holzer, ed., *The Lincoln-Douglas Debates*, 65. For another interpretation of Lincoln's use of metaphors, see James McPherson, "How Lincoln Won the War with Metaphors," R. Gerald McMurtry Lecture, Lincoln Museum, Ft. Wayne, Ind., 1985.

22. Holzer, *The Lincoln-Douglas Debates*, 60–61.

23. *Collected Works*, 3:547.

24. Holzer, *The Lincoln-Douglas Debates*, 290.

25. *Collected Works*, 2:453.

26. David Zaretsky, *Lincoln, Douglas and Slavery: In the Crucible of Public Debate* (Chicago: University of Chicago Press, 1990), 103–7.

27. Holzer, *The Lincoln-Douglas Debates*, 65; *Collected Works*, 3:20.

28. Ibid., 4:233, 2:385.

29. Ibid., 1:451, 4:430–31, 437, 440.

30. Ibid., 4:426.

31. Ibid., 8:101.

32. Ibid., 8:333.

33. Ibid., 2:323.

34. Quoted in Harry V. Jaffa, *Crisis of the House Divided: An Interpretation of the Issues in the Lincoln-Douglas Debates* (New York: Doubleday, 1959), 83.

35. Paul Nagel, *One Nation Indivisible: The Union in American Thought* (New York: Oxford University Press, 1964), 81.

36. *Collected Works*, 4:236.

37. Ibid., 4:236.

38. Ibid., 1:438.

39. Gabor Boritt, "Abraham Lincoln: War Opponent and War President," in *Lincoln the War President* (New York: Oxford University Press, 1992), 181–211.

Chapter Three

🦋

Emancipating the Republic: Lincoln and the Means and Ends of Antislavery

PHILLIP SHAW PALUDAN

It is one of the commonplaces of Lincoln scholarship that each generation seeks to "get right with Lincoln."[1] David Donald, Don Fehrenbacher, Mark Neely, Gabor Boritt, and most thoroughly now Merrill Peterson, have all demonstrated the ways in which Americans have turned to Lincoln over the years to support their political positions or to anoint and exemplify their hopes and dreams.[2]

Yet this ongoing struggle for Lincoln's blessing has often resulted in a series of alternate Lincolns, either/or Lincolns. This may simply be a result of the fact that emphases change over time; and one aspect of Lincoln seems more relevant or more appealing at any one time. But too often one finds publicists, politicians and scholars not just revealing one of many sides of a complex man, rather one finds them insisting that they have the true Lincoln which others distort or ignore. Lincoln is found, rather than sought. He becomes part of a polemic rather than an inquiry. When that happens, I believe, this very complex and admirable man becomes part of the problem, rather than part of the solution. Instead of providing, out the rich and subtle complexity of thought that he generated, new ways of seeing and solving problems, he helps adversaries dig in and reinforce their positions.

In such an environment, when factions use the nation's most subtle thinkers to reinforce their polemics, societies can get stuck. They get stuck because they are unable to think clearly about how to achieve their best hopes. Their ideas and institutions have been captured by ways of thinking that do not allow new paths and saving directions. William Butler Yeats knew such a time when "the falcon cannot hear the falconer" when "the best lack all conviction while the worst are full of passionate intensity." Voices rise and the politics of fear replaces the politics of hope. Lacking positive and protean visions we know the weakness of every alternative. The cacophony rises: "liberals are liars"; "conservatives are extremists"; vote against this, vote against that. It is a familiar song. It is at such times, as E. J. Dionne has noted, that Americans hate politics and politicians. They also fear and distrust lawyers as standing for the worst of the nation's values.[3]

Lincoln lived in a time somewhat like this, and he was a politician and a lawyer. His nation was stuck on the issue of slavery. Lincoln's task was to get it unstuck—to find a way for the nation to think about its hopes, ideals, and institutions in better ways. We might say new and better ways, but I think he might have said older and better ways. He looked for ways that fulfilled the nation's promises. He would have to show the nation that law and politics—what I call the political constitutional system—could work to fulfill the best hopes of this land. Being the kind of man he was, he had no alternative but to embrace the political constitutional system to achieve the ideal of equality and thus kill slavery.

I think that Harry Jaffa understood this Lincoln best. Speaking of the Emancipation Proclamation, he observes, "In a sense it is true that Lincoln never intended to emancipate the Negro: what he intended was to emancipate the American republic from the curse of slavery, a curse which lay upon both races, and which in different ways enslaved them both."[4]

Jaffa is clearly right about Lincoln's actions during the war, but the insight applies equally well to Lincoln's efforts before Sumter. It was then that he developed a way of thinking about the nation and about slavery that would ultimately free the Republic. To understand that emancipation, it is necessary to understand the powerful and wide-ranging impact of slavery. The power of slavery consisted of more than the immediate force that whites could use upon blacks, more than whips and guns and shackles and threats to separate families. The power was sustained by "a lock with a hundred keys," as Lincoln said. And the keys were held throughout the nation in the form of ideas that whites held that protected slavery. Racism was the most potent of these ideas, yet equally potent was the belief, in North and South, that the rule of law, and hence the Constitution itself, somehow protected slavery. Reinforcing that belief were the arguments, by Stephen Douglas especially, that democracy was compatible with slavery. Two ideas and institutions that whites treasured, that were part of their daily experience and enduring self-image, had thus been almost captured by slavery. Unless slavery could be separated from them, it might endure forever. It was Lincoln's prewar task to emancipate whites from these ideas.[5]

Before the conflict began, Lincoln had begun the process of emancipating the Republic. What he did before the war made it possible to free the slaves during the war and connect emancipation with the other goals of the war, saving the Union and preserving the Constitution. But connecting Lincoln to both equal liberty and the rule of law, especially in the prewar years, is not an easy task because there is a powerful Lincoln who stands in the way. Lincoln's words and deeds make him compelling, and we not only want to get right with Lincoln, but we also want him to guide us as we face our problems.

There is no more compelling contemporary problem than defining and securing equality. And because he was the great emancipator, nothing seems more natural than to turn to Lincoln on the topic, as historians and the general public have done so passionately. Historians and the public have created and admired a man whose foremost contribution was freeing the slaves, overcoming constitutional obstacles and transcending the conservative impulses of mere Union-saving as he did so.[6]

In Garry Wills's view, he is the idealist for equality whose "words . . . remade America" by changing the way Americans think about the meaning of the nation and the Constitution. Wills believes that Lincoln thought that the "Declaration somehow escaped the constraints that bound the Constitution. It was free to state an ideal that transcended its age, one that serves as a touchstone for later strivings." Wills sees Lincoln as a twentieth-century egalitarian, a champion who could master modern states' rights advocates, from Wilmore Kendall in 1963 to Robert Bork, Edward Meese, and Ronald Reagan in the 1980s, who denied that equality was a national commitment. Wills argues that the Gettysburg Address made advancing equality a federal responsibility. The instrument of that advance was the use of the "Declaration. . . . as a way of correcting the Constitution itself." The flawed Constitution must be redeemed by a glorified Declaration that would advance the modern struggle for equality. The rule of law must be rescued by an appeal to something nobler.[7]

Understandably, Lincoln the egalitarian, not the constitutionalist, is compelling in the age of the Second Reconstruction. Americans in the last third of the twentieth century live in a world of 'Freedom Now.' Equality's greatest modern hero, Martin Luther King, Jr., spoke for a higher law and met often bloody opposition from those who wrapped themselves in the constitutional rhetoric of states' rights and interposition. When the specific words of segregation were stricken from constitutional law, "institutional racism" remained, perhaps even more insidious than its blatant, ugly, brutal parent. In 1987, as the nation celebrated the bicentennial of the Constitution, the contrast between constitutionalism and a commitment to equality may have reached its most respectable peak. Thurgood Marshall, who was the first black justice of the Supreme Court and who had fought racism from within the legal system for decades, publicly doubted that blacks should rejoice: "Commemorating the Wrong Document?" he asked. Here was a disturbing and forceful contrast between constitutional order and equality.[8]

Historians contributed to the contrast. They had been engaged in discussions that split Lincoln the constitutionalist from Lincoln the liberator. They debated whether Lincoln was devoted to the Declaration of Independence *or* to the Constitution. The two documents stand at the foundation of what the country is and define the terms and possibilities for the polity. The Constitution is admired for the machinery that established national supremacy and preserved a Union, the Declaration for proclaiming the ideal that "all men are created equal" and resting legitimate government on that ideal. Reflecting the modern egalitarian consensus, the authoritative *Abraham Lincoln Encyclopedia* says, "As an antislavery man, Lincoln had a natural affinity not for the Constitution (with its compromising protections of the slave interest) but for the Declaration of Independence."[9] The powerful Lincoln that stands in our way is Lincoln the egalitarian, the defender of the Declaration rather than the Constitution.

I think this view of Lincoln is wrong. And I think that if we accept it without qualification we weaken our faith in the ability of political-constitutional institutions to achieve our egalitarian ideals. When we lose that faith, we have seriously crippled our ability to reach such ideals at all. Ironically, if Lincoln the emancipator overcomes Lincoln the constitutionalist, the possibility for securing equality will be weakened.

The point to remember, if we wish to understand the past and enhance Lincoln's relevance to modern times, is this: He was equally committed to the political constitutional system and to the ideal of equality. Both mattered profoundly to him, and he believed that one could not be achieved without the other. He fashioned a connection between them, not during the war years, but before.[10]

Before the war, the nation witnessed a great debate about the viability of its institutions, a discussion provoked by the presence of slavery in a nation that proclaimed equality. Of course, the debates between Lincoln and Douglas are well known, but during the late 1850s the nation experienced a three-cornered debate. Lincoln faced Douglas, but Douglas introduced a third party—Roger Taney and the Supreme Court's Dred Scott decision. Douglas and Taney represented two ideas. Douglas represented himself as the spokesman for democracy. He argued that the people of a territory or state could decide for themselves whether they wanted slavery. The great principle of self-government, of democracy in action, was the sovereignty of the people. He called it "popular sovereignty." Democracy, Douglas said, could legitimately endorse slavery. And, turning the proposition around, if someone attacked the people's decision about slavery, that someone—Lincoln, for example—would be challenging democratic self-government.

Then Douglas injected Roger Taney into the debate, and Taney, as chief justice of the U.S. Supreme Court, represented the voice of the Constitution. Douglas pointed out that the nation's highest tribunal in the Dred Scott decision had protected slavery in the territories. According to the Dred Scott decision, the Framers of the Constitution believed in slavery and endorsed its expansion. Again turning the proposition around, if someone—Lincoln, for example—attacked slavery, he attacked the Constitution.

Faced with the propositions that democratic self-government and the Constitution protected slavery, some turned against this debased rule of law. Demanding the equality of all people as promised in the Declaration of Independence, abolitionists such as William Lloyd Garrison said, "To Hell with the Constitution." Garrison burned copies of the Constitution in public, and some of the era's best and brightest agreed that law-breaking was necessary to attack slavery. Harriet Beecher Stowe indicted lawyers along with politicians and market-driven flesh peddlers as responsible for slavery. Emerson called the fugitive slave law a "filthy enactment," and vowed, "I will not obey it by God!" Thoreau wrote Civil Disobedience to insist that breaking the law was the only recourse in a society in which respecting the law meant protecting slavery.

The ideas were noble, but dangerous in a society that respected law so passionately. The Constitution, almost since its creation, has been the nation's "uncrowned king." Americans overwhelmingly have debated alternatives in constitutional terms. To call a law unconstitutional has either ended the debate or inspired a countercharge also made in constitutional terms. Few people in the nation's history have ever successfully answered the argument that a position is constitutional by saying, "Big deal!" or "So what?" Burning the Constitution, whether literally or figuratively, is like burning the flag. It burns people up. Respect for the Constitution and the processes it establishes are basic to being an American. However divided we may be by race, class, gender, or ethnicity, the one thing that unites and defines Americans is the political-constitutional process. As Senator Christopher Dodd, among others, has said, "Our means are our ends." There is, therefore, a great deal at stake in the process of getting right with the Constitution and the rule of law.

Lincoln faced the formidable challenge of proving Taney and Douglas wrong. He had to show that the Constitution and the democratic process supported his position and that of his party, that "all men are created equal" included, to some degree or other, black people as well as whites. The alternative to slavery did not have to be law-breaking or anarchy. Douglas and the Democratic party he represented insisted at almost every opportunity that Lincoln and the Republican party were abolitionists who threatened the established order and endangered the constitutional process. Lincoln's job was to refute that assertion and show how order and justice, the Constitution and the Declaration's faith in equal liberty, could be reconciled.

Although the dominant modern writing about Lincoln has emphasized his egalitarian ideas, a truer Lincoln is found by revealing his more dominant side. That does not mean that we must substitute Lincoln the lawyer for Lincoln the emancipator. It does mean that we must respect the fact that this very complex man was both, and one depended on the other. Lincoln's commitment to the existing order shaped the way he integrated the Declaration's ideals into the system of order at the core of his personality and beliefs. It is a story of evolution.

In the early days of his life, Lincoln paid minimal attention to the Declaration's ideals. He was working his way into, and then shaping, the institutions that defined the status quo. He was part of the establishment in at least two critical senses. Economically, he was a successful lawyer whom the major business in the state, the Illinois Central Railroad, hired to defend its interests. More viscerally, Lincoln had worked his way up to this position from the bottom. Starting as a landless, uneducated laborer separated by choice from his father's support and backing, such as it was, he advanced in the system whose major myths eulogized just such a rise. His personal experience both validated and personified that myth.[11]

Lincoln built his economic security on the two occupations most entwined with the system: He was a lawyer and he was a politician. His law practice required that he know the rules and procedures that settled disputes and distributed resources. For years of his life he traveled the circuit in Illinois, without the respite of home for many weeks at a time, absorbed in the camaraderie and the contests of argument and negotiation, and he learned to link fellowship and vocation. Because he was the most admired and welcomed of his colleagues in this arena, he could hardly escape believing that things went well there. The law and the environment of lawyering, of making the system work, were integral to Lincoln's life.

And, as Herndon said, "Politics were his life." He spent seven formative years in the Illinois state legislature, one term in Congress, and maneuvered and manipulated the political system throughout his mature years, working out political bargains in which ambitious men might take turns holding public office. His papers are interwoven with lists and evaluations of vote totals as well as letters discussing which candidates would get the most votes where and why. And he reveled in it. There, in the public sphere, doing the public's business, Lincoln replicated his legal career—admired and enjoyed by colleagues, forming coalitions, logrolling, forging majorities, compromising, and cajoling. He had seen and shaped politics with considerable pleasure and frequent success.

Lincoln's private and personal values strongly emphasized order. The climb out of rural poverty had shown him the need for the mind to overcome a life controlled by nature and circumstance. His experiences showed the terror of the loss of reason. He had been present, and only sixteen, when young Matthew Gentry, a companion in Indiana, suddenly went insane. The memory haunted him for years. He did not drink alcohol because it made him feel "flabby and undone." He studied the six books of Euclid's *Geometry* in order to train himself to think carefully and keenly, a regimen that paralleled his reading of the law. Thus the utopia he envisioned was of a "happy day when all appetites controlled, all passions subdued, all matters subjected, *mind*, all conquering *mind* shall live and move." If ever a man had reason for devotion to the system, the establishment in all of its manifestations, it was Abraham Lincoln.[12]

The public political environment in which he matured also inspired commitment to order. As Jacksonian democracy rose it was accompanied by mob rule and by vigilante attacks on abolitionists, bank officers, gamblers, and blacks. Jackson inspired establishment leaders to fear that things were not going their way; one in fact called Jackson "a concentrated mob." In this environment Alexis de Tocqueville worried about "the tyranny of the majority" and lauded local self-government institutions as a remedy. Anti-Jackson politicians formed the Whig party, built on challenges to Jackson's "mobocracy" as well as in support of government aid for economic development. Although President Jackson had said, "Never for a moment believe that the great body of the citizens . . . can deliberately intend to do wrong," Lincoln was dubious. His view of "the people" consistently was cast within discussions of government, laws, and the need for restraint. He was so little committed to Jackson's shibboleth that although he analyzed other political concepts at length he gave posterity a thirty-three-*word* definition of democracy. Lincoln was no democrat as the word was understood in his century. It is not surprising that he left the Democratic party his father had supported and joined the Whigs.[13] This anti-Jacksonian frame of mind positioned Lincoln to not be disarmed by Douglas's incantations about popular sovereignty.

Thus young Lawyer Lincoln cast the balance between the accomplishments of 1776 and those of 1787 by arguing that the Constitution and the institutions it established were fundamental. Speaking in early 1838 at the Young Men's Lyceum of Springfield on "the perpetuation of our political institutions," he noted that with Jefferson and the other Framers dead a new generation had to achieve their ideals by respecting the institutions the Founders had made, not simply by proclaiming their principles. With the men of the Revolution gone, succeeding generations could fulfill their mission by making reverence for the Constitution and the laws "the political religion of the nation. . . . as the patriots of seventy six did to support the Declaration of Independence. . . . so to the support of the Constitution and the Laws, let every American pledge his life, his property and his sacred honor."[14]

The Constitution was thus the means to the Declaration's ends. But how? At first Lincoln was not very clear about that. He was not even very clear about what the ends of the Declaration might be with respect to equality. During the 1840s and early 1850s he was essentially satisfied with the course of events, too busy building a career to attend to the issue seriously.

Clearly, Lincoln hated slavery in principle. "If slavery is not wrong, nothing is wrong," he told a correspondent in 1864. "I cannot remember when I did not so think, and feel." He cared about the suffering of the slaves, but his sympathy was held in check by other commitments. Until the institution reached out to trouble and threaten the overall operation of the polity, he was content to stick to his law business, and even within that business to defend at least one slave-chaser's right to his chattel.[15]

He understood, but would not join, abolitionist organizations that attacked the personal and human horrors of the institution. Lincoln first spoke publicly against slavery in 1837. He joined another Springfield lawyer and Whig to protest against resolutions that attacked abolition societies and defended states' rights to property in slaves. Lincoln called slavery unjust and bad policy but asserted that abolition societies "tend[ed] rather to increase than to abate its evils." In July 1848 he supported the Wilmot Proviso and challenged the expansion of slavery into the territories. But his challenges to that expansion came while defending the Whig party's overall program against charges that the Free-Soil party was a better choice than his own. The existing party system was adequate to deal with all the evils of society. In 1852 Lincoln was still defending the established polity, emphasizing that devotion to the rule of law would somehow keep alive the Declaration's principles. In his eulogy to Henry Clay he applauded his "beau ideal of a statesman" for both opposing slavery and maintaining respect for the Union and the laws. In the campaign of that year Lincoln again linked his opposition to slavery with respect for the political-constitutional system. Arguing that the Whig party would oppose slavery more faithfully than the Democrats, he still disavowed opposition outside existing institutional channels. Noting that Democrats were trying to use Seward's inflated rhetoric to discredit the Whigs, Lincoln embraced order. He said that if Seward's "higher law" speech "may attempt to foment a disobedience to the constitution or to the constitutional laws of the country, it has my unqualified condemnation." Lincoln did hate slavery, but he was aroused to passionate opposition only when it threatened the constitutional-political system.[16]

Until 1854 Lincoln saw little threat. It was enough to decry democratic excesses, to deflate occasional overenthusiastic bombast, to temper abolitionist zeal with rather standard admonitions about respecting order, and to deplore slavery but basically to let the issue alone. It is likely that Lincoln believed that the processes begun in 1787 were quietly and inevitably keeping the promises of 1776.

But on May 22, 1854, everything changed. The House of Representatives passed the Kansas-Nebraska bill, repealed the Missouri Compromise, and opened a million square miles of territory to slavery. More than that, it proclaimed loudly that the constitutional system no longer incorporated promises of equal liberty. Stephen Douglas had found that popular sovereignty justified repealing the Missouri Compromise. The Illinois senator argued that the people of a territory could do whatever they chose about slavery there. The law of the land was now neutral on equal rights. Popular government meant that some men could deny equal liberty to others because of the color of their skin. The Declaration's idea that "all men are created equal" had been banished from its constitutional context.

Lincoln's task was to put it back into that context, to retain the ties between declaring ideals and constituting a political-constitutional culture to realize them. Throughout the 1850s he began to think more deeply about the interrelationships between the documents and principles of 1776 and 1787. The result would be an even greater interconnection between constitutional process and egalitarian promises. But creating that interconnection would have a consequence. It would require that Lincoln change the nature of Jefferson's 1776 promise.

Lincoln's reconciliation of the Constitution and the Declaration rested on both logic and history. In the first place, he simply equated self-government with equality. Challenging the Kansas-Nebraska bill, he wrote, "At the foundation of the sense of justice there is in me" is the "proposition that each man should do precisely what he pleases with all that is exclusively his own." That was at the core of self-government. "No man is good enough to govern another man, *without that other's consent.*" And this principle, "the sheet anchor of American republicanism," rested on the ideals of the Declaration that "all men are created equal," which meant that governments had to rest on the consent of those men. "Allow all the governed an equal voice in the government, and that, and that only is self government." The ideal of equality was manifested in acts of self-government. Ideal depended on process. Expanding slavery imperiled process and ideal.[17]

Lincoln also used history to integrate ideals and institutions. Douglas had employed history to show that the Framers wanted to leave slavery alone and hence had no moral objection to it. Chief Justice Taney in the Dred Scott case had used history (Harold Hyman calls it "twistory") to argue that the Declaration of Independence revealed the proslavery ideals of the Framers. Both Taney and Douglas thus created a proslavery founding and a proslavery Constitution.

When Lincoln turned historian, the past that he found and fashioned revealed freedom's Constitution, not slavery's. The angle of vision he adopted was to look into the founding years and see not two founding events but one founding age. The age of the Founders that Lincoln found turned the writing of the Declaration in 1776 and the writing of the Constitution in 1787 into one event. Eleven years passed between the two gatherings in Independence Hall, and only six men who signed the Declaration signed the Constitution. For Lincoln, however, they were essentially one meeting, bonded in the act of founding the country. In the entire corpus of his writing he never separated the two events.

And he insisted that the egalitarian principles that animated the Declaration abided in the writers of the Constitution. Speaking against the Kansas-Nebraska bill in October 1854, he noted that the writers of the Constitution thought that slavery violated basic principles, and so they never mentioned slavery in the document. And "the earliest Congress, under the constitution, took the same view of slavery. They hedged and hemmed it in to the narrowest limits of necessity." In his February 1860 Cooper Union Address, he researched the history of the Framers' world extensively to prove that they had wanted to place slavery in the course of ultimate extinction. Because almost all the Framers thought slavery was an evil that contradicted the ideal of equality, they voted frequently and consistently throughout the 1780s and 1790s, Lincoln said, to prohibit slavery in the territories. At Gettysburg he would envision a nation born in 1776 and dedicated to equality, but it was "*government* of the people by the people and for the people" that would bring to life the "equality proposition." The government he had in mind was that created by the Constitution in 1787.[18]

Lincoln stepped over the constitutional fences of the Taney Court; he moved beyond guidelines proclaimed by his Democratic opponents. And they indicted him as an enemy of the Constitution. But this was an accusation, not a legitimate verdict. Lincoln operated within the constitutional possibilities of the founding years. For him, achieving the ideals of the Declaration meant preserving the government brought forth in 1787. He referred to the idea of "Liberty to all" in the Declaration as an "apple of gold," and to the "Union and the Constitution" as "the picture of silver." Although asserting that the picture was made for the apple and not vice-versa, he also said, "Let us act, that neither picture, or apple shall ever be bruised or broken."[19]

Lincoln insisted on his devotion to the Declaration's basic ideal that all men are created equal. "I have never had a feeling politically," he said, "that did not spring from the sentiments embodied in the Declaration of Independence." His strongest charge against the expansion of slavery was that it showed how far the nation had fallen from its founding ideals. "Near eighty years ago we began by declaring that all men are created equal," he observed, "but now from that beginning we have run down to the other declaration, that for SOME men to enslave others is 'a sacred right of self government.'" Thus the rise of proslavery sentiment revealed a decline of the nation from a purer past in which the constitutional system had put slavery on a course to ultimate extinction.[20]

But if the basic ideal abided, Lincoln's political environment required changes in what the Framers meant by that ideal. These changes would highlight constitutional process. Illinois in Lincoln's time was hardly committed to racial equality; a state law of 1853 kept blacks out. The Illinois legal code forbade interracial marriage, kept blacks off juries and out of the state militia, banned black testimony against whites, denied blacks the vote, and made no provision for black schools. Racism, especially in the southern half of Illinois, predominantly settled from slave-holding states, was a powerful and practically unchallengeable notion.[21]

Thus when Lincoln challenged the expansion of slavery by proclaiming that all men were created equal, Douglas and other Democrats played the race card. They howled miscegenation and named Republicans "Black Republicans." To counter the charge Lincoln had to reassure constituents, first in Illinois, then in the Midwest and beyond as his political horizons expanded, that he did not favor Negroes voting, performing jury service, or holding office. He did believe that the Declaration's promise of equality extended to life, liberty, and the pursuit of happiness. To Lincoln in the prewar years that meant that blacks had "the right to eat the bread, without leave of anybody else, which his own hand earns." And he mocked Douglas's charges by noting that treating blacks as human beings, with rights to keep the fruits of their own labor, hardly required intermarriage. But he also knew the dangers of advocating full equality and so was pushed to temporize by speaking of an equality to come. It was clearly a more respectable position than slavery forever and the assertion that blacks were inalterably inferior in everything, but it pandered. Political prejudice on race thus played its role in moving Lincoln to a new, or at least more well-defined, position not only on what equality might mean but also on how and when it would be achieved.[22]

So did the charges that Republicans were disunionists. At times Lincoln fed those allegations—his House Divided speech spoke of the nation split in two and suggested the threat in that division by noting that *either* freedom *or* slavery must triumph. But the future president was quick to deny this accusation. What was at stake, he claimed, was a struggle for the minds of men over the question of whether slavery or freedom controlled the territories and hence the future. It was a debate that would be resolved not with invasion or threat, but through political discourse that would create a return to idealism. This reassurance actually only promised Dixie a slow death for slavery if people like Lincoln won office. But it also suggested how a healthy political-constitutional process could bring the Declaration's egalitarian promise to life. This too pushed Lincoln toward redefining the meaning of 1776.[23]

Lincoln built another element of his evolving constitutional egalitarianism thanks to Chief Justice Roger Taney. When the Supreme Court issued its Dred Scott decision Lincoln again was forced to ponder new directions. Less than a year earlier he had spoken of trusting the Court to decide the constitutional question of the exclusion of slavery from the territories. But when the decision was handed down, Lincoln enlarged his ground and expanded the arena of constitutional discussion. He flanked the decision on two sides. First, Lincoln adopted Andrew Jackson's argument that the Court did not stand alone as interpreter of the Constitution. "The Congress, the executive and the court, must each for itself be guided by its own opinion of the Constitution." Congressmen and chief executive now joined judges in the constitutional debate. The meaning of the Constitution was too important to be left to judges. Second, Lincoln posited a discussion expanded in time as well as numbers. An important judicial decision would be binding, Lincoln said, only after a long process of discussion and litigation had taken place. What legitimized such a decision was "the steady practice of the departments throughout our history," arguments in previous courts in which the decision "had been affirmed and reaffirmed though a course of years." This process of determining what the Constitution meant also involved electing to office men who would reflect public opinion on such questions. The people would join the debate to instruct their leaders and to maintain their own authority as ultimate sovereigns. The electoral process set up by the Constitution would, in time, overcome the flawed constitutional vision of the Supreme Court.[24]

Having formulated a vigorous and involved political-constitutional debate that responded to the political imperatives of his age, Lincoln was now ready to evoke a new Declaration, one demanded by the system he envisioned and the world he occupied. He did not change his commitment to equality. But where the Founders had declared all men are created equal to be a "self-evident truth" Lincoln envisioned it as a "proposition"—the word would wait until Gettysburg, the idea was present in 1857. Equality was a "standard maxim for a free society, which should be familiar to all and revered by all; constantly looked to, constantly labored for, and even though never perfectly attained, constantly approximated, and constantly spreading and deepening its influence, and augmenting the happiness and value of life to all people of all colors everywhere." And the only way for that process to occur was for constitutional government to endure. Equal liberty and the order of law were thus intertwined and interdependent.[25]

"A house divided against itself cannot stand" Lincoln had said. Yet equally destructive were conflicting national ideals: democracy and the rule of law set against equality. But Lincoln had integrated these widespread and deeply felt ideals by showing that equality could only be achieved within their institutions of self-government. The beloved Constitution was not the property of Taney and the slave owners for whom he spoke any more than the democratic self-government that Douglas endorsed required implacable racism. Lincoln had helped the nation to become "unstuck"; he had provided a way of thinking about the sectional crisis that united the nation's best and most inescapable qualities in the struggle to free the nation from slavery.

Lincoln so interwove the ideals of the Declaration with the Constitution, with the processes of self-government, that attempts to unravel the threads dissolve his thought. And such efforts also obscure the meaning of his presidency. Saving the Union and ending slavery and defending the right of the people to change governments by ballots not bullets, and thus show the world that self-government worked, were interrelated parts of what Lincoln wanted to do. And as he assumed office he took "the most solemn oath" to preserve protect and defend a Constitution that in his view embodied all of those parts.

There was irony in the fact that Lincoln in the White House had more power to preserve the Declaration's ideal than any other person in the country and had made a clearer promise to do so than almost any other public official. His attacks on slavery were eloquent enough to rally an electoral majority behind him. He had gained their support in perhaps the only way that the age permitted, by appealing to their faith that the system would work for the best of their ideals. If Taney or Breckenridge or Bell or even Stephen Douglas had his way, freedom moved to a future so distant as to be unimaginable and unacceptable to most whites and blacks. Lincoln countered that. But his process-based egalitarianism made only long-term promises. If he would have his way, he said in August 1858, "The crisis would be past and the institution might be let alone for a hundred years, if it should live so long, in the States where it exists, yet it would be gone out of existence in the way best for both the black and the white races." Somehow, the process would work for the ideal; somehow, the Constitution would implement the Declaration. The North now had the vision to believe that, but achieving it would be a complex and agonizing process for the people and the president who assumed power in 1861.[26]

Yet at least Lincoln's thought—and his education of the public in that thought—had laid the foundation for making a struggle for the Union simultaneously a struggle for the ideal of equality. The people of the North were passionate in their commitment to self-government and devoted to the Constitution as they understood it. Lincoln made it possible for that devotion to incorporate the promises of 1776 within the processes of 1787. He had begun the process of emancipating the Republic from slavery. He had suggested how the best might regain their conviction that their most admirable hopes could be achieved within the system of order they were devoted to. War might accelerate this union of equality with the rule of law even as Lincoln and the North fought to save the Union.

Notes

1. A more extended form of this essay appears in the *Journal of the Abraham Lincoln Association* 15 (Summer 1994).

2. Merrill Peterson, *Lincoln in American Memory* (New York: Oxford University Press, 1994); David Donald, *Lincoln Reconsidered: Essays on the Civil War Era* (New York: Knopf, 1956); Don Fehrenbacher, *Lincoln in Text and Context* (Stanford: Stanford University Press, 1987); Mark Neely, Jr., "The Lincoln Theme since Randall's Call," *Papers of the Abraham Lincoln Association* (1979); Gabor Boritt, *Lincoln and the Economics of the American Dream* (1978; rpt. Urbana: University of Illinois Press, 1994).

3. E. J. Dionne, Jr., *Why Americans Hate Politics* (New York: Simon and Schuster, 1991).

4. Harry V. Jaffa, "The Emancipation Proclamation," in *One Hundred Years of Emancipation,* ed. Robert Goldwin (Chicago: Rand McNally, 1964), 23.

5. Lincoln's comment about the keys is in *The Collected Works of Abraham Lincoln,* ed. Roy P. Baslez, Marion Delores Pratt and Lloyd P. Dunlap, asst. eds., 9 vols. (New Brunswick: Rutgers University Press, 1953–55), 2:403–4 (hereafter cited as *Collected Works*).

6. See my "Toward a Lincoln Conversation," *Reviews in American History* 16 (March 1988): 35–42 for literature on Lincoln the egalitarian. James McPherson, in *Battle Cry of Freedom* (New York: Oxford University Press, 1988), presents the egalitarian Lincoln. However, in "Hedgehog and the Foxes," in *Abraham Lincoln and the Second American Revolution* (New York: Oxford University Press, 1992), 128, McPherson is ambiguous on the relationship between slavery and the Constitution. On the one hand, he says that Lincoln's major belief was that constitutional

government rested on the Declaration's principle of equal liberty. Yet McPherson also argues that Lincoln's oath to protect the Constitution meant that he could not attack slavery directly because "the Constitution protected slavery" (128). In one sense this is true. It stopped federal action in time of peace from interfering with slavery in slave states. When Lincoln interfered in time of war he performed an act that would have been unconstitutional in peacetime, but the need to preserve the union made the act lawful. Yet McPherson, like most modern historians, does not note that the other elements of the constitutional system had already put slavery in peril—for example, eleven southern states in 1860–61 were very sure that the electoral process endangered slavery.

7. Garry Wills, *Lincoln at Gettysburg: The Words That Remade America* (New York: Simon and Schuster, 1992) 102, 129–47.

8. Thurgood Marshall, "The Constitution's Bicentennial: Commemorating the Wrong Document?" *Vanderbilt Law Review* 40 (1987): 1337–42.

9. Mark E. Neely, Jr., *The Abraham Lincoln Encyclopedia* (New York: McGraw-Hill, 1982), 70. Examples of arguments that Lincoln chose one of the documents over the other are found in William Gienapp, "Lincoln and Slavery," in *Lincoln on Democracy,* ed. Mario Cuomo and Harold Holtzer (New York: HarperCollins, 1990), 57; Harry Jaffa, *Crisis of the House Divided: An Interpretation of the Lincoln-Douglas Debates* (Chicago: University of Chicago Press, 1982); and Gary Jacobson, "Abraham Lincoln 'On This Question of Judicial Authority'," *Western Political Quarterly* 36 (1984): 52–70.

10. See Jaffa, "The Emancipation Proclamation," 5: "There has been a tendency to see the two phases of the war as corresponding to the phases in which, first the Constitution, and then the Declaration of Independence, were looked to for the principles which needed to be vindicated. Needless to say, this implies a tension, if not a contradiction, between these two documents, as sources and statements of moral and political obligation. But there is no evidence that Lincoln himself was ever aware of any such tension or contradiction." Jaffa also says that "there is no evidence that Lincoln . . . was ever aware of any . . . tension or contradiction between [the Declaration and the Constitution]." By that I think he means that during the war Lincoln integrated the ideals and institutions of the nation's founding. In this chapter, I provide what Jaffa omits, a description of how and why Lincoln felt that way.

11. *Collected Works,* 3:478–79: Summoning the tale in many speeches Lincoln was defining self and polity when he said, "The penniless beginner in the world labors for wages awhile, saves a surplus with which to buy tools or land for himself; then labors on his own account for another while, and at length hires another new beginner to help him." On Lincoln's climb, see Richard Hofstadter, "Abraham Lincoln and the Self-Made Myth," in *American Political Tradition and the Men Who Made It* (1948; rpt. New York: Knopf, 1973), and Boritt, *Lincoln and the Economics of the American Dream.*

12. *Herndon quoted in J. G. Randall, Lincoln: The President,* 4 vols. (New York: Dodd, Mead, 1945), 1:40n.; Stephen B. Oates, *With Malice toward None: The Life of Abraham Lincoln* (New York: Harper and Row, 1977), 13–21, 75, 77; Albert Bev-

eridge, *Abraham Lincoln, 1809–1858* (Boston: Houghton Mifflin, 1928), 533–34; *Collected Works,* 1:279 (Feb. 22, 1841).

13. See Phillip S. Paludan, " 'The Better Angels of Our Nature': Lincoln Propaganda and Public Opinion in the North during the Civil War," (Gerald McMurtry Lecture, Lincoln Museum, Ft. Wayne, Ind., 1992.

14. *Collected Works,* 1:112. By focusing on the question of Lincoln's relationship to "the fathers" that has skewed discussion of the Lyceum Address, Wills ignores the importance of the speech as illustrating Lincoln's view of law and the Constitution. See *Lincoln at Gettysburg,* 79–87.

15. *Collected Works,* 7:281 (to Albert Hodges, April 4, 1864).

16. Ibid., 1:74, 126, 260, 2:3, 5, 7–9, 11, 14, 121–30, 136, 156.

17. Ibid., 2:265–66 (Oct. 16, 1854). Jaffa, in *Crisis of the House Divided,* analyzes this argument more completely.

18. *Collected Works,* 2:247–83, esp. 274–75 (Peoria Speech), 3:522–50 (Cooper Union), 2:274–75, 318, 403–5, 453–54, 491–92, 499–501, 546, 3:29, 92–93. "Neither the word 'slave' nor 'slavery' is to be found in the Constitution," a device "employed on purpose to exclude from the Constitution the idea that there could be property in men," Lincoln said at Cooper Union.

19. *Collected Works,* 4:168–69.

20. Ibid., 4:240 (Feb. 22, 1861), 2:275 (Oct. 16, 1854).

21. V. Jacques Voegeli, *Free but Not Equal: The Midwest and the Negro during the Civil War* (Chicago: University of Chicago Press, 1967), 1–2.

22. *Collected Works,* 3:400–403.

23. Ibid., 2:461–69 (June 16, 1858).

24. Ibid., 2:354–55 (July 23, 1856), 400–403 (June 26, 1857).

25. Ibid., 2:406 (June 26, 1857). In *Lincoln at Gettysburg,* Wills has things just right with his observation that what Lincoln fears (among other things) was that Douglas would succeed in preparting the public mind for giving up the "proposition" that all men are created equal. " 'Preparing the public mind' is a thing of great importance in an age of Transcendentalism. To fall silent, or to silence others, on the very notion of equality is the ultimate self betrayal of a land that was dedicated to a *proposition*" (120). What needs to be added is that the Constitution set up the system whereby that proposition would be realized. By demonstrating that, Lincoln made even more important the open political discussion that the polity secured and by which it was nurtured.

26. *Collected Works,* 3:18 (Aug. 21, 1858).

Part Two

LINCOLN'S LEADERSHIP

Chapter Four

🏵

Abraham Lincoln and Presidential Leadership

WILLIAM E. GIENAPP

"The Presidency," Abraham Lincoln once observed, "even to the most experienced politicians, is no bed of roses. No human being can fill that station and escape censure." He was referring to Zachary Taylor's controversy-wracked tenure, but his comment aptly foreshadowed his own experience in the office a decade later. It is safe to say that the office does not hold the same appeal for a president at the end of his administration as it did when he first took the oath of office. Often the capstone of a long career in public life, the presidency brings with it not only significant responsibilities and substantial personal power, but also, even under the best of circumstances, a multitude of problems and headaches. Yet for all its trials and tribulations, the presidency remains the focus of the American political system and the most important source of national leadership.

Because of the office's importance, the problem of evaluating presidential leadership has long attracted the attention of historians and political scientists. What makes a person a successful president, what constitutes the nature of presidential leadership, and what effect a president has on the course of historical events are all critical questions. The main conclusion to be drawn from these studies is that there are no hard and fast rules for evaluating presidential performance. Similar action in a different context can often lead to strikingly dissimilar results. Efforts to predict presidential performance, based on some mixture of personality traits and prior experience, have proven misguided and fruitless. Moreover, qualities that made a president unpopular at the time often take on a glittering sheen in retrospect. One thinks of the contemporary nostalgia for Harry Truman, who left office devoid of popularity and widely denounced, but who a few years ago was being touted by, of all things, a Republican president as the exemplar of presidential leadership. Evaluating presidents is never easy, for occupants of the office confront different problems, and none presents a record of either unbroken successes or unrelieved failure. Moreover, subsequent events modify historians' attitudes toward a particular chief executive, since anticipation of future developments is a vital component of national leadership.

While the manifold difficulties of evaluating presidential leadership should not be minimized, the problem can be divided into five categories. At least since the acceptance of political parties in the Jacksonian era, a president must be the leader of his party. He relies on his party for regular support at all levels of our federal system: in Congress, at the state and local level, and in the electorate. As the chief executive officer, he is also the leader of the administration, including the cabinet, which has played widely varying roles under different presidents. Today this problem is complicated by the existence of a vast, nonpartisan, independent federal bureaucracy, but this was not the case in the Civil War era. The bureaucracy was small by modern standards, and all federal offices were appointive, so in theory the president could wield decisive control over the executive branch. The third area of presidential leadership is as head of the government. Here, relations with Congress are crucial. Whatever his role in shaping legislation, a president needs to maintain a good working relationship with Congress. Fourth, the president is responsible for the conduct of diplomatic relations and military affairs. In the twentieth century, foreign affairs have become increasingly a major area of presidential initiative, but in the nineteenth century this role was less important because the United States was not a major world power. The country fought four significant wars during that century, however, and in these conflicts the president's role in determining war policy and his performance as commander-in-chief were crucial matters. And finally, the president is the leader of the American people. As such, he has a unique opportunity to mold public opinion, rally popular support, and shape America's destiny. It is essential that a president lead public opinion, yet he must be careful as opinion changes not to be too far in front or lag too far behind the popular will. Reading and anticipating public opinion, while at the same time shaping it to political ends, is one of the most critical challenges confronting a president. Together, these categories—the president as leader of his party, his administration, the government, the military, and the people—provide a framework to assess presidential leadership.

No president has held power during a greater national crisis than Abraham Lincoln; none has made decisions that had more far-ranging significance for the nation. His election in 1860 precipitated the secession of the states of the Deep South, and shortly after he took office the Civil War erupted. His entire presidency was dominated by the monumental challenge of leading the Republic safely through a costly war of unprecedented magnitude to preserve the Union.

In evaluating presidential performance, historians have invariably placed Lincoln in the highest category, and most put him at the very top of the list, ranking him as the greatest president in American history. Yet his contemporaries did not share this opinion. Scorned and ridiculed by Democrats, he encountered hostility even from Republican leaders who denounced him as weak and ignorant. As late as the summer of 1864 a majority of Republican congressmen believed that he was unsuited to be president and doubted that he had the ability to win the war. Voicing the view of these many critics, Senator James W. Grimes of Iowa proclaimed Lincoln's administration "a disgrace from the very beginning to every one who had any thing to do with bringing it to power."[1]

And indeed, if prior experience was any guide, Lincoln seemed woefully overmatched by the crisis he faced. One of the least experienced presidents in American history, he had served one undistinguished term in the 1840s in the House of Representatives, and upon retiring failed in his effort to obtain an appointive position in Illinois from the Taylor administration. He had never held an administrative post, had made two unsuccessful attempts, in 1855 and again in 1858, to win a seat in the United States Senate, and had been out of public office for more than a decade prior to his nomination for president. For a variety of reasons, however, the delegates at the 1860 Republican national convention believed that he was the strongest candidate they could run, and that none of the other leading contenders could be elected. Dismissing the possibility of secession, the delegates and party leaders gave little consideration to Lincoln's qualifications or his ability to lead the country. Republicans concluded that Lincoln had the best chance of winning, and that was sufficient.

Lincoln's prepresidential career, while undistinguished by national standards, nevertheless offered evidence of the abilities he would bring to the presidential office. He had worked diligently to hold the badly factionalized Republican party together in Illinois; his moderation and conciliatory approach made him a force of unity within its ranks, and as a result he enjoyed a broad base of popular support within the state. He had also observed James K. Polk's controversial presidency while serving in Congress, from which he had absorbed some crucial lessons about presidential leadership and partisanship in wartime. Polk's administration also offered instructive lessons concerning presidential-congressional relations. Finally, Lincoln had been an effective spokesman for the Republican party in Illinois politics and had run a particularly skillful campaign in 1858 when he challenged Stephen A. Douglas for his seat in the Senate; although defeated in that race, he championed fundamental party principles while simultaneously displaying great skill at maneuvering for political advantage. During these years of preparation, he developed the personal and political qualities that would be so important to his accomplishments as president.

When he assumed the presidency, Lincoln faced one overriding challenge: to preserve the Union. By the time he was inaugurated, seven southern states—the entire Deep South—had seceded from the Union and established a rival government, the Confederate States of America. Unwilling to recognize the legality of secession, Lincoln tried to continue the existing stalemate over Fort Sumter in Charleston harbor, but his decision to send a relief expedition to the besieged federal garrison led instead to war. In response to the attack on Fort Sumter, Lincoln adopted the policy of using whatever military force was necessary to maintain the Union. Like Confederate leaders, he initially anticipated that the war would be short and require only limited use of force, but by the time the conflict ended four years later, it had cost more than 620,000 American lives and billions of dollars of national treasure.

Presiding over the government during the greatest crisis in the nation's history, a crisis entirely without precedent, Lincoln had to feel his way as he went, adopting and altering policies as he thought best. "The dogmas of the quiet past, are inadequate to the stormy present," he told Congress in 1862. "As our case is new, so we must think anew, and act anew."[2] Still, his fundamental goal remained to save the Union without destroying democracy in the process. That he succeeded was his greatest accomplishment as president.

I

Abraham Lincoln's folksy wit, rollicking sense of humor, and gift for storytelling are well known, yet he was also a brooding, introspective individual with a deep sense of personal reserve. He had only one intimate friend in his entire adult life, Joshua Speed, who left Springfield and moved back to Kentucky when Lincoln was thirty-two, after which the intensity of their friendship waned. He had many acquaintances but few friends, bared his soul to no one, and throughout his political career made crucial decisions alone. These qualities continued after he went to Washington. As president, he did not surround himself with a group of political cronies and had no close personal associates or intimate advisers. Instead, he gathered advice from various quarters, listened patiently to friend and foe, and then made up his mind in solitude.

Lincoln entered the White House determined to be his own man. In organizing his administration, Lincoln confronted the thorny problem of selecting a cabinet. Because Lincoln appointed all of his major rivals for the 1860 Republican nomination to his cabinet—probably in part so he could keep an eye on them—it was considerably a more distinguished collection of individuals than most cabinets in American history. It had two outstanding members in Secretary of State William H. Seward and Secretary of the Treasury Salmon P. Chase; Caleb B. Smith in the Interior Department was the sole nonentity, and only one member, the incompetent Secretary of War Simon Cameron, brought disgrace upon himself. Censored by the House for the widespread corruption in his department, Cameron eventually resigned and was replaced by Edwin Stanton, a far abler man.

One reason Lincoln appointed so many rivals to cabinet posts is that he intended to rely on his own judgment rather than that of his advisers. Unlike the presidencies of James Monroe or Franklin Pierce, to take two examples, the cabinet was never a policymaking body under Lincoln, who looked to its members more to administer than to determine policy, especially with respect to the conduct of the war. Cabinet meetings often seemed to have no particular point, discussions frequently meandered without any clear focus, and Lincoln rarely took votes on any matters under deliberation. Secretary of the Navy Gideon Welles grumbled that cabinet meetings were "infrequent, irregular, and without system." Seward was frequently absent, preferring to deal with the president privately, and Secretary of War Stanton, fearing leaks, refused to discuss matters concerning the war in the presence of other members. The self-righteous Chase, convinced that his talents eclipsed those of all other members of the administration, including the president, was especially irritated by this state of affairs. He complained that "we . . . are called members of the Cabinet, but are in reality only separate heads of departments, meeting now and then for talk on whatever happens to come uppermost, not for grave consultation on matters concerning the salvation of the country."[3]

Confident in his ability to decide on the correct policy, Lincoln never felt bound by the prevailing opinion in the cabinet, and he rarely revealed his thoughts until he had made up his mind. Leonard Swett, an Illinois political associate, commented, "He always told only enough of his plans and purposes to induce the belief that he had communicated all; yet he reserved enough to have communicated nothing."[4] In its first meeting, a majority of the cabinet favored abandoning Fort Sumter, yet Lincoln kept his thoughts to himself and reserved judgment. On April Fool's day, when Seward modestly offered to be the premier of the administration and assume the burden of leadership, Lincoln tactfully but firmly rebuked his secretary's pretensions by affirming that *he* intended to fulfill that responsibility. Critical decisions such as army commands and military strategy were not discussed by the cabinet. Nor was the decision to issue the Emancipation Proclamation, the most crucial decision Lincoln made in the entire war, a collaborative one. When he presented a draft of the proclamation to the cabinet on July 22, 1862, Lincoln prefaced the discussion by telling its members: "I have got you together to hear what I have written down. I do not wish your advice about the main matter—for that I have determined for myself. . . . If there is anything in the expressions I use, or in any other minor matter, which anyone of you thinks had best be changed, I shall be glad to receive the suggestions."[5]

With the exception of Chase, Lincoln remained on good personal terms with his cabinet members, but he relied on them as advisers only selectively. He sought their advice on matters germane to their department, and usually deferred to their judgment, but on other questions consulted them sporadically if at all. Welles confessed that "of the policy of the administration, if there be one, I am not advised beyond what is published and known to all," and Chase fumed that if he wanted to know what was going on elsewhere in the administration, he had to send a clerk to get a copy of the New York *Herald*.[6] After his initial misjudgment, Seward became a loyal supporter and Lincoln's most intimate official adviser. Welles, who was jealous of Seward's relationship with Lincoln, reported that the secretary of state spent "a considerable portion of every day with the President, patronizing and instructing him, hearing and telling anecdotes, relating interesting details of occurrences in the Senate, and inculcating his political party notions."[7] Yet there was no doubt that as with the other members of the cabinet, Lincoln kept the upper hand with Seward and retained the final authority for himself. Soon Seward was singing the praises of the president he had at first so badly underestimated. "Executive force and vigor are rare qualities," he noted. "The President is the best of us."[8]

Although Lincoln took a strong lead in establishing policy, he never shut himself off from dissenting points of view and was not inflexibly wedded to particular means to achieve his goals. He exposed himself to a wide range of opinion, delegated authority effectively to subordinates, and took the lead in establishing policies on matters that he considered presidential responsibility. His cabinet represented all the major factions in the party and contained the full spectrum of Republican opinion, from the radical Salmon P. Chase to the ultra-conservative Gideon Welles. Carefully balanced between former Whigs and Democrats, it included members from the Northeast, the West, and the border states.

Nor did Lincoln allow personal feelings to determine his decisions. Lincoln was "a very poor hater," a longtime Illinois associate remarked, and he was always ready to work with anyone who agreed with him on a particular matter, whatever their other differences, including men he did not like personally.[9] He kept Chase in the cabinet until 1864, despite their increasingly icy personal relations, because of the secretary's valuable service to the Union. Unlike presidents who personalized political differences, Lincoln treated each problem separately and sought to build workable coalitions around each. Lincoln's philosophy was well summarized by his advice in the 1850s to Whigs who resisted joining with abolitionists in opposing the Kansas-Nebraska bill: "Stand with anybody that stands RIGHT. Stand with him while he is right and PART with him when he goes wrong."[10] Jealousy and touchy dignity, so common among leading figures in the capital, exerted no influence on Lincoln.

Lincoln dominated and controlled his cabinet, a fact that is all the more remarkable given its distinguished members. "I never knew with what tyrannous authority he rules the Cabinet till now," John Hay, his private secretary, wrote approvingly in 1863. "The most important things he decides & there is no cavil." Even the normally crotchety Gideon Welles concluded that Lincoln alone was indispensable to the war effort. "He could have dispensed with any one of his cabinet and the administration [would] not have been impaired," the secretary observed, "but it would have been difficult if not impossible to have selected anyone who would have filled the office of chief magistrate as successfully as Mr. Lincoln."[11]

II

Lincoln also excelled as a leader of his party because he knew how to maintain good personal relations with individuals and because he paid close attention to organizational details. Political parties in the nineteenth century were held together by the glue of patronage: "to the victor belong the spoils," a New York politician once proclaimed. Consequently, Lincoln devoted considerable attention to federal appointments. On occasion he pretended to be above such sordid political details, as for example when he told a group of Pennsylvania party leaders, "You know I was never a contriver; I don't know much about how things are done in politics."[12] In truth, Lincoln probably devoted more time and energy to patronage matters than any other concern except the military. A president never has enough offices to satisfy every office-seeker, but Lincoln made effective use of the patronage because under his policy of "justice to all" he recognized all party factions in his appointments.

Lincoln had to adjudicate disputes constantly among various Republican factions in the different states, but at no time did he single out his critics for political annihilation. Even after Chase left the cabinet following his clumsy attempt to challenge the president for the 1864 nomination, Lincoln did not purge the federal bureaucracy of Chase's allies, and indeed he eventually appointed Chase chief justice of the Supreme Court. Similarly, Lincoln was caught up in the increasingly bitter fight in Maryland between Henry Winter Davis and Montgomery Blair, yet Blair remained loyal even after Lincoln, out of political necessity, dropped him from the cabinet in 1864. Despite Davis's vituperative denunciation of the president for refusing to sign the Wade-Davis bill on Reconstruction in 1864, Lincoln, sensing the shifting tide in the state's politics, extended greater recognition to Davis and the Radicals in Maryland appointments. Lincoln's adroit handling of party critics was crucial in holding the Republican party together during the war.

Lincoln possessed another vital quality for party leadership: he could take the political pounding and could not be intimidated. He stood up to an avalanche of criticism after rescinding John C. Frémont's emancipation edict in Missouri in 1861. He refused to let the radicals force his hand on emancipation in 1862 or on his policy of reconstruction in 1864. He resisted the growing popular cry for peace negotiations in 1864 and effectively deflected the issue by permitting unofficial peace commissioners to go to Richmond, a move that exposed the unwillingness of Jefferson Davis to consider anything less than southern independence. He endured calculated personal slights, social humiliation, unprecedented ridicule, and vicious criticism without descending to pettiness or vindictiveness.

Lincoln confronted a deepening division in his party, especially over the issues of slavery, war policy, and reconstruction. As the war dragged on, the Radicals became more vociferous in their condemnation of the president and his policies. But Lincoln handled this division effectively. With an eye to party harmony, he granted the Radicals honesty of purpose. As he explained to Hay, "They are nearer to me than the other side, in thought and sentiment, though bitterly hostile to me personally. They are utterly lawless—the unhandiest devils in the world to deal with—but after all their faces are set Zionwards."[13] Moreover, time and again he effectively outmaneuvered the Radicals and defeated their efforts to dictate policy. As agitation to make emancipation a Union war aim intensified in the party, Lincoln undercut the Radicals by signing the First and then the Second Confiscation Act. After signing the second act, which provided for the emancipation of any slave owned by a disloyal master, Lincoln ignored the law and continued to pursue his policy of compensated emancipation under state auspices. Radicals might fume privately, or grumble about Lincoln's lack of purpose, but they were powerless to check him. Few participated in the movement to nominate a separate ticket in 1864, and any hope to prevent Lincoln's nomination at the Union convention quickly ended with the selection of so many federal officeholders, all loyal Lincoln men, as delegates. Despite more than three years of criticism that Lincoln was too indecisive and not up to the task before him, the president was easily renominated by the Republican convention in 1864. Lincoln's ability to keep policy firmly in his hands, to retain the support of the federal bureaucracy, and gain renomination were all testimony to his effective party leadership.

III

Another critical component of presidential leadership is relations with Congress. In dealing with the legislative branch, Lincoln, despite his forceful leadership in other areas, was not an activist president in the modern sense of the term. While he recommended general policies, he normally did not submit legislation to Congress.

Lincoln's philosophy harked back to the principles of the Whig party. "My political education strongly inclines me against a very free use of any . . . means, by the Executive, to control the legislation of the country," he affirmed in a speech as president-elect. "As a rule, I think it better that congress should originate, as well as perfect its measures, without external bias."[14] Thus, although he was a firm believer in using government power to promote economic development, he showed little interest in the precise form of economic legislation passed during the war, leaving it largely to Congress to frame such important legislation as the Homestead Act, the Land Grant College Act, the protective tariff, and the national banking laws. He delegated Chase to deal with Congress on matters of taxes, bonds, and banking. Once, when the secretary of the treasury sought his advice on a financial matter, Lincoln replied with less than complete candor, "You understand these things. I do not."[15] Only Chase's insistence that the outcome in Congress hinged on presidential action induced Lincoln to lobby personally for passage of the National Banking Act of 1863, one of the few times Lincoln directly intervened to get legislation through Congress.

Lincoln's most active role in legislative matters occurred on the issue of slavery. Again, this behavior reflected his basic belief that the question of emancipation and Union war aims was his responsibility as commander-in-chief, and not that of Congress, because the Constitution gave Congress no jurisdiction over slavery in the states. As Lincoln expressed his constitutional view on one occasion, "I conceive that I may in an emergency do things on military grounds which cannot be done constitutionally by Congress."[16] In his annual message in 1861, Lincoln urged Congress to adopt a plan to finance gradual emancipation in the border states. When Congress failed to act on the matter, he sent specific legislation to Congress. In the summer of that year, when Congress passed the Second Confiscation Act, Lincoln forced a modification of the act by threatening to veto it until Congress passed an explanatory resolution meeting his objections, which it did (although he then signed the bill, he sent the veto message he had drafted to Congress anyway to indicate his unhappiness). Finally, following his reelection, he threw all of his influence behind the drive to gain the last few votes needed in the House of Representatives to pass the proposed Thirteenth Amendment abolishing slavery. He made lavish use of patronage to win the votes of a handful of northern Democrats, which enabled the amendment to pass and be sent to the states for ratification. Never before had he taken such an active role in securing legislation.

Like modern presidents, Lincoln found Congress a severe trial. Once a senator came to the White House and launched into a vituperative denunciation of the president and his policies that ended with the warning, "Sir you are within one mile of Hell!" To which a smiling Lincoln replied, "Yes, . . . it is just one mile to the Capitol!"[17] Determined from the beginning to conduct the war on policies he set, he had no illusions about the role of Congress. When the war began, he called Congress into special session to meet on July 4, thereby giving himself a free hand for more than two months. Lincoln took full advantage of this period, taking a series of steps by executive edict that clearly exceeded his legal authority. Lincoln felt he had to act decisively, which was true, but it is clear he also did not want any interference from Congress. When Congress convened, it had little choice but to ratify Lincoln's actions after the fact. Indeed, it was not just coincidence that Lincoln's most decisive assertions of presidential power usually occurred when Congress was not in session: the initial call for troops, the institution of the blockade, the revocation of Frémont's proclamation, the suspension of the writ of habeas corpus, and the announcement of the preliminary emancipation proclamation.

Still, Lincoln's relations with the legislative branch, while at times strained, never broke down completely, and in particular they were better than under either his predecessor, James Buchanan, or his successor, Andrew Johnson. This more harmonious relationship reflected in part the fact that Lincoln was much more tactful and flexible in his approach. As a minority president and the Republicans' first chief executive, Lincoln was particularly sensitive to the need to maintain party unity. He shrewdly steered a middle ground between the conservatives and Radicals in his party, satisfying neither fully but keeping both united in their opposition to the Democrats. Had he lived, he certainly would have reached some accommodation with his party critics over the question of Reconstruction. Relations between the president and Congress no doubt would have been strained at times, but they never would have reached the paralysis of the final months of Buchanan's administration or the complete rupture that occurred under Johnson.

A striking example of Lincoln's ability to outmaneuver his congressional critics was the cabinet crisis in December 1862. Egged on by Chase's allegations that Lincoln was controlled by Seward, who allegedly opposed a vigorous prosecution of the war, and that the rest of the cabinet was ignored, a committee of Republican senators came to the White House to demand a shake-up of the cabinet. Aware of the origins of this movement, Lincoln arranged for the delegation to meet with him in the presence of the entire cabinet except for Seward. With his cabinet colleagues as witnesses, Chase was forced to declare that the cabinet was in basic agreement on war policy, thus directly contradicting what he had been telling members of Congress privately. Seward had already submitted his resignation, and the next day, when a disconcerted Chase hesitantly offered his, the president eagerly snatched it from his hands. "Now I can ride," Lincoln subsequently commented, "I have got a pumpkin in each end of my bag."[18] Assuming the pose of acting in the country's best interest, he then proceeded to reject both resignations, thereby stymieing the congressional movement to reorganize the cabinet. The crisis ended with Lincoln in firm control of his administration and free of congressional dictation. As Leonard Swett, who had observed Lincoln closely for many years in Illinois politics, remarked, "He handled and moved men remotely as we do pieces upon a chessboard."[19]

Unlike a number of his predecessors, Lincoln lacked diplomatic training and took little interest in foreign affairs. Instead, he left the conduct of diplomacy largely in the hands of his able secretary of state, William Henry Seward. Occasionally Lincoln took a more active role, as, for example, when he toned down the language of Seward's instructions to Charles Francis Adams, the American minister to Great Britain, following the outbreak of war, but such action was an exception. After a rocky beginning, when Seward proposed fighting a war against a European power as the means to reunite the country, the secretary soon won the president's confidence.

Lincoln devoted his attention instead to military affairs. Taking the term *commander-in-chief* literally, he assumed an active role in the conduct of the war, both in the selection of commanders and in the determination of strategy. When the Civil War began, he was not well versed in military strategy; his military experience was limited to brief service in the Illinois militia during the Black Hawk War, which he justly lampooned in a famous congressional speech. But as the saying goes, he was a quick learner.

Lincoln was a much more activist president on military affairs than on domestic policies. His activity grew out of the sobering effect of the Union army's disastrous performance at the beginning of the war and his recognition that any blame would ultimately fall on him as commander-in-chief. As his self-confidence grew he became increasingly independent of his military advisers. This process began after the Battle of Bull Run and came to full development following the removal of George McClellan from command in the fall of 1862. As was the case with his cabinet, the president listened to advice from his generals but made strategic decisions himself.

Lincoln took control of the war effort almost in desperation. He quickly lost faith in Winfield Scott, the commanding general at the beginning of the war, who was an imposing military figure but now well past his prime. After trying the hesitant McClellan as general-in-chief, he brought Henry Halleck, the army's top theoretician who was known as Old Brains, to Washington to assume this position. Halleck's nerve failed after the second Battle of Bull Run, when, as Lincoln explained to John Hay, "he broke down—nerve and pluck all gone—and has ever since evaded all possible responsibility—[he is] little more than a first rate clerk." Henceforth Halleck limited his activity to writing orders as directed.[20] In this situation, Lincoln provided what coordination there was among the Union's armies until Ulysses S. Grant became general-in-chief in 1864.

Despite his limited military background, Lincoln displayed a keen insight into strategic questions, and his aptitude increased as the war continued. He immediately recognized the importance of the navy, and at the start of the war he imposed a blockade on the Confederacy without consulting his military advisers. Shortly thereafter, he rejected Scott's famous Anaconda Plan, which proposed to strangle the Confederacy to death by blockading the coast and seizing control of the Mississippi River; nevertheless, in contemplating it he began to develop an appreciation of the significance of the western theater in the conflict. Moreover, unlike his generals who continued to think in terms of territory, he increasingly recognized that Confederate armies and not Richmond were the Union's army main objective in Virginia. He reluctantly approved of McClellan's plan to strike at Richmond from the east in 1862 but preferred a direct thrust at the Confederate army at Manassas. A year later, now firm in his conviction and more self-confident, he instructed General Joseph Hooker, "I think *Lee's* Army, and not *Richmond,* is your true objective point."[21]

His most important insight was that the Union's strategy had to take advantage of the North's numerical superiority. In January 1862 he outlined his fundamental strategy in a letter to General Don Carlos Buell. The "general idea of this war is that we have the greater numbers, and the enemy has the *greater* facility of concentrating forces upon points of collision; that we must fail, unless we can find some way of making *our* advantage an over-match for *his;* and that this can only be done by menacing him with superior forces at *different* points, at the *same* time."[22] Unlike some of his generals, most notably the cautious George McClellan, he recognized that the war could not be won by maneuver and that hard fighting was required. And despite his reputation for being tenderhearted, he could face the arithmetic the war entailed. W. O. Stoddard recalled that in the gloom in December 1862 following General Ambrose Burnside's devastating defeat at Fredricksburg, in which the Union's casualties were 50 percent higher than Lee's, the president observed (in Stoddard's words) that "if the same battle were to be fought over again, every day, through a week of days, with the same relative results, the army under Lee would be wiped out to its last man, [but] the Army of the Potomac would still be a mighty host, the war would be over, the Confederacy gone, and peace would be won at a smaller cost of life than it will be if the week of lost battles must be dragged out through yet another year of camps and marches."[23] In essence, Lincoln's search for a suitable commander was a search for a general who understood how to make the North's numerical superiority count. When he found such a commander in Grant, he steadfastly stood by him despite the torrent of northern criticism over Grant's heavy losses in 1864 in Virginia.

Lincoln's interference with his generals' plans varied according to his personal faith in an individual. While prodding his often sluggish generals forward, he did not hesitate to intervene and counteract their plans. A good example was when he detached part of McClellan's army during the ill-fated peninsular campaign to protect Washington. He was less active in dealing with Ulysses S. Grant and William Tecumseh Sherman, who shared his fundamental strategic outlook, than he was with more laggard generals such as McClellan, Buell, and William Rosecrans. Yet even with Grant he was not reluctant to voice his opinions, and Grant's claim in his *Memoirs* that Lincoln left all military decisions to him is demonstrably false. He demurred from Grant's plan to make an overland push against Mobile and showed no interest in the general's idea of a seaborne invasion of North Carolina to disrupt Richmond's communications (Lincoln continued to insist, correctly, that Lee's army should be the Union's target in the eastern theater).

Lincoln also displayed enormous skill in his personal dealings with his generals. Nowhere was this more apparent than in his relationship with George McClellan. Cautious and indecisive, McClellan masked his deeply rooted self-doubt behind a false bravado and soaring vanity. He refused to reveal his plans and scarcely disguised his contempt for the president, whom he referred to privately as "the original Gorilla." Yet Lincoln understood that McClellan possessed organizational abilities and by instilling much-needed discipline was fashioning the Army of the Potomac into an efficient fighting force. Thus he was willing to overlook personal slights. In November 1861 he called at the general's home in Washington accompanied by Seward and John Hay. McClellan was out, and upon returning he went

to bed without receiving the waiting president. Lincoln failed to take offense, and when Hay commented afterward on McClellan's insolence, the
president quietly observed that "it was better at this time not to be making
points of etiquette & personal dignity."[24] Time and again, Lincoln displayed
extraordinary tact in dealing with his military commanders, as, for example,
in his delicate handling of prickly George Meade after the battle of Gettysburg. Lincoln was chagrined at Meade's failure to pursue Lee aggressively
after the battle, but when word of his displeasure got back to Meade, the
president soothed the general's ruffled feathers and kept him in command
of the Army of Potomac, where he continued to render vital service throughout the duration of the war.

Military performance, not personal relations or partisan affiliations,
counted most with Lincoln. He never shared the widespread hostility in
Washington to West Point men; he rejected the obtuse view of many Radicals in his party, including the leading members of the Joint Committee on
the Conduct of the War, that Democratic generals lacked the commitment
necessary to win the war; and he resisted their relentless pressure to remove
McClellan and other Democrats from command. When Ben Wade of Ohio,
one of the leading Radicals in the Senate, demanded that Lincoln remove
McClellan, the president asked whom Wade would replace him with.
"Anybody," blustered the senator. "Wade, anybody will do for you," Lincoln pointedly replied, "but I must have somebody."[25] He insisted to Republican leader Carl Schurz, who upbraided the president after the 1862
elections for giving Democrats military commands, that the war "should
be conducted on military knowledge" and not "on political affinity." Noting
that many Republicans had also received such commands, Lincoln tren-
chantly observed, "I do not see that their superiority of success has been so
marked as to throw great suspicion on the good faith of those who are not
Republicans."[26] Similarly, Lincoln displayed no concern that Grant had
been a Democrat before the war. When pious critics pressed Lincoln to
remove Grant because of his alleged drinking, he responded succinctly, "I
can't spare this man. He fights."[27]

To be sure, Lincoln's military leadership was not without its faults. He
was excessively concerned with the defense of Washington and did not
always appreciate how various forces dispersed throughout Virginia helped
defend the capital. He placed too much emphasis on liberating east Tennessee, which was a stronghold of Unionism, from Confederate control
for political rather than military reasons. His General Order No. One,
ordering all Union forces to advance on January 31, 1862, although eventually withdrawn, was so impractical as to be embarrassing. Clinging to
ineffective generals such as Buell and Rosecrans long after their shortcomings were obvious, he was also slow to recognize Grant's ability and had to

be persuaded to give Grant command in the Mississippi theater. (He subsequently acknowledged his error, however, hailing Grant's Vicksburg campaign as "one of the most brilliant in the world.")[28]

Worse, he gave too many important field commands to men appointed for political reasons. John McClernand, Nathaniel Banks, Franz Siegel, John C. Frémont, and Benjamin F. Butler were all political generals, appointed to appease various factions and gain support for the administration. To some degree, such appointments were necessary, but it was one thing to appoint these men, another to give them vital field commands. All of these individuals failed miserably in battle, and they should have been relegated to other duties more suited to their talents. It was a terrible mistake to allow Banks to head the Red River expedition, or to let Butler direct the bungled attack on Wilmington. Yet Lincoln resisted pressure from Grant to remove Butler (who was the darling of the Radicals in Congress) and, in contrast to his usual forthright acceptance of responsibility, insisted that Grant assume responsibility for sacking Butler.

On the whole, however, Lincoln was an excellent military leader. While he displayed a sound understanding of what was required to win the war, it took him time to find generals who could put these ideas into practice, and thus throughout most of the war Lincoln served as the Union's chief military strategist.

V

Another major source of power is the president's position as leader of the American people. As the only member of the federal government elected by all the people, the president is in a unique position to shape and mobilize public opinion; his relationship with the people can provide a great reservoir of strength in any clash with the legislative branch. Lincoln was a master in these matters, displaying an uncanny ability to read the public mood.

One of the most surprising aspects of Lincoln's tenure as president was his failure to make more speeches in order to rouse popular support for his policies. In this regard, he was entirely conventional, adhering to the tradition that a president refrain from campaigning or stump speaking. His reticence stood in sharp contrast to Confederate president Jefferson Davis, who embarked on several tours through the South and gave a number of speeches to strengthen southern popular resolve. Nor did Lincoln deliver any speeches to Congress; instead, he adhered to the tradition of sending his annual messages to Congress in writing. He was probably hurt by his failure to make more public speeches, since they could have been justified in terms of the great national emergency, and his career in Illinois politics made him well versed in appealing to ordinary folk. Most of his speeches were short addresses at the White House on various occasions. Longer and more frequent speeches would have provided him with an effective means to rally public opinion and win popular support.

Eschewing presidential speeches, Lincoln relied instead on the written word to convey his ideas to the people. Although he was largely self-educated, having by his calculation less than a year of formal schooling, Abraham Lincoln was an accomplished literary craftsman. His speeches and writings possess an eloquence few presidents have ever approached. Time and again during the war, in his public documents, he displayed unrivaled ability to rouse popular emotions by placing the struggle in its broadest context and rooting it in the most basic American values. In his special message to Congress on July 4, 1861, he described the war as part of the larger struggle for democracy and opportunity throughout the world: "This is essentially a People's contest. On the side of the Union, it is a struggle for maintaining in the world, that form, and substance of government, whose leading object is, to elevate the condition of men—to lift artificial weights from all shoulders—to clear the paths of laudable pursuit for all—to afford all, an unfettered start, and a fair chance, in the race of life."[29] His letter to James Conkling on emancipation and to Erastus Corning on civil liberties demonstrated his fundamental decency and good sense. The Gettysburg Address, the most famous presidential speech ever delivered, concisely stated the meaning of the war, and the Second Inaugural, given on the eve of victory, was remarkable for its humility and its compassion. Lincoln's ability to reach out to the common people of his society, from whose ranks he had risen, was manifested throughout his presidency and provided him a solid base of popular support. In fact, Lincoln was probably more popular with the people than he was with the leaders of his party.

Lincoln also possessed a sure sense of political timing, a quality aptly demonstrated by his eventual adoption of emancipation as a war aim. He avoided endorsing this policy prematurely, waiting for popular sentiment to develop while subtly leading the public mind toward the policy of emancipation. Thus in 1861 he revoked Frémont's emancipation edict in Missouri, citing its adverse effect on opinion in Kentucky and the other border states. He took similar action in 1862 when another of his generals, David C. Hunter, freed the slaves in South Carolina, Georgia, and Florida. Nevertheless, Lincoln was not significantly trailing Congress on this matter, and he was probably substantially ahead of northern public opinion. His famous public letter to Horace Greeley at the end of August 1862 declaring "I would save the Union" was actually designed to prepare the public mind for a change in policy, a change he had already decided on but announced only a month later. The black abolitionist leader Frederick Douglass appreciated Lincoln's situation. Had he immediately attacked slavery, Douglass later explained, "He would have inevitably driven from him a powerful class of the American people and rendered resistance to the rebellion impossible." To abolitionists, the president had seemed tardy, Douglass continued, but within the context of public sentiment, "a sentiment he was bound as a statesman to consult," Lincoln had acted on slavery as swiftly as possible.[30]

Throughout the war, Lincoln was guided by an understanding of the larger issues of the struggle. Instead of catering to popular passions or inflaming sectional hatreds, he upheld the ideal that this was a war to preserve democracy, not just in this country but throughout the world. He was driven by his vision of America as a land of opportunity, where everyone had the right to rise by developing their abilities to the fullest. His most fundamental belief was that equality was the nation's paramount ideal.

As the war continued, however, Lincoln embraced an expanded view of the conflict. He now saw the end of slavery as necessary to fulfill the country's destiny, and at Gettysburg he called for a new birth of freedom that would redeem the unprecedented sacrifices of the war. Just as he insisted that emancipation was a fundamental requirement for peace, so he adopted a more expansive view of black Americans' rights in the new Union. By the end of his life, he had endorsed limited black suffrage in the defeated South, although he had not accepted full equality. Still, Lincoln's capacity for growth was striking. While he never lost sight of his vision of the nation's future, that vision was not unchanging, but rather evolved and expanded in response to the war.

VI

In every regard, Lincoln was a superior president. An extraordinary politician, he knew how to assess men's character and was a master of the details of party organization. Tolerant and forbearing, he possessed a genius for getting individuals of diverse viewpoints to work together on a broad range of issues. Manifesting an uncanny feel for public opinion, he displayed a sure sense of timing, always crucial in politics. Flexible in his approach, he possessed the ability to weigh alternatives and to perceive clearly the consequences of his actions. Never losing sight of his larger objectives, he knew when to stand firm and when to compromise. Not tied to the past, he was willing to try new policies to achieve his ends, and, always ready to shoulder responsibility, he was not afraid to change his mind or admit that he had been wrong. His two secretaries, John Nicolay and John Hay, marveled over his unsurpassed ability "to still the quarrels of factions, to allay the jealousies of statesmen, to compose the rivalries of generals, to soothe the vanity of officials, to prompt the laggard, to curb the ardent, [and] to sustain the faltering."[31]

Throughout the war, in even its darkest hours, he never lost sight of why the war was being fought or lacked faith in his ability to lead the nation through the crisis. Indeed, probably his most remarkable quality as president was his unwavering belief in himself, what Welles called his "wonderful self-reliance."

Like other strong presidents, Lincoln took an expansive view of his powers. Whether he would have been as active a president had the war not occurred is doubtful since he grounded his claim of special powers on his role as commander-in-chief. The powers Lincoln exercised were breathtaking in their extent and significance. He spent money without congressional authorization, suspended the writ of habeas corpus throughout the Union, authorized military trials of civilians, proclaimed a blockade, initiated a program of Reconstruction, dictated the terms for peace, and abolished slavery by presidential edict. With remarkable deftness, he walked the thin line between failing to respond vigorously and abuse of power. Exercising unprecedented power, he was neither corrupted by it nor viewed it as an end in itself.

In contrast to modern historians, however, contemporaries did not hold Lincoln's leadership in high regard. Following the defeat at the Battle of Bull Run, Lyman Trumbull pronounced Lincoln unequal to the task before him. Three years later he had not changed his mind. Writing from Washington in February 1864, he reported that few party leaders were for Lincoln's reelection for "there is a distrust and a fear that he is too undecided and inefficient to put down the rebellion." The conservative Orville Browning, another associate from Illinois, concurred. In the same year he wrote, "I am personally attached to the President, and have . . . tried to . . . make him respectable; tho' I never have been able to persuade myself that he was big enough for his position. Still, I thought he might get through, as many a boy has got through college, without disgrace, and without knowledge; but I fear he is a failure."[32]

The contrast between historians' assessment of Lincoln and his reputation during his lifetime could not be more stark. The question arises, Why didn't Lincoln's contemporaries recognize his greatness? Why weren't the qualities historians cite as evidence of his superb leadership perceived in the same way by those who knew him personally and witnessed his presidency firsthand?

The contemporary view of Lincoln was strongly influenced by his undistinguished background. With an unexceptional political career and little national experience, he lacked presidential stature when he entered the White House. His limited education, backwoods stories, peculiar accent, awkward manner, and homely face all reinforced this image and undercut his prestige. Many observers could not get beyond his physical appearance, taking him to be nothing more than a prairie lawyer, and leading politicians in Washington, many of whom had careers at least as distinguished as his, saw no reason to hold him in awe.

In addition, as president Lincoln had to deal with some of the most divisive issues in our history, including secession, slavery, and traditional civil liberties in wartime. His policies were bound to offend large numbers of people, since passions were strong on both sides. When he tried to pursue a middle course, he ran the danger of alienating both extremes, as, for example, on emancipation. When he took a hard line, as on the draft or civil liberties, his stance intensified emotions in the electorate. Moreover, his policies were susceptible to widely varying interpretations. For example, his basic conciliatory nature could be seen as a sign of weakness or temporizing; his moderation could be interpreted as indecisiveness.

But the major handicap Lincoln labored under was the staggering cost of the war and his failure to end the conflict. Repeatedly, northern hopes for a decisive breakthrough and quick end to the war had been disappointed. The death toll mounted, the destruction escalated, generals came and went, and still the fighting continued. Always a realist, Lincoln observed at one point, "I do not need sympathy nearly so much as I need success."[33] Indeed, in the summer of 1864, with the military situation still bleak, Lincoln was certain that he would be defeated in the November election. Only Sherman's capture of Atlanta in September placed the contest beyond all doubt.

Had Lincoln been defeated in 1864, he would have gone down in history as a failure—an ineffective president who was unable to win the war, dealt ineptly with the major issues he confronted, declined to provide any direction to his squabbling cabinet, failed to heal the widening breach in his party, and headed an incompetent, corrupt, and divided administration.[34] His shortcomings would be attributed to his lack of experience and while perhaps given good marks for being sincere and well meaning, he would be dismissed as hopelessly overshadowed by the magnitude of the task before him, a glaring example of the folly of nominating such an unqualified man for president.

Historians, of course, approach Lincoln from a different perspective. They know the outcome of events and never question, as people at the time did repeatedly, Lincoln's ability to lead the nation through the most severe trial in its history. They recognize the magnitude of the problems he confronted and realize that solutions were anything but simple. They are captivated by the magic of his life, with its path from log cabin to White House, and his ultimate triumph over adversity and defeat. They are influenced by the favorable reminiscences of the Civil War generation, all written in the glow of Lincoln's sainthood following his tragic death. And try as they might, they can never fully comprehend the popular passions the war and Lincoln's policies aroused.

More fundamentally, historians' favorable assessments of Lincoln's leadership also reflect their understanding of the military difficulties confronting the Union. Not only did the Union have to overcome white southerners' nationalist commitment and break their will to fight, but it also had to wage a war over a geographic expanse greater than that of Western Europe. The southern terrain was extraordinarily varied, heavily wooded (particularly in the western theater), and traversed by poor roads. The Union navy was charged with blockading some 3,500 miles of coastline, while the army had to surmount the strategic complexities of fighting along a line of more than a thousand miles (a distance greater than from the Franco-German border to that of modern Russia). Moreover, the swampy areas in the lower Mississippi Valley and along the Atlantic Coast were very unhealthy in the summer, especially for unseasoned Union soldiers, a fact that regularly cut manpower strength in half and rendered military operations much more difficult. And, finally, the country's military leaders were not prepared to fight the kind of war the Civil War became. Their education at West Point and their experience in the Mexican War, which were based on what were by now obsolete military theories, had not trained them in the concepts of modern warfare. Thus it took time for Lincoln to find generals who saw that new strategic thinking was required. In sum, defeating the Confederacy was no simple matter, and it required not just a fearsome sacrifice—it also required time.[35]

Northern public opinion, in contrast, persistently underestimated the military challenge of defeating the Confederacy and anticipated a quick end to the fighting. Unlike modern historians, Lincoln's contemporaries failed to grasp the extent to which technology had made the defense significantly stronger than the offense, and they never perceived that as a result it was now virtually impossible to annihilate an army in battle. Instead, influenced by the Napoleonic wars early in the century, northerners expected a war of maneuver leading to a decisive battle that would bring the war to a close. Each spring northerners hailed the newest Union offensive as the campaign that would defeat the Confederacy and end the war. Even in 1864, after having these expectations repeatedly dashed, "most people," Noah Brooks recalled, "thought that General Grant would close the war and enter Richmond before the autumn leaves began to fall." Keenly aware of the public's attitude, Lincoln commented in June of that year, "The most trying thing of all this war is that the people are too sanguine; they expect too much at once."[36]

Lincoln's political standing was also hurt by popular fixation on the Virginia theater. From the beginning of the war, when Horace Greeley emblazoned "Forward to Richmond!" on the masthead of the New York *Tribune*, northerners placed an undue emphasis on the fighting in Virginia. Historians recognize that the war was won in the West, and that the Union victories there in 1862 and 1863 were serious setbacks for the Confederacy. But northerners, dazzled by Lee's military brilliance and frustrated over the Army of the Potomac's repeated failures, gave insufficient weight to the Union's victories in the western theater. They never comprehended how the Union ultimately won, and Lincoln's reputation suffered accordingly. Lincoln was not blind to this situation. Noting that northern public opinion attached more significance to the Seven Days' battles than it did to Union successes at Shiloh, New Orleans, Nashville, and Memphis, he complained in early August 1862, "It seems unreasonable that a series of successes, extending through half-a-year, and clearing more than a hundred thousand square miles of country, should help us so little, while a single half-defeat should hurt us so much."[37] With a better understanding of the military situation, historians give Lincoln's leadership as commander-in-chief much higher marks than did his contemporaries.

The final reason for Lincoln's appeal to historians is the power of his words. Historians inevitably know Lincoln through his words, through the speeches and written documents he left behind. Lincoln's gift for language was marvelous, even poetic, so much so that he is the only American president other than Thomas Jefferson whose writings can be considered literature. In his language Lincoln is at his finest. His letter to the Widow Bixby revealed his magnanimous temper and deep compassion; his Gettysburg Address is considered the supreme statement of the meaning of America; his second inaugural address displayed a profound understanding of the role of slavery in the war and the magnitude of the tragedy the nation had endured. Lincoln never lost his faith in democracy and the American people. Noting that he had "a patient confidence in the ultimate justice of the people," he asked: "Is there any better, or equal hope, in the world?" He was certain that "truth and . . . justice will surely prevail, by the judgment of this great tribunal, the American people."[38] His utterances established him as democracy's most eloquent spokesman.

Through four years of civil war, he remained immune to the war's searing hatreds. Even the most cynical critic is completely disarmed by the closing words of the Second Inaugural: "With malice toward none; with charity for all; with firmness in the right, as God gives us to see the right, let us strive to finish the work we are in; to bind up the nation's wounds; to care for him who shall have borne the battle, and for his widow, and his orphan —to do all which may achieve and cherish a just, and a lasting peace, among ourselves, and with all nations."[39] His words are like a soaring comet streaking across the humdrum political sky. More than a century after his death, the words of Abraham Lincoln still shine brightly and continue to illuminate our lives.

Notes

An earlier version of this chapter was presented at the seventh annual Lincoln Colloquium, sponsored by the Lincoln Home National Historic Site, Springfield, Illinois. I wish to thank Mark E. Neely, Jr. for a number of helpful suggestions.

1. Quoted in David Donald, *Lincoln Reconsidered*, 2d ed. (New York: Alfred A. Knopf, 1965), 63.

2. Roy P. Basler, ed., Marion Delores Pratt and Lloyd P. Dunlap, asst. eds., *The Collected Works of Abraham Lincoln*, 9 vols. (New Brunswick: Rutgers University Press, 1953–55), 5:537 (hereafter cited as *Collected Works*).

3. Quoted in David Donald, ed., *Inside Lincoln's Cabinet: The Civil War Diaries of Salmon P. Chase* (New York: Longmans, Green, 1954), 16–17.

4. Quoted in Richard N. Current, *The Lincoln Nobody Knows* (New York: McGraw-Hill, 1958), 12–13.

5. Donald, *Lincoln Reconsidered*, 201.

6. *Ibid.*, 67; Allan Nevins, *Statesmanship of the Civil War*, rev. ed. (New York: Macmillan, 1962), 121.

7. Donald, *Inside Lincoln's Cabinet*, 16–17.

8. Stephen B. Oates, *With Malice Toward None: The Life of Abraham Lincoln* (New York: Harper and Row, 1977), 105.

9. Leonard Swett, quoted in *Herndon's Life of Lincoln*, ed. Paul Angle (Cleveland: World Publishing, 1942), 431.

10. Donald, *Lincoln Reconsidered*, 132–33.

11. Hay to John Nicolay, Aug. 7, 1863, in *Lincoln and the Civil War in the Diaries and Letters of John Hay*, ed. Tyler Dennett (New York: Dodd, Mead, 1939), 76; Welles quoted in Nevins, *Statesmanship of the Civil War*, 123.

12. Donald, *Lincoln Reconsidered*, 66.

13. Dennett, ed., *Lincoln and the Civil War*, 108.

14. *Collected Works*, 4:214.

15. Frederick Blue, *Salmon P. Chase: A Life in Politics* (Kent: Kent State University Press, 1987), 171.

16. Dennett, ed., *Lincoln in the Civil War*, 204.

17. James G. Randall, *Lincoln the President*, 4 vols. (New York: Dodd, Mead, 1945–55), 3:132.

18. John Nicolay and John Hay, *Abraham Lincoln*, 10 vols. (New York: Century, 1886–90), 6:271.

19. Donald, *Lincoln Reconsidered*, 67.

20. Dennett, ed., *Lincoln and the Civil War*, 176, 167.

21. *Collected Works*, 6:257.

22. Ibid., 5:98.

23. William O. Stoddard, *Inside the White House in War Times* (New York: C. L. Webster, 1890), 179. See also 199.

24. Dennett, ed., *Lincoln and the Civil War*, 35.

25. Benjamin P. Thomas, *Abraham Lincoln: A Biography* (New York: Knopf, 1952), 307.

26. *Collected Works*, 5:493–95 (Lincoln to Carl Schurz, Nov. 10, 1862).

27. Shelby Foote, *The Civil War: A Narrative*, 3 vols. (New York: Random House, 1986), 2:625.

28. Foote, *The Civil War*, 2:625.

29. *Collected Works*, 4:438.

30. Frederick Douglass, *Life and Times of Frederick Douglass* (1892; rpt. New York: Collier, 1962), 489; *Collected Works*, 4:531-33, 5:388–89.

31. Nevins, *Statesmanship of the Civil War*, 126.

32. James G. Randall, *Lincoln the Liberal Statesman* (New York: Dodd, Mead, 1947), 81.

33. Nevins, *Statesmanship of the Civil War*, 117.

34. Donald, *Lincoln Reconsidered*, 57.

35. Williamson Murray, "What Took the North So Long?" in *Experience of War*, ed. Robert Cowley (New York: Norton, 1992), 177–86.

36. Noah Brooks, *Washington D.C. in Lincoln's Time*, ed. Herbert Mitgang (1895; rpt. Chicago: Quadrangle, 1971), 137–38.

37. *Collected Works*, 5:355–56.

38. Donald, *Lincoln Reconsidered*, 142.

39. *Collected Works*, 8:333.

Chapter Five

🌲

The Civil War and
the Two-Party System

MARK E. NEELY, JR.

"A free people, in times of peace and quiet—when pressed by no common danger—naturally divide into parties. At such times, the man who is of neither party, is not—cannot be, of any consequence." That observation, made in a speech in 1852, is Abraham Lincoln's only recorded assertion of the necessity of a two-party system in a republic.[1] In light of his later career, it contains a troubling qualification: "when pressed by no common danger." For it fell Lincoln's lot to be president during the greatest war in American history, when the country was dangerously pressed. And the doubt about the role of parties in times of war apparent in Lincoln's 1852 statement was widely shared in nineteenth-century America. The effect of that uncertainty on the political history of the Civil War remains largely unexplored.

The two-party system's survival of the ordeal of civil war has long been regarded as a triumph of the American political tradition, but the self-congratulatory tone of historians who described American history as a great continuing consensus seems inadequate to explain the raw and bloody politics of the Civil War. I first noticed this disparity while studying the problem of civil liberties in the North during the Civil War. Wondering where the political parties stood on the civil liberties issues, I naturally consulted the standard work on the role of parties in the war, a long article by the historian Eric McKitrick written in the late sixties and entitled "Party Politics and the Union and Confederate War Efforts." I was surprised by what I read:

> The very existence of the Democratic party provided the authorities-
> . . . with a ready-made device for making the first rough approximation
> in the identification of actual disloyalty. It also provided a kind of built-in
> guarantee against irrevocable personal damage should the guess turn

out to be wrong. When in doubt they could always round up the local Democrats, as many a time they did, and in case of error there was always a formula for saving face all around: it was "just politics." There was, in short, a kind of middle way, an intermediate standard that had its lighter side and alleviated such extremes in security policy as, on the one hand, the paralysis and frustration of doing nothing, and, on the other, the perversions of power that accompany political blood-baths.[2]

In ten years' research, in which I examined almost fifteen thousand cases of civilians arrested by military authority during the Civil War, I never saw an instance in which the inmates of the "American Bastille," as the Democrats dubbed military prisons, or their jailors, regarded internal security as a wartime version of electioneering high jinks. The authorities were uniformly grave, and the victims, every one, regarded the experience as harrowing.

There is a hopeless disjunction between the existing analytical categories of political history, which can turn the bitterest of party conflicts into "dialogue," "conversation," or "discourse," and the actual experience of party politics in the Civil War. Much of this can be traced to the influence of McKitrick's work. From it, historians have woven an interpretation that attributes northern victory in the war in part to the superiority of their two-party political system. The system energized government and smoothed federal-state relations, it is said, even while providing the salutary checks of an organized loyal opposition. Elections managed by parties are supposed to have refined issues and, at bottom, continually reaffirmed national purpose. By contrast, the Confederacy, lacking political parties, suffered from debilitating states' rights disputes, shrill opposition to the executive, and meaningless elections that failed to enlist the popular will in the war effort. In the North, elections tested policies and perfected them in debate while a legitimate opposition put forward serious alternatives. Disgruntlement was kept within manageable limits, and party loyalty and organization sustained the war effort across the nation.[3]

In this chapter, I will start bridging the gap between that roseate historical description and the political reality of ugly party conflict that at times threatened the very life of the nation. I will first examine the Civil War generation's idea of the proper role of political parties in war, then describe the extent and nature of party political activity during the war, and finally focus on Illinois as an example of the extremes of party behavior that, far from strengthening the northern war effort, threatened the continuing existence of republican government in what was then called the Old Northwest.

The Idea of Party in the Civil War Era

Nearly everyone at the time who voiced an opinion believed what few historians believe now, that a two-party system was at best inconvenient during a great war.[4] The assumptions of the age came to light at the moment of war's outbreak, when politicians of both parties rushed to pledge their fealty to the Union and noisily denounced any continuation of partisanship during the nation's life struggle. The most famous of these statements issued from the leader of the opposition party, Stephen A. Douglas, who, after the fall of Fort Sumter, thundered, "There are but two parties, the party of patriots and the party of traitors. [Democrats] belong to the first." Even New York Democrat Fernando Wood, whose name would later become a byword for Copperhead obstructionism, relied at first upon the unspoken assumptions of the age and vowed, "I know no party now." The Republican gesture to the era's ideals was to talk of forming a "Union" party. However anemic these Union-party movements were, some politicians, at least, briefly put stock in them. How else could a historian explain the following phenomenon? Early in September 1862, Republican Senator Lyman Trumbull of Illinois wrote President Lincoln to inform him of what would not have been news in any other season of preparation for off-year elections: "The Democrats are organizing for a party contest this Fall. They have called a state convention and are calling congressional and county conventions of a purely party character throughout the state."[5]

Still, avowals of temporary suppression of party spirit from politicians were mostly talk, and the pace of partisanship hardly broke stride. Occasionally, there were more analytical discussions of the role of free politics in war. Harper's Weekly, for example, published an article called "Our Institutions on Their Trial" on August 3, 1861, in the sobering wake of the Union defeat at Bull Run two weeks earlier, and the first sentence stated what then seemed obvious: "The most convenient government for a nation at war is a despotic monarchy; the most inconvenient—according to general opinion—a democratic republic."[6]

Observers in the Confederacy saw it the same way. Thus the famous diarist Mary Boykin Chesnut, for example, writing on August 29, 1861, refused to grow overconfident because of the recent Confederate victory at Bull Run. She mused on the latest news, "Capital article in the [New York] Albion to day—on the lettre de cachet system, passport system & suppression of the press at the north. Freedom[']s gone there in the hope to subjugate us. [William Howard] Russell [of the London Times says] the tramp of the man, who ever he may be (McClellan?) is already heard who is to be their despot. Then our trouble comes. We can easily fight the 'many headed monster thing' now pretending to govern." That autumn, after enduring in silence some abusive criticism of President Jefferson Davis by one of her relatives, Mrs. Chesnut ran up to her room to write in her diary what she could not say in the parlor: "Republics won't do. I am a strong government woman."[7]

Confederate citizens apparently took pride in the absence of political parties from their wartime government and regarded the continuance of the two-party system in the North as a weakness. Indeed, Jefferson Davis, Robert E. Lee, and Richmond newspaper editor Edward A. Pollard all considered ways of exploiting that presumed weakness to Confederate advantage. Davis, writing after the war, recalled that "political developments at the North [in 1864] . . . favored the adoption of some action that might influence popular sentiment in the hostile section. The aspect of the peace party was quite encouraging, and it seemed that the real issue to be decided in the Presidential election of that year was the continuance or cessation of the war."[8] Pollard was Davis's most unrelenting critic, but on this point the newspaperman essentially agreed with the Confederate president:

> The North, in conducting the war, had constantly the disadvantage of a divided public sentiment; and there was a near prospect in the approaching Presidential election that this occasion of a great popular dissent might be turned to the account of the South, and increase the encouragement which it had already greatly derived from the political controversies of the enemy. In fact, . . . the division of public opinion in the North . . . was an advantage [of the South] . . . that has not been justly estimated in . . . comparisons . . . between the resources of the contestants. It reduced them to something like equality, when we consider that the political division in the North must have detracted from its power to make war in proportion to the numbers that it carried off from the support of the government.[9]

Even the seemingly unpolitical General Robert E. Lee premised his grand strategy on the continuing party divisions in the North. In the spring of 1863, at the height of southern optimism about the war, Lee told his wife that the Confederacy must "establish" its "supplies on a firm basis" in 1863 (hence his invasion of Pennsylvania in the summer), and then, "if successful this year, next fall there will be a great change in public opinion at the North. The Republicans will be destroyed & I think the friends of peace will become so strong that the next administration will go in on that basis."[10]

Such incidental observations from people who were not systematic political thinkers are revealing, but it would aid modern understanding to know what the political scientists of the era said on the subject. Unfortunately, the Civil War predated the dawn of political science, and few theoretical

works were available. The most famous of these, however, expressed doubts
about the role of political parties in wartime. Francis Lieber's *Manual of
Political Ethics*, published in two volumes in 1838 and 1839, may well have
been the first systematic work on politics in the world to recognize that
parties were essential to liberty in a republic.[11] Lieber's study of history led
him to state that he knew "of no instance of a free state without parties."
Moreover, he argued in a forward-looking section of this otherwise rather
conservative book that it was not "desirable that no parties should exist."
"Without parties," he insisted, "there could be no loyal, steady, lasting and
effective opposition, one of the surest safeguards of public peace. . . . Without
parties many of the wisest measures could never be carried, and many of
the best intended measures would remain harsh, unmodified, absolute."[12]

Thus Lieber anticipated two of three virtues customarily ascribed to
party systems by modern political scientists and historians—their vigilance
over the party in power and their role in refining policy within the party.
That was no mean feat for a Whig intellectual suffering through the hey-
day of Jacksonian Democracy, and we should not be too quick to criticize
him for ignoring a third crucial role of parties, that of exciting the electorate to vote or to take action or to protest.

Lieber's discussion of the role of a loyal opposition proved so effective
that twenty-five years later, during the war, when Democrats sought to
protest Lincoln's policy of military arrests of civilians, they could cite Lieber
on their side. Thus in 1863 Samuel Sullivan "Sunset" Cox, a prominent
Ohio Democratic congressman, forwarded a letter from an Ohio convention protesting the military arrest of politician Clement L. Vallandigham
to Lincoln with the careful admonition that the convention "based all their
action on the principle laid down by Doctor Lieber" that "a constitutional
opposition was one of the estates of the realm; which no free government
would seek to ostracize. Their resolutions . . . all proceed upon the idea of
sustaining the fundamental and all other laws, and obedience to the constituted authorities of the United States."[13] Cox surely took delight in using
the Republicans' favorite political theorist to prove that the Democrats
formed a loyal opposition during the war.

By the time of Cox's letter to Lincoln, however, Francis Lieber had all
but given up on the utility of political parties in time of war. The *Manual*
had hedged the point earlier when considering the "great question how
far an opposition ought not only to yield, after war has once been declared,
but, to aid patriotically in carrying it to a glorious end."

If your *nation* engages in the war, and not simply a preposterous *administration*, against your opinion, you may act as private citizen as you like,
provided always you do in no sort or manner aid directly or indirectly

the enemy, . . . but if you are a representative or officer, you are bound first of all to bring the war to a happy and glorious end, and not to cripple the administration. The latter would be treasonable. Remember that it is your state, your nation, that declares and fights out the war, not this or that minister; remember that the honor and history of your country are engaged; that however conscientious you may be in your opposition, you may err after all; that you cannot oppose the administration without strengthening the enemy, who has unsheathed his sword against your kindred, and that whatever your opinion was as to the beginning of the war, all considerations absolutely cease, when the enemy approaches your own country. . . . If an opposition feels really and conscientiously convinced that the war is inexpedient, let them follow the old Roman rule: treat after victory, but fight until then.[14]

As time passed, Lieber grew less enamored of the antics of American political parties, even in peacetime. In his 1853 treatise *On Civil Liberty and Self-Government*, written at a time of widespread voter disgust with what historians now call the Second American Party System, Lieber noted that "if by party be understood a despicable union of men, to turn out a certain set of office-holders merely to obtain the lucrative places, and, when they are obtained, a union to keep them, it becomes an odious faction of placemen or office-hunters, the last of those citizens to whom the government ought to be entrusted."[15]

When war came, Lieber further changed his mind and wrote a broadly circulated pamphlet entitled "No Party Now but All for Our Country." He now argued that

Parties are unavoidable in free countries, and may be useful if they acknowledge the country far above themselves, and remain within the sanctity of the fundamental law. . . . But Party has no meaning in far the greater number of the highest and the common relations of human life. When we are ailing, we do not take medicine by party prescription. We do not build ships by party measurement. . . . We do not pursue truth, or cultivate science, by party dogmas; and we do not, we must not, love and defend our country and our liberty . . . , according to party rules. . . . When a house is on fire, and a mother with her child cries for help at the window above, shall the firemen at the engine be allowed to trifle away the precious time in party bickerings, or is then the only word—"Water! pump away!; up with the ladder!"[16]

The Extent and Nature of Party Activity during the War

By the assumptions of that era, the role of political parties in wartime was uncertain at best, and the prevailing wisdom saw them as a great inconvenience. Confederates seemed grateful that parties had yet to appear in their fledgling country, and there were those in the North who apparently thought that parties should properly disappear until the war was over. That did not happen. The parties did not diminish their partisan activities in the least. In fact, they increased them, and with that continuing partisanship in the midst of war came extreme denunciations of divisiveness and fear of disloyalty.

One of the most important differences between the American political system and parliamentary systems remains the inexorability of the American electoral process. Elections come by the clock in the United States; we have them whether we need them or not. At the legally prescribed time an election is held; whether the president's popularity is high or low, Americans hold a presidential election every four years. Even if there is a war on, Americans have presidential elections, congressional elections, state elections, and many others.[17]

In the Civil War era, elections not only marched inexorably to their own calendar, but that calendar was also not nearly as standardized and rationalized as today's political schedule. Only the presidential election came at a standard time in all the states. Other elections were not necessarily tied in with the presidential one held in early November. General election day in New Hampshire fell on the second Tuesday in March; in Connecticut, on the first Monday in April; in Rhode Island, the first Wednesday in April; in Kentucky, the first Monday in August; in Maine, the second Tuesday in September; and in Indiana, the second Tuesday in October.[18]

Not all elections came in even-numbered years, either. In 1861 all the New England states held gubernatorial elections; New York City elected a mayor; New Hampshire, Maryland, and Kentucky elected U.S. congressmen; Maryland, Ohio, Kansas, Wisconsin, California, Minnesota, and Iowa chose governors; Pennsylvania elected most of a new state legislature; and Illinois chose a constitutional convention to revise the state's fundamental political document in the midst of war.[19] Off-year congressional elections of the sort with which we are familiar today, but freighted with the additional significance of a referendum on the war in many districts, were offered in 1862. In 1863 New England chose governors again (and three New England states chose their congressmen); New York chose state officers and New York City a mayor; Pennsylvania chose a governor, along with California, Wisconsin, Ohio, and Kentucky; Maryland, Delaware, and Kentucky chose congressional delegations; Michigan chose a state regent; and New Jersey chose state senators and county officers.[20] The Civil War lasted forty-eight months, and in half of those months—twenty-four at least—major elections occurred in the North.

Such an undisciplined political calendar meant that politicking was a constant during the war. Preoccupation with civil war by no means altered the politicians' informal timetable for electioneering. They began thinking about elections early and prepared for them long. Thus Lincoln's old Springfield friend James C. Conkling wrote to the president as early as August 21, 1863, to inform him that the "presidential campaign for your successor (*if any*) has already commenced in Illinois." Public meetings of supporters and opponents were already being held fifteen months in advance of the presidential election—and ten months ahead of Lincoln's renomination.[21]

The public letter Lincoln eventually sent in response to Conkling's invitation to speak in Illinois was put to immediate use by politicians in the 1863 election season. Israel Washburn, one of a famous band of political brothers, wrote to the president from Maine on September 15, 1863, announcing Republican victory in the state election just held. "The victory," Washburn reported, "was won upon the question of the square and unqualified support of your administration & its policy. . . . [it revealed] earnest approval—& especially of your recent letter—It (the letter) aided not a little in swelling our wonderful majority."[22] Lincoln's modern biographer, J. G. Randall, who had a gentle academic's distaste for electioneering antics, tried his best to dignify Lincoln's letter to Conkling. Lincoln, he argued, did not once "claim credit for his party or use the language of partisanship," although Republican partisans "appropriated" it for political "advantage." Conkling read the letter aloud at a mass meeting in Illinois advertised as one for "unconditional Union men . . . without regard to former party associations," but in Randall's view the venue was unfairly put to partisan use by local and smaller-minded Republicans, who did not live up to the spirit of the occasion.[23] In truth, Conkling got Lincoln's attention in the initial letter of contact by forthrightly describing the occasion in the narrowest of political terms as a meeting that would promote Abraham Lincoln's chances for renomination on the Republican ticket and reelection as president.

Because of the unremitting calendar of important elections, President Lincoln had already issued a key political pamphlet earlier in the summer of 1863. Although not usually thought of as a campaign document—J. G. Randall called it "one of those dignified, carefully worded statements addressed to a person or occasion, but intended as a kind of state paper"— Lincoln's famous letter of June 12, 1863, to Erastus Corning and other New York politicians who had protested the military arrest of the Ohio Democrat Clement L. Vallandigham was handled as electioneering documents were.[24] After issuing the public letter, the president then had copies of it printed and mailed across the country on the frank of his private secretary John G. Nicolay. This kept the president above the appearance of self-promotion and electioneering, but the recipients knew exactly what it meant to receive a copy of a presidential position paper sent to them at tax-payers' expense by the private secretary of the head of the Republican party. The recipients thanked the president for the pamphlet, and some assured him they knew its proper use.[25] Thus Roscoe Conkling of New York replied, "I received a pamphlet copy under Nicolay's frank, & it makes the best Campaign document we can have in this state."[26] William A. Hall of New York thanked the president for the pamphlet and informed him that the political machine in the state had churned into action: "There has at this time been ordered 50,000 copies of your letter in pamphlet form from the 'Tribune' and before the present week closes there will have been printed and circulated of this letter at least 500,000 copies. . . . Your friends in New York are taking steps to give every Soldier in the field a copy of it."[27] Francis Lieber, who served during the war as an officer in the Loyal Publication Society, also thanked the president for the printed copy franked from Nicolay and assured the president, "I shall propose to our Loyal Publication Society to print some 10000 copies of it, which will certainly be done, if we are not out of all money."[28]

Such impressive print runs were associated mainly with political movements in the nineteenth century, and, indeed, if we are to judge by the amount of campaign literature and ephemera produced, by the resulting voter enthusiasm, or by the stridency of the rhetoric, the political parties redoubled their efforts during the war and created more partisan spectacle than ever. The number of copies of the president's Corning letter printed in the relatively quiet 1863 election season foreshadowed the tremendous electioneering effort the party put forth for the presidential election in 1864. In fact, both parties chose to run more issues-oriented campaigns than they had in 1860, and during the course of it they produced a staggering amount of campaign literature that still litters the shelves of used-book stores. The National Union Congressional Committee distributed for the Republicans some six million printed items, almost three for every vote Lincoln received in November 1864. And if one adds the nearly half-million pamphlets produced by the privately funded Loyal Publication Society, then there were more than three for every Lincoln voter.[29]

The voters responded with alacrity: Voting actually increased in 1864, above the numbers reached in the election of 1860 with its incredible turnout—sometimes estimated at 82 percent in northern states.[30] Voting rose above the remarkable levels of 1860 despite the absence of tens of thousands of potential voters soldiering in the South. Overall, voting rose in the North by 3.1 percent in 1864 from its 1860 level (not counting the vote of new states).[31] The number of voters rose in every state except Kentucky, Missouri, Maryland, Michigan, Wisconsin, and California, and the only significant declines came in the border states. The reasons for those declines seem obvious. Missouri and Kentucky, where voting fell by 37 percent, were ravaged by internal civil war and extreme social disorder. If one removes Kentucky and Missouri from the comparison, then voting in the northern states rose almost 6.7 percent in 1864 above the already high level reached in 1860.[32]

For the most part, voters turned out in record numbers. Voting jumped 20 percent in giant Pennsylvania. It rose 22.6 percent in Maine, and 12.6 percent in Connecticut. It rose 8.2 percent in New York. It rose more than 3 percent out west in Indiana and in Illinois. In fact, the northern vote in 1864 was so great that the totals for the whole nation hardly look as though a third of the states had left the Union![33]

Party electioneering rhetoric, always heated in peacetime, reverted in wartime to the shrieking accusations of treason and ugly threats of lynching associated with the party contests of the early republic, in the era *before* political parties were thought to be legitimate. Even intellectuals, like Pennsylvania's Charles Janeway Stillé, whose pamphlet entitled "How a Free People Conduct a Long War" may have been the most widely circulated piece of political literature of the Civil War North, routinely referred to "the . . . factious and disloyal opposition on the part of a powerful party."[34]

Americans in Lincoln's era did not find it easy to reconcile continuing partisanship with the sense of national crisis, especially given the theoretical assumptions about political parties then prevalent. Instead of a decline in partisan activities in recognition of a united war effort, Americans witnessed increased electioneering activity, increased voting, and the most strident political rhetoric employed since the War of 1812.[35] These activities may have constituted little more than politics as usual in a wartime setting, but the setting made all the difference in perception of the legitimacy of the activities. Many were the calls for Union parties, discarding old labels and old issues, and many were the complaints against destructive partisanship. Thus the New York State Chamber of Commerce complained in formal resolutions adopted on February 5, 1863, that "the spirit of party which stifles love of country is too manifest at the present time, and through the divisions it creates, and the animosities it awakens is to be feared and deprecated as the ally of rebellion; and it should be rebuked, discouraged, and banished from our midst."[36]

Partisanship persisted, nonetheless, and that led in turn to still more heated rhetoric, as ordinary political activity in the context of war was easily mistaken for indifference to or hostility toward the unified war effort. It was easy to draw the line in theory but impossible to discern it in practice. Thus the abolitionist Gerrit Smith, in a stunning oration called "Stand by the Government," delivered in Albany, New York, on February 27, 1863, asserted that the "Republicans, Democrats, and Abolitionists must all help, be it at whatever risk to their respective parties. Indeed, so far as the Rebellion is concerned, they must all give up their parties, and become one party. Outside of this one party they may still maintain old party names and old party aims."[37] Instead, the parties continued to call each other names in a way now heated to the boiling point by war issues.

In describing that partisan name-calling, it becomes extremely difficult to avoid the impression that from time to time one party gave and the other took, that one tyrannized and the other suffered. But in such a competitive system of give-and-take, each gave as good as it got. It is also difficult not to misinterpret the shrill language customary in nineteenth-century partisanship as indicating more extreme threats than were really intended. There were, however, examples that clearly went beyond the bounds of ordinary partisanship and seemed to threaten the very existence of republican government.

The Case of Illinois

The excesses of wartime politics in Lincoln's home state created a raw and near-bloody situation that has repeatedly tempted historians to depict Republicans as excitable tyrants (especially tempting because they were led by the explosive alcoholic governor Richard Yates) or Democrats as disloyal to the Union cause. A balanced appraisal, however, suggests that Democrats and Republicans were tempted to the same excesses—they simply lacked equal opportunity to exploit the institutions of state government. In the most famous and dangerous episode, Democrats, after capturing the state legislature in the elections of 1862, attempted the next year to limit the governor's military powers. In response Governor Yates found an obscure provision of the constitution that allowed him to "prorogue" the legislature if the two houses failed to agree on a date for adjournment. He invoked it, and thus for much of the war Illinois was governed without a legislature. A similar situation prevailed in neighboring Indiana after Democrats captured their state legislature in 1862; Republicans bolted and denied a quorum. J. G. Randall, who did not mince words on constitutional issues, called the predicament of these midwestern states "a collapse of representative government." And the historian Kenneth Stampp termed the conflict in Indiana "the collapse of constitutional government."[38]

Before he dismissed the legislature in 1863, Yates had been faced with a constitutional convention meeting in Springfield. In the midst of war, this was trying, and the Democrats, who dominated the convention, did nothing to make it less so. They did not yet have control of the legislature, so they attempted to use the constitutional convention to reach for powers no one ever dreamed such a convention should have. The convention did not confine itself to the task of drafting a document for submission to the people. On the contrary, it attempted to act more or less as a legislature, establishing committees to investigate the Republican governor's programs and issuing inflammatory and embarrassing reports on the administration.[39] There was no precedent for such behavior. But political parties in the Civil War sought to use to advantage any popularly elected assembly that might be thought to represent the sovereign people. In neighboring Missouri, the Republicans, after toppling the legal government in Jefferson City with a coup d'etat, then revived the secession convention (now that southern sympathizers had departed, it was dominated by Unionists) and used this improbable mechanism to choose a governor and legislature to govern the state until 1865.[40]

The example of party strife in Illinois vividly illustrates the brink to which the parties sometimes took the Republic during the war: The governor ruled without a legislature for well over a year. It was not illegal, as the government of Missouri was, nor did Yates resort to the illegal methods that Governor Oliver P. Morton used in a similar situation in Indiana.[41] But there is chilling evidence of potential for further collapse of representative government that has heretofore been neglected. It comes in the form of resolutions drawn up by midwestern regiments stationed in Tennessee and Mississippi in 1863. For example, "The Resolutions on the Conduct of the War, Adopted by the Officers and Enlisted Men from Illinois, stationed at Bolivar, Tennessee, February 13th, 1863" commented bitterly on the party strife between Yates and the Democrats in Illinois:

> We have witnessed with shame and indignation, the efforts recently made in our State, to resist the Governments of the Nation and the State, in their noble and patriotic efforts to restore the public peace. We had hoped that . . . the voices of faction and the clamor of parties would have given way to a united effort to maintain the Executive of our Government and the honor of our State. But a horde of traitors have dared to come forth, even into Legislative Halls, and then perpetrate upon us and our cause, by *voting*, what their Southern allies have the courage and honor to do by *fighting*. . . . We came to this war from all parties, but know only one party now, that which has sworn to maintain the union. . . .
> . . . should treason rear its monstrous form at home—if it be found that our own beloved State harbors in her bosom, men who dare to consort with the public enemy and become the . . . tools of traitors in arms against us, we will only wait for the first base act of treason, to turn back and crush them, as we do those in front, beneath the heel of war.[42]

Any fair-minded historian must pay serious attention to threats to turn Illinois regiments around and march on Springfield rather than on Vicksburg, threats that came from specific regiments and were signed by officers who did not hide behind anonymity.

Frightening as they may seem, the resolutions of the Bolivar soldiers did say they would await "the first base act of treason" before marching on Springfield. From Corinth, Mississippi, came more frightening resolutions drawn up by seven Illinois regiments on January 30, 1863. These resolutions also lamented "the bitter partisan spirit that is becoming dangerously vindictive and malicious in our state, the tendency of which is to paralise and frustrate the plans of the federal and state authorities in their efforts to suppress this infamous Rebellion." Like many others during the war, these Illinois soldiers asked their "friends and neighbors at home to lay aside all petty jealousies and party animosities and as one man stand by us in upholding the president in his war measures." But they were most specific in identifying what would cause them to turn on the enemy in the rear: "Should the loathsome treason of the madmen who are trying to wrest from [Governor Yates] . . . a fraction of his just authority render it necessary in his opinion for us to return and crush out Treason there, we will promptly obey a proper order to do so." All it required, apparently, was an order from Governor Yates.[43]

In every case, the initiative in getting up the resolutions came from officers, who were not, as modern American officers are, strictly forbidden from political activities while on active service.[44] Officers drafted the Corinth resolutions at a meeting held at the music hall in that town on January 29, 1863. One of those who spearheaded the movement was Augustus Chetlain, an abolitionist officer of the Seventh Illinois Volunteer Infantry. He recalled after the war that "a large meeting of officers was held," over which he, who was in command of all the troops at Corinth, presided. Colonel Chetlain preferred to describe the purpose of the meeting in his *Recollections* as an attempt "to arouse the people of the western states to the importance of filling up the depleted ranks of the Western Army."[45] In fact, none of the resolutions mentioned recruiting; they were more political than that. The historian of the Seventh Regiment was more honest when he wrote in the regimental history that the resolutions gave "expression to [the soldiers'] views upon modern democracy, and their bitter detestation of the treasonable element . . . becoming so prevalent in Illinois."[46]

On the next day, Friday the 30, the resolutions were presented to the men, who were assembled for that purpose on dress parade. The regimental historian recalled that the men said "amen to every word" of the resolutions, and perhaps they did, but the conditions of dress parade should be kept in mind in evaluating the resolutions.[47] "Dress parade" is a ceremony, usually held at retreat, when the men are in formation, in dress uniforms, and under arms.[48] It is a distinctly military ritual, with nothing of the freewheeling or raucous atmosphere of a civilian political meeting about it. The soldiers were under military discipline, and free speech did not obtain. During the Civil War they were still governed by the military code of 1806 and in particular by a regulation originally drawn up by two thin-skinned politicians who would later become presidents, John Adams and Thomas Jefferson. They drafted the regulation in an era when most Americans did not believe in the idea of a legitimate opposition. By 1806 it stated that "any officer or soldier who shall use contemptuous or disrespectful words against the President of the United States, against the Vice-President thereof, against the Congress of the United States or against the Chief Magistrate or legislature of any of the United States in which he may be quartered" could be cashiered or courtmartialed.[49]

The soldiers' resolutions did not—almost certainly could not—well up from the ranks. The common soldiers enjoyed only the privilege of voting yea or nay, and the resolutions were drafted under conditions that made criticism of the president impossible. The meeting of the Ninety-sixth Illinois Volunteer Infantry Regiment was most revealing. Stirred by a mass meeting held in occupied Nashville to celebrate George Washington's birthday, where the famous Tennessee refugee "Parson" William G. Brownlow spoke, a number of men in the regiment were aroused to political action. A week later, on March 1, at a brigade dress parade of five regiments, the brigade commander, Colonel Smith D. Atkins, made a "patriotic speech." On Monday, March 2, the officers met, prompted by discussions of the Emancipation Proclamation among the men and by desertions and loss of morale attributed to those discussions. The officers gathered at brigade headquarters at 9 in the morning, and then that night, at dress parade, the regiment was formed "in a hollow square" and a captain, described as "a good elocutionist," read the resolutions to the men. Colonel Thomas E. Champion followed with "a brief but earnest address, and then called out: 'As many of the soldiers of the Ninety-Sixth Illinois as endorse the resolutions just read, will manifest it by saying "aye." ' " The regimental historian described the rest of the memorable day this way:

> The ayes were numerous and enthusiastic, but strange to say, not universal. In an instant the Colonel commanded: "Sergeants, take your Companies to quarters." The officers were kept together for a few moments and then went to their tents. That night, in every tent, there was a long discussion of the resolutions. In the light of after events it is difficult to comprehend how it was that any union soldier should think for a moment of opposing them, but the fact remains that there was most strenuous objections on the part of a few, quite a percentage, even of the members of the Illinois regiments, not favoring the absolute emancipation of the slaves. Colonel Champion caused to be forwarded to the Chicago

papers, and also to the papers in Lake and Jo Daviess Counties, copies of the resolutions, and stated that they were adopted by the NINETY- SIXTH Regiment "without a dissenting voice." This was literally true, but the Colonel afterward declared that he dared not put the negative for fear the nays would be so numerous as not to look well for a Regiment from the State which was President Lincoln's home.[50]

This set of resolutions denounced demagogues at home who interfered with the midwestern governors; three more Illinois infantry regiments, one from Indiana, and an Ohio battery signed. They did not include threats to march on Springfield, Indianapolis, or Columbus. However, preliminary versions came from each regiment, and those of the Ninety-second Illinois, for example, urged their friends at home to "mark" the Copperheads "for future reference—shoot them, if need be," and vowed " 'that hemp be not created in vain.' "[51]

Political resolutions from the army were not and could not of necessity be nonpartisan. To criticize the president was a court-martial offense, as was criticism of Congress. Had these Illinois regiments still been in training in their home state rather than stationed in Mississippi or Tennessee, the resolutions they passed would have been, arguably, a court-martial offense, because they might easily be construed as criticism of the state legislature itself. In short, only Democrats, under the circumstances of the Civil War, stood much risk of being criticized in army political statements.

These ominous threats of diverting military forces to repress civilian political movements in Illinois, issued under distressingly unfree and partisan conditions, would have been welcome to Governor Yates and other Republican leaders in Springfield. Yates was ready to give the word that would trigger the threatened about-face of the Illinois regiments. At the very same time the resolutions were being drafted, he was engaged in a concerted effort to persuade Abraham Lincoln to send troops to Illinois to overawe the peace Democrats. The same day that the Corinth officers' resolutions were passed, Yates and a number of Lincoln's more excitable political friends in the state asked the president to send four regiments to Illinois "under pretence of recruiting" to keep an eye on the legislature when it reconvened in June and possibly then "to declare the State under martial law . . . and disperse the Legislature."[52] Lincoln refused the request, Yates did not go outside the chain of command to solicit mutiny in the Illinois regiments, and instead he eventually found a nonmilitary solution that allowed him to eliminate the state legislature in the constitutional provision mentioned earlier. But it was a closer call than anyone has heretofore noticed. The ground had been sewn to reap a bloody harvest of political usurpation and perhaps slaughter.

In the end, Illinois witnessed no political slaughter, and the parties confined their activities to violent denunciations and eager voting. The ultimate loyalty of Democrats, established by historians decades ago, is not the question at hand here. The question is, Were there instances when the two-party system impeded the war effort? Obviously, there were, but a more difficult question remains: Were such instances outweighed or at least counterbalanced by the more wholesome, more restraining, and more widely celebrated party influences traditionally referred to in the historical literature?

That is a question answerable only in a book, not a chapter. But it is a question worth asking. Despite the beneficial role usually attributed to the two-party system in the northern war effort, the heretofore unmentioned excesses of the Illinois regiments' resolutions offer unsettling proof that the political parties' continuing conflicts occasionally threatened the Union cause. In some instances at least, the two-party system was precisely what Lincoln and the American people at the time thought: a great inconvenience when the country was "pressed by . . . common danger."

Notes

1. Roy P. Basler, ed., Marion Dolores Pratt and Lloyd P. Dunlop, asst. eds., *The Collected Works of Abraham Lincoln*, 9 vols. (New Brunswick: Rutgers University Press, 1953–55), 2:126.

2. Eric L. McKitrick, "Party Politics and the Union and Confederate War Efforts," in *The American Party Systems: Stages of Political Development*, ed. William Nisbet Chambers and Walter Dean Burnham (New York: Oxford University Press, 1967), 141. Michael F. Holt terms McKitrick's essay "brilliant" and "one of the most stimulating analyses of Civil War politics ever written." See Holt, "Abraham Lincoln and the Politics of Union," in *Abraham Lincoln and the American Political Tradition*, ed. John L. Thomas (Amherst: University of Massachusetts Press, 1986), 111. Phillip S. Paludan calls McKitrick's article "seminal" and "relies heavily" on it in *"A People's Contest": The Union and Civil War, 1861–1865* (New York: Harper and Row, 1988), 407n. That in turn leads him to seeing Civil War politics as a "dialogue" and observing, for example, "Democratic strength molded Republican unity and energized party institutions, providing the benefits of party that had evoked so much admiration before the war" (89). Harold Hyman also depends on the essay to shape his important article on the "Election of 1864," in *History of American Presidential Elections*, ed. Arthur M. Schlesinger, Jr., and Fred L. Israel, 4 vols. (New York: Chelsea House, 1971), 2:1161–62. Such reliance on McKitrick's essay has given it the status of virtually unquestioned authority.

3. McKitrick, "Party Politics and the Union and Confederate War Efforts," esp. 132–34, 137–39, 141–42, 144–45, 149–51.

4. McKitrick admits this, saying that the two-party system was "not, either North or South," regarded as "a positive value" and adding, "Nobody at the time, so far as

is known, ever explicitly thanked the Almighty for parties." Ibid., 120–21. But he attributes to the attitude no causal abilities; in fact, he glosses over it.

5. Paludan, "A People's Contest," 85–86; Joel H. Silbey, A Respectable Minority: The Democratic Party in the Civil War Era, 1860–1868 (New York: W. W. Norton, 1977), 39–49; Lyman Trumbull to Abraham Lincoln, Sept. 7, 1862, Abraham Lincoln Papers, Library of Congress (microfilm). Conservative Republicans were still overestimating Democratic support of the administration in the late summer of 1862; see Orville H. Browning to Abraham Lincoln, Sept. 10, 1862, Abraham Lincoln Papers. The impulse to form "Union" parties is problematic for McKitrick. See "Party Politics and the Union and Confederate War Efforts," 148n. Holt attempts a solution that boils down to a sort of neorevisionism in "Abraham Lincoln and the Politics of Union."

6. "Our Institutions on Their Trial," Harper's Weekly, Aug. 3, 1861, 482. The article did not specifically mention political parties but focused instead on constitutionally limited government, Congress, and, especially, a free press. See also Michael C. C. Adams, Fighting for Defeat: Union Military Failure in the East, 1861–1865 (orig. pub. as Our Masters the Rebels, 1978; rpt. Lincoln: University of Nebraska Press, 1992), 83 and passim.

7. C. Vann Woodward and Elisabeth Muhlenfeld, eds., The Private Mary Chesnut: The Unpublished Civil War Diaries (New York: Oxford University Press, 1984), 146, 167.

8. Jefferson Davis, Rise and Fall of the Confederate Government, 2 vols. (New York: Appleton, 1881), 2:611.

9. Edward A. Pollard, Life of Jefferson Davis with a Secret History of the Southern Confederacy. . . . (Philadelphia: National Register Publishing Company, 1869), 351–52. Pollard made the point as implicit criticism of Davis: Here was yet another advantage the Confederacy enjoyed that should have enabled the inept Davis to win southern independence.

10. Alan T. Nolan, Lee Reconsidered: General Robert E. Lee in Civil War History (Chapel Hill: University of North Carolina Press, 1991), 87–88.

11. Richard Hofstadter, The Idea of a Party System: The Rise of Legitimate Opposition in the United States, 1780–1840 (Berkeley: University of California Press, 1969), 258–59. Hofstadter is wrong to say "he continued to hold the pro-party position he had arrived at by 1839" (258n).

12. Francis Lieber, Manual of Political Ethics, 2 vols. (Boston: Charles C. Little and James Brown, 1838–39), 2:414, 415.

13. Samuel S. Cox to Abraham Lincoln, June 14, 1863, Abraham Lincoln Papers.

14. Lieber, Manual of Political Ethics, 2:444–45.

15. Francis Lieber, On Civil Liberty and Self-Government, enlarged ed. in one vol. (Philadelphia: J. B. Lippincott, 1859), 153. On antiparty sentiment in the early 1850s see Michael F. Holt, The Political Crisis of the 1850s (New York: W. W. Norton, 1978), 130–34.

16. Francis Lieber, "No Party Now but All for Our Country," reprinted in History of American Presidential Elections, ed. Schlesinger and Israel, 2:1183.

17. Roy F. Nichols, The Disruption of American Democracy (New York: Macmillan, 1948), 5–6. Nichols made the point for the 1850s.

18. *The Tribune Almanac and Political Register for 1861* (New York: The Tribune Association, 1861), 64.

19. *The Tribune Almanac and Political Register for 1862* (New York: The Tribune Association, 1862), 56–63.

20. *The Tribune Almanac and Political Register for 1864* (New York: The Tribune Association, 1864), 55–67.

21. James C. Conkling to Abraham Lincoln, Aug. 21, 1864, Abraham Lincoln Papers.

22. Israel Washburn to Abraham Lincoln, Sept. 15, 1863, Abraham Lincoln Papers.

23. James G. Randall, *Lincoln the President: Midstream* (New York: Dodd, Mead, 1953), 261, 253.

24. Randall, *Lincoln the President*, 226.

25. See letters (all in Abraham Lincoln Papers) to Lincoln from John W. Forney, June 14; David Paul Brown, June 15; Edwin D. Morgan, June 15; Edward Everett, June 16; Samuel A. Foot, June 16; Hugh McCulloch, June 16; John Ten Eyck, June 16; George Francis Train, June 16; Benjamin H. Brewster, June 18; Horace Maynard, June 16; Mark Delahay, June 19; Daniel S. Dickinson, June 19; James M. Ashley, June 23; and Jacob M. Howard, July 8, 1863.

26. Roscoe Conkling to Abraham Lincoln, June 16, 1863, Abraham Lincoln Papers.

27. William A. Hall to Abraham Lincoln, June 15, 1863.

28. Francis Lieber to Abraham Lincoln, June 16, 1863, Abraham Lincoln Papers.

29. William F. Zornow, *Lincoln and the Party Divided* (Norman: University of Oklahoma Press, 1964), 180–82.

30. Joel H. Silbey, *The American Political Nation, 1838–1893* (Stanford: Stanford University Press, 1991), 145.

31. Based on Schlesinger and Israel, eds., *History of American Presidential Elections*, 2:1152, 1244, and *The Tribune Almanac and Political Register for 1865* (New York: The Tribune Association, 1865), 46–66.

32. "Abraham Lincoln and the Politics of Union," 132, Michael F. Holt attributes the decline in border-state voting to military arrests of Confederate sympathizers and to military intimidation of Democratic voters at the polls.

33. Based on Schlesinger and Israel, eds., *History of American Presidential Elections*, 2:1152, 1244. With a third fewer states, voting fell off by only 13.9 percent (new states excluded).

34. Charles Janeway Stille, "How a Free People Conduct a Long War," reprinted in *Union Pamphlets of the Civil War, 1861–1865*, ed. Frank Freidel, 2 vols. (Cambridge: Harvard University Press, 1967), 384.

35. See especially Samuel Eliot Morrison, "Dissent in the War of 1812," in Morrison, Frederick Merk, and Frank Freidel, *Dissent in Three American Wars* (Cambridge: Harvard University Press, 1970), 3–31; Donald R. Hickey, *The War of 1812: A Forgotten Conflict* (Urbana: University of Illinois Press, 1989), 52–71.

36. "Chamber of Commerce of the State of New York. Preamble and Resolutions adopted . . . ," Feb. 5, 1863, Abraham Lincoln Papers.

37. Gerrit Smith, "Stand by the Government. Speech . . . in Albany . . . ," Feb. 27, 1863, Abraham Lincoln Papers.

38. Randall, *Lincoln the President: Midstream*, 253; Kenneth M. Stampp, *Indiana Politics during the Civil War* (1949; rpt. Bloomington: Indiana University Press, 1978), 158.

39. Jack Nortrup, "Yates, the Prorogued Legislature, and the Constitutional Convention," *Journal of the Illinois State Historical Society* 62 (Spring 1969): 5–17; Arthur Charles Cole, *The Era of the Civil War, 1848–1870* (1919; rpt. Urbana: University of Illinois Press, 1987), 268–69, 299.

40. Michael Fellman, *Inside War: The Guerrilla Conflict in Missouri in the American Civil War* (New York: Oxford University Press, 1989), 10–11.

41. Emma Lou Thornbrough, *Indiana in the Civil War Era, 1850–1880* (Indianapolis: Indiana Historical Bureau and Indiana Historical Society, 1965), 186–90; Stampp, *Indiana Politics during the Civil War*, 176–81.

42. "The Resolutions on the Conduct of the War, Adopted by the Officers and Enlisted Men from Illinois, stationed at Bolivar, Tennessee, . . . , Feb. 13th, 1863," Abraham Lincoln Papers.

43. "Patriotic Resolutions of the Officers & Men of Illinois Regiments Corinth, Miss.," Jan. 30, 1863, Abraham Lincoln Papers.

44. Lawrence P. Crocker, *Army Officer's Guide, Forty-fifth Edition* (Harrisburg: Stackpole Books, 1990), 443.

45. Augustus L. Chetlain, *Recollections of Seventy Years* (Galena: The Gazette Publishing Co., 1899), 96–97.

46. D. Leib Ambrose, *History of the Seventh Regiment Illinois Volunteer Infantry, from Its Muster into the U.S. Service, April 25, 1861, to Its Final Muster Out, July 9, 1865* (Springfield: Illinois Journal Co., 1868), 136.

47. Ambrose, *History of the Seventh Regiment*, 138.

48. Frank Gaynor, ed., *The New Military and Naval Dictionary* (New York: Philosophical Library, 1951), 87; Matt B. Garber and P. Bond, *A Modern Military Dictionary* (1942; rpt. Detroit: Gale Research, 1975), 85.

49. John F. Callan, *The Military Laws of the United States, Relating to the Army, Volunteers, Militia, and to Bounty Lands and Pensions, from the Foundation of the Government to the Year 1863* (Philadelphia: George W. Childs, 1863), 175; Leonard Levy, *Jefferson and Civil Liberties: The Darker Side* (1963; rpt. New York: Quadrangle/The New York Times Book Company, 1973), 26–28. Officers are still governed by that regulation, slightly revised. See Crocker, *Army Officer's Guide*, 446.

50. Charles A. Partridge, ed., *History of the Ninety-sixth Regiment Illinois Volunteer Infantry* (Chicago: n.p., 1887), 100–104.

51. *Ninety-second Illinois Volunteers* (Freeport: Journal Steam Publishing House, 1875), 72. The "hemp" phrase appeared in the final version. See "Preamble and Resolutions adopted by the Second Brigade, General Baird's Division, in Camp Near Nashville, Tenn. . . . ," March 2, 1863, Abraham Lincoln Papers.

52. William Butler, Ozias M. Hatch, and Jesse K. Dubois to Abraham Lincoln, March 1, 1863 (with Yates endorsement), Abraham Lincoln Papers.

🦋

Chapter Six

Avoid Saying "Foolish Things": The Legacy of Lincoln's Impromptu Oratory

HAROLD HOLZER

In 1862, a Union brigadier general named George Lucas Hartsuff was wounded at Antietam and sent to nearby Frederick, Maryland, to recover. There, on October 4, President Abraham Lincoln, en route home from a visit with the Army of the Potomac in the field, stopped to pay a visit to the general at his bedside.[1]

No one knows what the commander-in-chief whispered into the general's ear that day—although, conceivably, it inspired Hartsuff to his remarkable recovery. But what Lincoln said that same day to a group of well-wishers gathered outside the house where the general was recuperating was transcribed. Waiting until Lincoln emerged, they called for what well-wishers usually demanded when they saw Lincoln in the flesh. They demanded a speech. What is doubtful is that any of the townspeople who heard Lincoln that day were as inspired by his words as was the bedridden general, because Lincoln said, "In my present position it is hardly proper for me to make speeches. Every word is so closely noted that it will not do to make trivial ones, and I cannot be expected to be prepared to make a matured one just now. If I were as I have been for most of my life, I might perhaps talk amusing to you for half an hour, and it wouldn't hurt anybody, but as it is, I can only return my sincere thanks for the compliment paid our cause and our common country."[2] Neither Lincoln's ordeal—nor that of his listeners—was quite over. Minutes later, he arrived at the local railroad station, where he was compelled to orate again. "Fellow-Citizens," he began. "I see myself surrounded by soldiers and a little further off I note the citizens of this good city of Frederick anxious to hear something from me. I can only say, as I did five minutes ago, it is not proper for me to make speeches in my present position."³

Think of it: "*Not proper for me to make speeches!*" This, from the fabled orator who would deliver a Gettysburg Address and a Second Inaugural Address that would live in the annals of both history and literature; this from the westerner who had earned a huge reputation as an orator and debater back in Illinois. The voice was the same, but the syntax was different, along with the protestations that encouraged his listeners at Frederick to believe that he was inadequate to the task of public speaking—or that any effort at all smacked somehow of impropriety. There was still another obvious difference: preparation.

The fact is, Abraham Lincoln, whose ascent to the presidency owed a major debt to his accomplishments as a public speaker, was an oratorical enigma. He could, of course, soar. But he could also sink. And more often than not, he was little better than dreadful when he spoke extemporaneously. At least that is the inevitable conclusion after a careful review of Lincoln's impromptu talks *on paper*—the transcriptions stenographers recorded on the spot for publication in newspapers. With few exceptions, these show a Lincoln at the nadir of his oratorical skills. The surprise is that the worst of these talks proliferated at the peak of his powers as a writer, from 1860 to 1865.

Once he became president, the man who had inspired and amused audiences so successfully as a public speaker and courtroom lawyer back in Illinois decided it was no longer proper for him to make speeches at all, impromptu or prepared. And with rare exceptions, it is seldom remembered, he did not. As he said in Pittsburgh as president-elect, "I am rather inclined to silence, and whether that be wise or not, it is at least more unusual now-a-days to find a man who can hold his tongue than to find one who cannot." True, Lincoln was then and throughout the long and difficult interregnum between his election and his inauguration avoiding policy statements, trying through silence to keep the Union together—at least so some historians have concluded. But in so doing he was also forfeiting a precious opportunity to use his newly expanded rostrum—the bully pulpit of the presidency—to keep additional states from seceding. Lincoln either did not know of or ignored the precedents for so doing. Even George Washington, who had also wanted what he called "a quiet entry devoid of ceremony," was instead repeatedly honored and called upon to speak en route to his inaugural. The historian J. G. Randall argued that Lincoln instead sought to "make no mistakes before taking further bearings." What Randall did not add was that Lincoln undoubtedly knew all too well that when he spoke extemporaneously he was prone to "mistakes."⁴ The historian Garry Wills has contended that Lincoln's greatest words profoundly changed a nation that was already fourscore and seven years old; if so, then it is not altogether unreasonable to speculate that earlier words by Lincoln might have changed a nation—the Confederacy— that was only two months old. They did not.[5]

In his defense, Lincoln had spent days before leaving for the capital meticulously preparing the one speech he knew would be the most closely read and important of his career: his inaugural address. The result unquestionably benefited from the close attention he paid to its preparation. But it was too late to preserve the Union with words. His impromptu speeches en route to that inaugural were potentially more timely but nowhere near as effective, or so their transcripts suggest.

Of course not all of Lincoln's impromptu speeches were transcribed accurately. His legendary "Lost Speech" in Bloomington was not recorded at all, although most historians now doubt the stubborn myth that reporters dropped their pens in awe, transfixed by Lincoln's golden oratory. We cannot completely dismiss charges by Lincoln's supporters that Democratic party stenographers worked to "garble the speeches of Mr. Lincoln" at the 1858 debates with Douglas. But neither can we totally ignore the Democratic argument that in Lincoln Republicans had "a candidate for the Senate of whose bad rhetoric and horrible jargon they are ashamed, upon which before they would publish it, they called a council of 'literary' men to discuss, reconstruct, and re-write." Nor should it be forgotten that Lincoln once reacted to a supporter's, not an opponent's, transcript of an 1858 speech by admitting, "Well, those are my views, and if I said anything on the subject, I must have said substantially that, but not nearly so well as that." In other words, Lincoln's impromptu rhetoric often needed the ameliorating help of sympathetic transcribers, for which he might be grateful. Stenographic reports could surely distort, but they could also improve. Unfortunately, there is nothing better on which to rely.[6]

Admittedly, there are also qualities in spoken speech—especially extemporaneous speech—that no transcriber can record. Such idiosyncratic touches are apparent only to on-the-spot listeners but are unavoidably lost to time and history. Such words might sound perfectly lucid as they are spoken but later look garbled in print. The New York *Tribune,* for example, acknowledged after Cooper Union that Lincoln's "tones, [and] gestures, the kindling eye, and the mirth-provoking look defy the reporter's skill." John Locke Scripps remembered "the intense irony of his invective, and the deep earnestness . . . of his eloquence." And a Massachusetts newspaper marveled at "that perfect command of manner and matter which so eminently distinguishes the western orators." If accurately recalled, these were characteristics Lincoln may well have learned from one of his heroes. He believed that Henry Clay's eloquence consisted of a "deeply earnest and impassioned tone, and manner, which can proceed only from great sincerity." But if Lincoln tried to emulate Clay's style, his own manner often defeated him. A Cincinnati newspaper, for example, complained that Lincoln pronounced "words in a manner that puzzles the ear sometimes to determine whether he is speaking his own or a foreign tongue."[7]

Even with his unique accent tempered by the undeniable effects of gestures and expressions we cannot recreate, there is still little of a charitable nature that can be said about Lincoln's performances in the towns and cities on his inaugural train journey. "I do not . . . expect, on any occasion, till after I get to Washington, to attempt any lengthy speech," he vowed in Indianapolis. He might have extended his ban to speeches of any length at any of the stops where, as he put it during the trip, his "iron horse" stopped "to water himself." Journalist Henry Villard had perceptively noted as Lincoln prepared to depart Springfield that "the grandeur of the mission he will be called upon to fulfill" was more "a source of anxiety and embarrassment than of hopeful and exciting emotion to him." Villard believed that "his lips must be trained to less ready and unqualified responses." But the ensuing inaugural journey proved that Lincoln's "training" had been insufficient.[8]

At one of his first stops along the long rail trip he said, "I hope that our national difficulties will pass away, and I hope we shall see in the streets of Cincinnati—good old Cincinnati—for centuries to come, once every four years her people give such a reception as this to the constitutionally elected President of the whole United States." It was a noble thought, but a tortured one, too.[9] At Steubenville, he declared, "If anything goes wrong . . . and you find you have made a mistake, elect a better man next time. There are plenty of them." Listeners probably wondered whether they had made a mistake.[10] And in Columbus, Lincoln assessed the disunion crisis by declaring, "It is a good thing that there is no more than anxiety, for there is nothing going wrong . . . nothing that really hurts anybody," careless words that were widely reprinted in the newspapers to show that Lincoln was not up to the task before him. He preached merely "patience and a reliance on . . . God," and supposedly a local citizen approached him afterward and declared, "You've got to give them Rebels a hotter shot than that before they're licked." As Vanity Fair observed with perhaps more insight than they realized, "Abe is becoming more grave. He don't construct as many jokes as he did. He fears that he will get things mixed up if he don't look out."[11]

By the time Lincoln got to New York he had probably heard about such criticism, but if he sought to alleviate growing concern over his abilities with a reassuring address in that hostile city he did not succeed. Yet he did come close to excusing his lackluster, inconsistent performances by admitting the wide gulf of ability that separated Lincoln the Speech *Reader* from Lincoln the Speech *Giver:*

> I have been in the habit of thinking and speaking for some time upon political questions that have for some years past agitated the country, and if I were disposed to do so, and we could take up some of the issues as the lawyers call them, and I were called upon to make an argument about it to the best of my ability, I could do that without much preparation. But that is not what you desire. . . . I have been occupying a position, since the Presidential election, of silence, of avoiding public speaking . . . because I thought, upon full consideration, that was the proper course for me to take . . . not . . . for any party wantonness, or from my indifference to the anxiety that pervades the minds of men. . . . I have kept silence for the reason that I supposed it was peculiarly proper that I should do so until the time came, according to the customs of the country, I should speak officially.[12]

Here at least was insight into the "position" Lincoln would maintain throughout his presidency, even if he was unable to adhere to it on his inaugural journey: He believed that presidents properly spoke publicly, when they spoke publicly at all, "officially"—that is, from text. Issues might be debated by lawyers or politicians "without much preparation," but not by presidential candidates, presidents-elect, or presidents. For one thing, their words were watched too closely; for another, events moved too quickly. As Lincoln told his New York audience, the "political drama" was "shifting its scenes" so rapidly even then that if he did not hold his tongue he "might be disposed by the shifting . . . afterwards to shift" himself. Or perhaps Lincoln was telling the whole truth when he protested in Indiana that if he gave too many speeches he "should be entirely worn out."[13]

To be sure, Lincoln eventually did produce some fine oratorical moments as he neared Washington, although it is possible that by then he had learned the bitter lessons of Indianapolis, Columbus, and New York and had begun writing out his thoughts in advance or at least making notes, as he probably did for the best of his so-called extemporaneous speeches back in Illinois, including the Great Debates with Douglas. But by then the pro-secession Charleston *Mercury* had already dismissed Lincoln's cumulative efforts as mere "fiddle-faddle," a "weak compound of blockhead and blackguard," and even up north no less ardent a Unionist than Charles Francis Adams worried that Lincoln's talks had "fallen like a wet blanket," putting "to flight all notions of greatness."[14]

Those pre-inaugural speeches—Lincoln's last prolonged exercise in impromptu oratory—probably taught him a valuable lesson. Accepting his limitations as an extemporaneous speaker, he wisely curtailed such opportunities thereafter. Or, once spoken, he altered the results as he had done at the beginning of his inaugural journey, as perhaps he had first learned to do as a congressman by revising his remarks, as other congressmen did and do, for official publication. Proof that Lincoln subjected his extemporaneous remarks to after-the-fact editing was unearthed with the discovery of a long-lost scrapbook in which Lincoln's assistant private secretary, John M. Hay, meticulously pasted newspaper accounts of the president-elect's journey eastward. In one such clipping, headlined "Mr. Lincoln's Speeches at Indianapolis" the text is revealingly prefaced: "The following are the speeches delivered by Mr. Lincoln in Indianapolis, *as revised by himself* [emphasis added] for the Indianapolis Journal." Clearly, Lincoln was a willing conspirator in the effort to improve for posterity what he said extemporaneously.[15]

In another example, we all remember, or at least think we remember, the achingly beautiful words Lincoln spoke before his departure from Springfield. "No one, not in my situation, can appreciate my feeling of sadness at this parting," he began. Or did he? Not according to a stenographer whose version appeared the next morning in the *Illinois State Journal*. In that transcript, Lincoln began a good deal more awkwardly: "No one who has never been placed in a like position, can understand my feelings at this hour, nor the oppressive sadness I feel at this parting." The text admired by generations of readers continued: "Here I have lived a quarter of a century, and have passed from a young to an old man." As the stenographer recorded it: "For more than a quarter of a century, I have lived among you, and during all that time I have received nothing but kindness at your hands. Here I have lived from my youth until now I am an old man." And what about the famous peroration? The version most historians cite is, "To His care commending you, as I hope in your prayers you will commend me, I bid you an affectionate farewell." But the on-the-scene reporter heard the same expression and transcribed it as, "To Him I commend you all—permit me to ask that with equal security and faith, you will all invoke His wisdom and guidance for me. With these few words I must leave you—for how long I know not. Friends, one and all, I must now bid you an affectionate farewell."[16]

There is nothing wrong with this more prosaic version. But it is hardly the heartfelt elegy most of us have been led to recall. And it is not the speech Lincoln would have delivered had he taken the time to write it beforehand. So he did the next best thing. He wrote it afterward. This superlative writer, whose words Harriet Beecher Stowe thought "worthy to be inscribed in letters of gold," wisely occupied the first few minutes aboard his inaugural train obliging those reporters traveling with him who had failed to record the speech as it poured forth from him, and he wrote it as he perhaps wished he had delivered it. The text of the revised version survives, and from it we can deduce precisely how and when Lincoln prepared it. The manuscript begins in his hand, and after a few lines that famous, clear penmanship begins to sway and jolt with the jostling of the speeding train. Then Lincoln's handwriting is replaced by that of his secretary, John G. Nicolay—the president-elect evidently finding that writing speeches on a moving train was unpleasant (and so much for another indelible legend, that Lincoln wrote his Gettysburg Address on board a train a few years later). So he handed his paper to his secretary and dictated. The result was beautiful words—but not the words he had delivered spontaneously.[17] Harriet Beecher Stowe could hardly have known the genesis of this particular speech, but she did know enough to realize of Lincoln's speeches that they evidenced "a greater power in writing than the most artful devices of rhetoric." For Lincoln, the most artful rhetoric was always written. It could not be spoken nearly as well—not without preparation.[18]

No event of Lincoln's lifetime ever inspired him more unforgettably than the sacrifice and victory at Gettysburg. We all know what that battle moved him to say—or we think we know. To serenaders who gathered outside the White House on July 7, 1863, to celebrate that victory, Lincoln responded with a tribute to the living and dead who gave their lives that the nation might live. In effect, this was Lincoln's first Gettysburg Address —the one he gave spontaneously and fumblingly. He said, "How long ago is it?—eighty odd years—since on the Fourth of July for the first time in the history of the world a nation by its representatives, assembled and declared as a self-evident truth that 'all men are created equal.' That was the birthday of the United States of America." Not for another four months were these stumbling thoughts refined into what may be the most famous opening line of any speech ever delivered in America: "Fourscore and seven years ago our fathers brought forth on this continent a new nation conceived in liberty and dedicated to the proposition that all men are created equal"—words delivered, marveled John Hay, who heard both versions, "with more grace than is his wont." Translation: Lincoln seldom orated so gracefully, especially extemporaneously.[19]

Gettysburg also proved an exception to Lincoln's rule of silence. By then, he had made it his practice to refuse even the most compelling speaking opportunities and remain close to Washington, a seclusion that in today's presidents would undoubtedly arouse suspicions of some devious "rose garden strategy" or worse. But the political culture required fewer appearances of nineteenth-century presidents, and Lincoln appeared genuinely to believe that a president belonged at his White House desk where the voters or, more to the point, the elite and remote Electoral College, had sent him. Besides, his most famous and successful extemporaneous effort,

the Lincoln-Douglas Debates, had been rewarded by a popular vote majority but an electoral loss. His silence as presidential candidate may have
generated less than 40 percent of the popular vote, but it also produced an
electoral majority.

Silence, he may well have concluded, was more rewarding than stump
speaking. Others agreed. Stephen A. Douglas, who shattered tradition by
speaking on his own behalf in 1860, was vilified simply for refusing, as he
put it (with a sly shot at his opponent), "to put a padlock on my lips or to
appoint a committee to . . . explain that I did not think it proper to express
any opinion." "No other candidate for the presidency ever degraded himself by . . . delivering partisan harangues," the Republican press jeered in
response, "Mr. Douglas is doing what Mr. Lincoln would scorn to do. . . .
May he be the last as he is the first." In truth, Douglas was neither. Winfield
Scott had been attacked eight years earlier for taking the stump in the
1852 presidential campaign "contrary to the taste of all good men." Henry
Clay had been castigated for similar transgressions. Thus one paper could
declare itself "disgusted" by the mere "spectacle" of President Buchanan
speaking openly in the 1860 campaign. As Lincoln's hometown, pro-Repub-
lican newspaper, the *Illinois State Journal,* insisted, "The American people
have always believed it would be in exceedingly bad taste and censurable
in a candidate for the high office of President to . . . electioneer by making
political speeches." Lincoln the celebrated political orator now agreed that
the presidency was beyond both politics and oratory—"an office no man
should seek by direct means," in the words of the *State Journal.* His tongue
silenced by what he called "the lessons of the past," Lincoln's career as a
stump speaker came to an abrupt end.[20]

Yet his subsequent, stubborn determination to refuse presidential speaking opportunities cannot fully be explained, as some historians have, merely
as evidence of his desire to remain close to the White House to ensure unin-
terrupted communication with his generals in the field. Even if Lincoln's
White House, astonishingly, was not equipped with its own telegraph, there
were enough lines in the large cities of the East and at railroad stations all
along the way to provide a traveling president, out on the hustings to
inspire his people, all the assurances he needed that he would remain in
close contact with his government and that the government could, in effect,
travel with him.

Lincoln ignored this possibility. The historian Waldo Braden calculated
that he made ninety-five speeches in four years as president. That may
sound like a large number, but seventy-eight were delivered in or from the
White House. Most were not really speeches at all but formal remarks to
visiting delegations or brief responses to serenaders. Another seven talks
were delivered elsewhere in Washington. Of course, during this era even the

president's annual messages to Congress—the nineteenth-century equivalents of today's State of the Union messages—were by tradition written by the president and then delivered to Capitol Hill to be read by a clerk. But as president, Lincoln was more wary of making impromptu speeches than even tradition required. When, for example, a delegation of Missouri Radicals arrived at the White House and demanded a response to their disgust with military affairs in their home state, Lincoln told them that they would have to wait for his official answer. He was not willing to extemporize on so sensitive an issue as relations with the crucial border states. Not until several days later did Lincoln have his reply ready. He had carefully written it out and then sent it to his visitors.[21]

As for his remaining ten presidential addresses, just one—the Gettysburg Address—can truly be called a formal presidential speech, and perhaps Lincoln accepted the summons to Gettysburg precisely because it asked that he deliver not the main oration but merely "a few appropriate remarks." Even then he couched his effort with a caveat: "The world will little remember what we say here." Of the other Lincoln speeches, two impromptu talks were given the day he visited Frederick; two more were delivered bumblingly en route to and at Gettysburg before he appeared at the Soldiers' Cemetery; another five were given at two Sanitary Fairs in 1864; and another was delivered unexpectedly in Jersey City as Lincoln was returning to Washington from a brief conference with Winfield Scott at West Point. As Lincoln said in this typical impromptu effort, "When birds and animals are looked at through a fog they are seen to disadvantage, and so it might be with you if I were to attempt to tell you why I went to see Gen. Scott." He ended with a less-than-sublime coda: "The Secretary of War, you know, holds a pretty tight rein the press, so that they shall not tell more than they ought to, and I'm afraid that if I blab too much he might draw a tight rein on me."[22]

Uninspiring as it was, the talk revealed the extemporaneous Lincoln at his best—"talking amusing to you" as he put it, but without so rising to the occasion, back in Frederick. Lincoln generally felt that such "amusing" bursts of wit were not appropriate to his station, especially once his demeanor and dignity became subjects of campaign mockery back in 1860. So he would hold a tight rein on himself. He would not, if he could help it, "blab too much." Like Clay, he would never speak, as Lincoln had recalled admiringly, "merely to be heard."[23]

Sometimes he could not help it. At a banquet at the Philadelphia Sanitary Fair in June of 1864, the man who had already achieved sublime greatness at Gettysburg was called upon to make a speech. He said, "I do not really think it is proper in my position for me to make a political speech . . . and being more of a politician than anything else, and having exhausted that branch of the subject at the fair, and not being prepared to speak on the other, I am without anything to say. . . . I must beg of you to excuse me from saying anything further." This was the impromptu Lincoln at his most honest. He believed that it was inherently improper for him to deliver speeches, and he was "not prepared" to deliver a formal one. Unable to avoid making an impromptu speech, he could do no better than produce a disjointed one. But it is hardly surprising that a reporter for the anti-Lincoln *New York World* reported with mock seriousness on Lincoln's remarks in Philadelphia: "The second Washington did not, on this occasion . . . crack many jokes—smutty or otherwise. Whether the solemnity of the occasion overpowered him, or whether he felt bilious, I am uninformed."[24]

The double irony was that the roster of impromptu opportunities maimed was dwarfed by the list of opportunities for formal oratory Lincoln rejected in advance. During the war he turned down enticing invitations to speak at events honoring war heroes David Farragut and Ulysses S. Grant. He declined an invitation to return to New York's Cooper Union to rally northerners to enlist, despite its organizers' promise that he might thus "encourage, by your voice, the active efforts of the loyal men . . . in support of the Union Cause." And even when James Conkling invited Lincoln home to Springfield to address what promised to be "a Grand Mass Meeting" of "Unconditional union men . . . the most imposing demonstration that has ever been held in the Northwest," Lincoln could summon enough enthusiasm only to reply cautiously, "I think I will go, or send a letter—probably the latter." In the end, he chose the latter course. He constructed a majestic letter to be read aloud there: "You say you will not fight to free negroes. Some of them seem willing to fight for you, . . . Among free men, there can be no successful appeal from the ballot to the bullet." Had Lincoln chosen to deliver these carefully written remarks in person, the result might well be counted today as one of his great presidential orations.[25]

Lincoln surely knew how successful he could be when he could read his prewritten speeches rather than invent them on the scene. Writing home after his triumph at Cooper Union, he boasted that it "gave me no trouble whatever, being within my calculation before I started"—meaning that he had written the speech in advance and researched it exhaustively. William Herndon remembered that Lincoln worked on it for weeks: "He searched through the dusty volumes of Congressional proceedings in the state library, and dug deeply into political history. He was painstaking and thorough in the study of his subject." It was a thoroughness in speech preparation he no longer had the liberty—or desire—to practice as president.[26]

Still, even if Lincoln was following a tradition of silence he thought appropriate, it is worth recalling that, in stark contrast, his Confederate counterpart, who unlike Lincoln is seldom remembered as a great orator, undertook several morale-building speaking tours during the war. William C. Davis calls them evidence of "how conscious he had become of the need to reach out." Jefferson Davis even used a speech dramatically to quell the Richmond bread riot. Lincoln, by comparison, hardly rushed north to use personal persuasion to quiet a far more dangerous situation—the worst urban disturbance in American history—the New York draft riots. So by 1865, when the vice president recalled that the president's speeches had become "bold and undaunted," filled with "loftiness of sentiment and . . . magnetic . . . delivery," it comes as no surprise that it was Confederate Vice President Alexander H. Stephens talking, and about Jefferson Davis not Abraham Lincoln.[27]

Although there can be little dispute about the surprisingly hollow legacy of Lincoln's lackluster impromptu oratory, there remains a lingering mystery. How did a politician who earned fame as an orator and debater regress so dramatically as president? Was it a matter of declining skill, the pressures of running a government and a war, a stubborn belief in the impropriety of presidential oratory, a combination of all of these elements, or something more?

To understand the evolution of Lincoln's rhetorical skills, it is useful to begin virtually at the beginning, with his education as a public speaker.[28] One of the first primers Lincoln got hold of in New Salem was *A Guide to the English Tongue* by a schoolmaster named Thomas Dilworth. Here Lincoln found instruction on syntax, analogy, and comparison; lessons in effectively using monosyllables (perhaps the original inspiration for Lincoln's subsequent and effective use of one-syllable words in such masterpieces as the Gettysburg Address); a guide to pronunciation, perhaps the first he ever read; advice on debating ("upbraid no man's weakness to discomfit"); and stories in verse with which to practice oration ("On the Diligent Ants" was one, "Life is Short and Miserable" was another). Or, Lincoln could try reciting and gaining insight from an instructive verse:

> Henceforth our Youth, who tread thy flow'ry way,
> Shall ne'er from the roles of proper *Diction* stray!
> No more their speech with Barb'rous terms be fill'd;
> No more their pens a crop of nonsense yield;
> But chosen words in due arrangement stand,
> And *Sense* and *Eloquence* go hand in hand.

"Vain-glory destroys all the fruits of good action," warned Dilworth in another passage, adding in a fatuous rhyme entitled "On Ambition" (which Lincoln clearly ignored, perhaps to his own subsequent psychological detriment):

> When wild Ambition in the Heart we find,
> Farewell Content, and quiet of the mind:

> For glitt'ring Clouds, we leave the solid shore,
> And wonted Happiness returns no more.[29]

Lincoln also read William Scott's *Lessons in Elocution*. Perhaps no book more informed or influenced his early development as a public speaker. From its pages came specific instruction from which the roots of Lincoln's oratorical style can be glimpsed: "Let your articulation be Distinct and Deliberate. . . . Let your Pronunciation be Bold and Forcible. . . . Pitch your voice in Different Keys. . . . Acquire a just Variety of Pause and Cadence. . . . Pronounce your words with propriety and elegance." Readers were given practice passages from Hume, Sterne, and others; a series of famous sermons; and crowd-pleasing soliloquies from Shakespeare, some of the political kind, like the St. Crispian's Day call to arms from *Henry V* and Antony's funeral oration from *Julius Caesar*. There was even practical advice to debaters: "A wise man endeavors to shine in himself; a fool to outshine others."[30]

Here, too, was a specific lesson in which Lincoln apparently came to believe, although he clearly never adequately learned it: "It were much to be wished, that all public speakers would deliver their thoughts and sentiments, either from memory or immediate conception: For, besides that there is an artificial uniformity which almost always distinguishes reading from speaking, the fixed posture, and the bowing of the head, which reading requires, are inconsistent with the freedom, ease, and variety of just elocution."[31]

Scott's *Lessons* even offered specific instructions on how to accomplish that spontaneous-looking "ease" the author recommended so strongly. The book provided specific lessons on the art of gesture, complete with woodcut illustrations in which ludicrously portrayed long-haired boys in dandified, not to mention outmoded, eighteenth-century costume were shown raising their arms loftily or shifting daintily from hip to hip. Through these words and pictures, Lincoln learned, for example, that "a boy should . . . rest the whole weight of his body on his right leg . . . the knees should be straight . . . the right arm must be held out, with the palm open, and the fingers straight and close, the thumb almost distant from them as it will go . . . [and] the very moment the last accented word is pronounced . . . the hand, as if lifeless, must drop down to the side . . . as if dead." Then, the lesson continued, the "left hand raises itself, into exactly the same position as the right was before . . . and so on, from right to left, alternatively, till the speech is ended." Scott advised further that a bent arm could be employed for emphasis, an arm brought down suddenly could highlight a crucial word or expression. But at all costs, the book cautioned, "Great care must be taken . . . not to bend [one's arm] at the wrist." Proper gesture,

Scott preached, was essential "to keep the audience awake." It was important not to put one's hands in one's pockets, or stare at one's hat, or play with a spool of thread or other prop. "Avoid ridiculous gestures," the author warned, but don't be a "speaking statue," either.[32] "The arms are sometimes both thrown out . . . sometimes they are lifted up as high as the face. . . . With the hands we solicit, we refuse, we promise, we threaten, we dismiss, we invite, we entreat, we express aversion, fear, doubting, denial, asking, affirmation, negation, joy, grief, confusion, penitence. . . . The hands serve us instead of many sorts of words, and where the language of the tongue is unknown, that of the hands is understood, being universal." It was expected that the face also be used to express gravity, fear, remorse, gravity, fear, denial, exhortation ("a kind, compliant look"), judgment, pardon, veneration, and other emotions, including mirth, raillery, even flashing hatred, but never sloth, which yawning would inevitably suggest. Lincoln learned this lesson well. Years later a contemporary marveled that when Lincoln moved his head with "a quick jerk" for emphasis, it was like "throwing off electric sparks into combustible material."[33]

The author granted, in a cautionary note to teachers using his volume as a textbook, "The master will be a little discouraged, at the awkward figure his pupil makes, in his first attempts. . . . But this is no more than what happens in dancing, fencing, or any other exercise that depends on practice." And Lincoln surely practiced. By the time he was a matured stump speaker, engaging Stephen A. Douglas in head-to-head debate, observers were taking appreciative note of individualistic habits of gesture and expression that surely originated in Scott's primitive lessons. It was these gestures that came in large part to mark Lincoln as a unique orator— even if he never totally outgrew the awkwardness his old primer promised would eventually vanish.[34]

One observer remembered that Lincoln often "pointed his theories into his hearers' head with a long, bony forefinger." He could "fling both hands upward" or "clench his fists in silent condemnation." Still another recalled that every so often, to emphasize a point, Lincoln would suddenly "bend his knees so they would almost touch the platform, and then . . . shoot himself to his full height, emphasizing his utterances in a very forcible manner." And still, one eyewitness to the debates concluded, the overall result was that Lincoln remained strikingly "ungraceful in his gestures."[35]

Lincoln's law partner and biographer William H. Herndon concurred that "on the stump" Lincoln was "at first . . . very awkward, and it seemed a real labor to adjust himself to his surroundings. He struggled for a time under a feeling of apparent diffidence and sensitiveness, and these only added to his awkwardness." Herndon insisted that Lincoln "never sawed

From *Lessons in Elocution* by William Scott (Boston, 1811) (Rare Books and Manuscripts Division, The New York Public Library, Astor, Lenox, and Tilden Foundation)

the air nor rent space into tatters and rags as some orators do. He never acted for stage effect." Yet, he conceded that "to express joy or pleasure, he would raise both hands at an angle of about fifty degrees, the palms upwards, as if desirous of embracing the spirit of that which he loved. If the sentiment was one of detestation—denunciation of slavery, for example—both arms, thrown upward and fists clenched, swept through the air. . . . This was one of his most effective gestures."[36]

Thus Herndon and other onlookers recorded one explanation for Lincoln's early success as a stump speaker, even when he lacked the written text that so often elevated his performances into the realm of poetry. That quality was gesture—the unrecordable element of Lincoln's speaking style, now and forever lost, except through generic period description. But it may well have been that Lincoln's style of gesture, weaned through Scott's primer, developed on the stump, and refined in the Great Debates of 1858, set him apart from other speakers, as much as his direct, forthright style and his "illustrations," as one admirer called them, which boasted "romance and pathos and fun and logic all welded together." Here was an extremely tall man with a homely face whose expression could change with the toss of a head—whose eyes could flash, Herndon recalled, "in a face aglow with the fire of his profound thoughts"; whose long arms could sweep dramatically through the air; and who sometimes bent at the knee and shot upward, looking heaven only knows how tall on the platform. And he could be earnest and impassioned at one moment, scathingly sarcastic at another. His voice, even if high-pitched, as some contemporaries recalled, could be heard to the farthest reaches of large outdoor crowds. A worried Stephen A. Douglas conceded on the eve of their debates that his rival's "droll ways and dry jokes" made him nothing less than "the best stump speaker . . . in the West." Even so, unless they were edited by partisan reporters, Lincoln's riveting stump performances—characterized by explosions of humor and outlandish gestures—seldom scanned in newspaper reprints. However considerable his reputation as a stump speaker, the evidence suggests that his extemporaneous performances were, in terms of syntax and substance, far less effective than the orations he wrote in advance.[37]

And herein may very well lie the elusive explanation for Lincoln's diminishing skill as an impromptu speaker. There are no period descriptions of President-elect Lincoln or President Lincoln ever gesturing awkwardly, gesturing dramatically, or gesturing at all. Photographs show him clutching his manuscript as he reads his great Second Inaugural. Eyewitnesses recalled that he held either his manuscript or his lapels at Gettysburg. Hard experience had taught Lincoln to rethink the lessons of Scott's *Lessons in Elocution*. Although Lincoln surely never lost his ability to engage his audience with the twinkle of his eye or the tilt of his head, he volitionally abandoned the great prop he had learned in Scott and honed to perfection on the prairie: the dramatic use of gesture to engage the emotions as Scott had taught and keep audiences awake. After his election to the presidency, Lincoln the now-rigid, inhibited impromptu orator, was no longer entertaining. For the man who had once entertained courtroom juries and political rallies alike, the joke was now on him.

On the eve of his greatest speech, Lincoln responded to calls for a greeting by a crowd gathered outside the David Wills house in Gettysburg and appeared at the door to offer, as John Hay bluntly confided in his diary, "half a dozen words meaning nothing." "The inference is a very fair one," Lincoln said that evening, "that you would hear me for a little while, at least, were I to commence to make a speech. I do not appear before you for the purpose of doing so, and for several substantial reasons. The most substantial of these is that I have no speech to make. In my position, it is somewhat important that I should not say any foolish things." Just then a voice in the audience shot back: "*If* you can help it." Replied Lincoln, "It very often happens that the only way to help it is to say nothing at all."[38] And perhaps that is why, as president, Lincoln said nothing at all whenever he could and said as little as possible when he was unable to keep silent. More often than history has recalled, when he could not avoid speaking extemporaneously he could not avoid saying foolish things.

Tellingly, Lincoln's last response to a crowd of well-wishers gathered outside the White House, delivered a few days before his assassination, was anything but spontaneous. "The President had written out his speech," recalled the journalist Noah Brooks, "being well aware that the importance of the occasion would give it significance, and he was not willing to run the risk of being betrayed by the excitement of the occasion in saying anything which would make him sorry when he saw it in print." Lincoln had had much reason to be sorry in the past. His impromptu speeches probably read even worse than they sounded.[39]

He might have refined his skills at impromptu oratory, but he did not. He might have artfully used gestures to entertain his audiences, but apparently did not. He might have filled the void between expectation and performance by delivering more formal speeches, but he did not even do this. And he remained perpetually ambivalent about which form of expression was most proper. As he said in his second lecture on discoveries and inventions in 1859, "Speech alone, valuable as it ever has been, and is, has not advanced the condition of the world much. . . . *Writing* . . . is the great invention of the world." Yet in that very same lecture he contradicted himself. "*Writing,*" he said, "—although a wonderful auxiliary for speech, is no worthy substitute for it. . . . One always has one's tongue with him, and the breath of life is the ever-ready material with which it works."[40]

Lincoln once declared, "I shall never be old enough to speak without embarassment when I have nothing to talk about."[41] He lived to be fifty-six. And the man acknowledged as one of the greatest public speakers ever to occupy the White House must have been embarrassed many times. The leader often remembered as the first modern president apparently failed altogether to comprehend the power of oratory in molding public opinion and maintaining public support during a crisis. Instead, as he admitted in Chicago on November 21, 1860, and continued to believe for the next four-and-a-half years, "I am not in the habit of making speeches now." Perhaps he hinted at his rhetorical doubts most revealingly when he declared in his 1862 Message to Congress, "Men should utter nothing for which they would not be responsible through time and in eternity." The man who knew, as he put it in the same message, that he could not "escape history" found it prudent to escape the dangers of extemporaneous public speaking as often as possible. Had Lincoln been a better impromptu speaker, or had he taken advantage of the frequent opportunities offered him to make formal presidential speeches in public, he might well be remembered not only as the Great Emancipator but also as the Great Communicator.[42]

Notes

1. Washington *Star*, Oct. 6, 1862.

2. Roy P. Basler, ed., Marion Dolores Pratt and Lloyd P. Dunlap, asst. eds., *The Collected Works of Abraham Lincoln*, 9 vols. (New Brunswick: Rutgers University Press, 1953–55), 5:450 (hereafter cited as *Collected Works*).

3. *Collected Works*, 5:450.

4. *Collected Works*, 4:209; Barry Schwartz, *George Washington: The Making of an American Symbol* (New York: Free Press, 1987), 49.

5. See Garry Wills, *Lincoln at Gettysburg: The Words That Remade America* (New York: Simon and Schuster, 1992).

6. Harold Holzer, ed., *The Lincoln-Douglas Debates: The First Complete, Unexpurgated Text* (New York: HarperCollins, 1993), 13; Emanuel Hertz, ed., *The Hidden Lincoln: From the Letters and Papers of William H. Herndon* (New York: Viking Press, 1938), 271.

7. New York *Tribune*, Feb. 28, 1860, Lowell [Mass.] *Journal* (1848), and Cincinnati *Enquirer*, Sept. 18, 1859, quoted in Robert S. Harper, *Lincoln and the Press* (New York: McGraw-Hill, 1951), 11, 37, 46; Elwell Crissey, *Lincoln's Lost Speech: The Pivot of His Career* (New York: Hawthorn Books, 1967), 241; *Collected Works*, 2:126.

8. *Collected Works*, 4:193, 204; Harold G. Villard and Oswald Garrison Villard,

eds., *Lincoln on the Eve of '61: A Journalist's Story by Henry Villard* (New York: Alfred A. Knopf, 1941), 41, 48–49.

9. *Collected Works*, 4:198.

10. Ibid., 207.

11. Ibid., 204; Victor Searcher, *Lincoln's Journey to Greatness* (Philadelphia: John C. Winston, 1960), 134; Mark E. Neely, Jr., *The Abraham Lincoln Encyclopedia* (New York: McGraw-Hill, 1982), 159; Herbert Mitgang, ed., *Abraham Lincoln: A Press Portrait* (Chicago: Quadrangle Books, 1971), 229.

12. *Collected Works*, 4:230–31.

13. Ibid., 194.

14. See, for example, Lincoln's address before the New Jersey senate at Trenton, Feb. 21, 1861, and at Independence Hall, Philadelphia, Feb. 22, 1862, *Collected Works*, 4:235–36, 240–41; Searcher, *Lincoln's Journey to Greatness*, 35, 134.

15. Newspaper clipping, "Mr. Lincoln's Speeches at Indianapolis, as Revised by Himself," from John Hay's scrapbook, private collection.

16. For different versions of the Farewell Address, see *Collected Works*, 4:190–91.

17. Harriet Beecher Stowe's article about Lincoln appeared in *Littell's Living Age* on Feb. 6, 1864. See Mitgang, ed., *Abraham Lincoln*, 377; see also Villard and Villard, eds., *Lincoln on the Eve of '61*, 73; for a reproduction of the post-facto manuscript of Lincoln's Farewell Address, see Stefan Lorant, *Lincoln: A Picture History of His Life* (New York: W. W. Norton, 1969), 119.

18. Mitgang, ed., *Abraham Lincoln*, 377; Tyler Dennett, ed., *Lincoln and the Civil War in the Diaries and Letters of John Hay* (New York: Dodd, Mead, 1939), 120.

19. *Collected Works*, 6:319.

20. *Illinois State Journal*, June 19, 1860, July 24, 1860, Aug. 29, 1860; *Illinois State Register*, Oct. 7, 1860; Wayne C. Williams, *A Rail Splitter for President* (Denver: University of Denver Press, 1951), 24, 30.

21. Waldo C. Braden, *Abraham Lincoln: Public Speaker* (Baton Rouge: Louisiana State University Press, 1988), 95; Dennett, ed., *Diaries of John Hay*, 101; *Collected Works*, 6:499–504. Lincoln's letter to Charles D. Drake and others was written on Oct. 5, 1863, in response to a meeting held Sept. 30.

22. Ibid.; David Wills to Abraham Lincoln, Nov. 2, 1863, Abraham Lincoln Papers, Library of Congress; *Collected Works*, 5:284.

23. *Collected Works*, 2:126.

24. Ibid., 7:398; *New York World*, June 18, 1864, in *Abraham Lincoln*, ed. Mitgang, 405.

25. See Harold Holzer, ed., *Dear Mr. Lincoln: Letters to the President* (New York: Addison-Wesley, 1993), 280–81, 288–89, 292–93; *Collected Works*, 6:399, 406–10.

26. *Collected Works*, 3:555; William H. Herndon and Jesse Weik, *Abraham Lincoln: The True Story of a Great Life*, 3 vols. (Springfield: The Herndon's Lincoln Publishing Co., n.d.), 3:454, 478.

27. William C. Davis, *Jefferson Davis: The Man and His Hour* (New York: Harper-Collins, 1991), 466–69; Clement Eaton, *Jefferson Davis* (New York: Free Press, 1977), 27, 233.

28. See, for example, M. L. Houser, *Lincoln's Education* (New York: Bookman,

1957), 117; David C. Mearns, "Mr. Lincoln and the Books He Read," in *Three Presidents and What They Read*, ed. Arthur E. Bestor, David C. Mearns, and Jonathan Daniels (Urbana: University of Illinois Press, 1963), 54–57.

29. Thomas Dilworth, *A Guide to the English Tongue in Five Parts*... (Philadelphia: John Bioren, 1809), i, 74, 78, 97, 102–4; for confirmation that Lincoln read Scott, see Ward Hill Lamon, *The Life of Abraham Lincoln, from His Birth to His Inauguration as President* (Boston: Jas. R. Osgood, 1872), 37.

30. William Scott, *Lessons in Elocution; or, A Selection of Pieces in Prose and Verse for the Improvement of Youth in Reading and Speaking*... *to which are prefixed Elements of Gesture* (Boston: Isaiah Thomas Jun[.], 1811), 33–36, 40, 46, 48, 49, 381–82, 385–86, 393.

31. Scott, *Lessons*, 56.

32. Ibid., 12, 15–16, 19, 135–36.

33. Ibid., 28, 33–36; Herndon and Weik, *Abraham Lincoln*, 2:407.

34. Scott, *Lessons*, 19.

35. Rufus Rockwell Wilson, *Intimate Memories of Lincoln* (Elmira: Primavera Press, 1945), 173–74, 184–85.

36. Herndon and Weik, *Abraham Lincoln*, 2:405–7.

37. Ibid., 408; Robert W. Johannsen, *Stephen A. Douglas* (New York: Oxford University Press, 1973), 640–41.

38. *Collected Works*, 7:16–17.

39. P. J. Staudenraus, ed., *Mr. Lincoln's Washington: Selections from the Writings of Noah Brooks, Civil War Correspondent* (New York: Thomas Yoseloff, 1967), 388.

40. *Collected Works*, 3: 359–60.

41. Lois J. Einhorn, *Abraham Lincoln the Orator: Penetrating the Lincoln Legend* (Westport: Greenwood Press, 1992), 17.

42. *Collected Works*, 4:143, 5:535, 537.

Part Three

LINCOLN'S LEGACY

Chapter Seven

🦋

What Is an American?
Abraham Lincoln and Multiculturalism

RICHARD N. CURRENT

Abraham Lincoln is a dead white male. He was a honkey. He was a WASP. His world was quite different from the world we inhabit today. You might wonder, then, what relevance his memory could possibly have for the question of the validity and desirability of multiculturalism. The question is a serious one. It amounts to this: What is—and what should be—an American?

The current buzzword *multiculturalism* means different things to different people; the issue is, in part, semantic.[1] As some use the word, it refers to efforts to enhance recognition and respect for ethnic and racial minorities, as well as for women, homosexuals, and others who may feel marginalized or oppressed. To achieve these goals, schools and colleges are undertaking to broaden the curriculum, provide counseling in regard to "diversity," and prevent offensive speech. Advocates of such programs differ among themselves as to specifics, but they generally agree that multiculturalism is a good thing—even when others use the word to justify far more drastic measures.[2]

These others do not see multiculturalism as a means of enriching a culture that everyone shares or aspires to share. Instead, they question whether any such common culture is either possible or desirable. "Unlike earlier periods in the history of this country," says one multicultural pronouncement, the 1991 New York curriculum report, "the various peoples who make up our nation . . . seem determined to maintain and publicly celebrate much of that which is peculiar to the culture with which they identify." These various ethnic and racial groups "now insist . . . that their knowledge and perspective be treated with parity."[3] This New York multicultural manifesto continues:

Before this time [the 1960s] the dominant model of the typical American has been conditioned primarily by the need to shape a unified nation
out of a variety of contrasting and often conflicting European immigrant
communities. But following the struggle for civil rights, the unprecedented increase in non-European immigration over the last two decades
and the increasing recognition of our nation's indigenous heritage, there
has been a fundamental change in the image of what a resident of the
United States is. With this change . . . previous ideals of assimilation to
an Anglo-American model have been put in question and are being set
aside.[4]

According to this multiculturalist view, there is no longer a single, homo-
geneous American culture, if indeed there ever was one. Rather, there are
now five distinct and separate cultures in the United States: Indian or
Native American, African American, Asian American, Hispanic or Latino
American, and European American. These, it is argued, are all of exactly
the same intrinsic worth, have contributed equally to American life, and
must be "treated with parity." The traditionally predominant European-
American culture, the argument goes, has actually been Anglo-American,
and to allow it to continue to predominate is to be guilty of "Anglocentrism,"
which is the worst form of "Eurocentrism."

As proof of "the *Anglocentrism* of American culture so far," Ali A. Mazrui
of SUNY Binghamton points with alarm to the fairly obvious fact that
American "political culture" is similar to British, Canadian, Australian,
and New Zealand political culture.[5] An even more obvious sign of Anglocentrism is the prevalence of the English language in the United States.
All languages must be declared equal, it appears, and "language rights"
must be protected as if they were civil rights. Opponents of "parallel language rights in government"—proponents of making English the official
language of the country—are condemned as "mean-spirited" characters
who favor legislation that is "discriminatory and divisive." "The movement to repress undocumented people [illegal aliens] and the movement
to repress our language rights are the same movement," said a Hispanic
member of the Massachusetts legislature who recently filed a resolution to
declare Massachusetts a multicultural and multilingual state.[6]

When it comes to school and college curricula, not all reformers are
satisfied with such modest changes as broadening the Western civilization
course into a world civilizations course.[7] Some demand that American
history be taught strictly as ethnic history. New textbooks take this approach.
One of them bears the title *A Different Mirror: A History of Multicultural
America,* and its author is Ronald Takaki, a Japanese-American professor
at the University of California, Berkeley. Takaki focuses on blacks, Indians,
Chinese, Japanese, Mexicans, Irish, and Jews and their struggles for status

in this country. "What we need," he says, "is a new conceptualization [of American history], where there is no center." His book mentions Thomas Jefferson only as a slaveholder, not as an author of the Declaration of Independence. "There is little here," a reviewer points out, "about the drafting of the Constitution or the evolution of the Republic's democratic ideals."[8]

Multiculturalists aim to bring about a "radical rethinking of what being an American means," as Sau-Ling Wong, a Chinese-American professor at Berkeley, puts it.[9] Already (to repeat the words of the New York curriculum report) "there has been a fundamental change in the image of what a resident of the United States is." The state's curricular experts speak of a "resident," not a *citizen*, of the United States. They and other multiculturalists see each resident as belonging not to American society but only to one of the groups into which they divide that society. According to this view, there are no longer any Americans as such. There are only Native, African, Asian, Hispanic, and European Americans. Residents derive their identity from their ancestors; it is their inheritance; it is in their blood. Even though they may be third-generation residents—they and their parents born in this country—they cannot become culturally naturalized. Assimilation has never really worked; it has been nothing more than the imposition of "Anglo-conformity" on all the groups. Such is the conclusion that follows from a "radical rethinking of what being an American means."

There is no place for Abraham Lincoln in that kind of radical rethinking. He had a very different conception of what it means to be an American. For him, it was a matter of commitment to certain principles, not a matter of racial or cultural inheritance. The principles were those of "a new nation, conceived in Liberty, and dedicated to the proposition that all men are created equal."[10] Lincoln's most explicit statement of this idea was at an Independence Day celebration in Chicago in July 1858:

> We find a race of men living in that day [1776] whom we claim as our fathers and grandfathers. . . . We have besides these men—descended by blood from our ancestors—among us perhaps half our people who are not descendants at all of these men, they are men who have come from Europe—German, Irish, French and Scandinavian—men who have come from Europe themselves, or whose ancestors have come hither and settled here, finding themselves our equals in all things. If they look back through this history to trace their connection with those days by blood, they find they have none, they cannot carry themselves back into that glorious epoch and make themselves feel that they are part of us, but when they look through that old Declaration of Independence they find that these old men say that "We hold these truths to be self-evident, that all men are created equal," and then they feel that the moral senti-

ment taught in that day evidences their relation to those men, that it is
the father of all moral principle in them, and that they have a right to
claim it as though they were blood of the blood and flesh of the flesh of
the men who wrote that Declaration, and so they are.[11]

To become an American—to become a citizen of the United States—an
immigrant "should be put to some reasonable test of his [or her] fidelity to
our country and its institutions," and he or she "should first dwell among
us a reasonable time to become generally acquainted with the nature of
those institutions." So Lincoln believed. And the "naturalization laws should
be so framed as to render citizenship under them as convenient, cheap,
and expeditious as possible."[12] Thus, in Lincoln's view, it should be fairly
easy to become an American, regardless of an immigrant's inherited nationality or culture.

Lincoln therefore condemned the discriminatory immigration and naturalization policies that the Know-Nothings advocated. "As a nation, we
began by declaring that 'all men are created equal,'" he wrote. "We now
practically read it 'all men are created equal, except negroes.' When the
Know-Nothings get control, it will read, 'all men are created equal, except
negroes and foreigners and catholics.' When it comes to this I should prefer
emigrating to some country where they make no pretence of loving liberty—
to Russia, for instance, where despotism can be taken pure, and without
the base alloy of hypocracy."[13]

Disagreeing with Lincoln on this as on other matters was Stephen A.
Douglas, who insisted in the 1858 debates that Negroes were not included
in the Declaration of Independence. Lincoln replied:

> I think the authors of that notable instrument intended to include *all*
> men, but they did not mean to declare all men equal *in all respects*. They
> did not mean to say all men were equal in color, size, intellect, moral
> development or social capacity. They defined with tolerable distinctness
> in what they did consider all men created equal—equal in certain inal-
> ienable rights, among which are life, liberty and the pursuit of happiness.
> This they said, and this they meant. They did not mean to assert the
> obvious untruth, that all men were then actually enjoying that equality,
> nor yet that they were about to confer it immediately upon them. In fact
> they had no power to confer such a boon. They meant simply to declare
> the *right* so that the *enforcement* of it might follow as fast as circum-
> stances should permit.
>
> They meant to set up a standard maxim for free society which should
> be familiar to all: constantly looked to, constantly labored for, and even
> though never perfectly attained, constantly approximated and thereby
> constantly spreading and deepening its influence and augmenting the
> happiness and value of life to all people, of all colors, everywhere.[14]

The United States, based as it was on these principles, was unique in the history of the world. Here was a "system of political institutions conducing more essentially to the ends of civil and religious liberty than any of which the history of former times tells us."[15] In his very first political statement, as a young man of twenty-three, Lincoln proposed that everyone "receive at least a moderate education and thereby be enabled to read the histories of his own and other countries, by which he may duly appreciate the value of our free institutions."[16]

That kind of comparative history might well be recommended to the multicultural curriculum-makers of today. Such a history would be especially appropriate for the education of those who pontificated that "African-Americans, Asian Americans, Puerto Rican/Latinos and Native Americans have all been the victims of an intellectual and educational oppression that has characterized the culture and institutions of the United States and the European American world for centuries."[17] As a comparison of the United States with other countries would have shown, none of the others has welcomed so many and such diverse newcomers, none has enabled the various peoples to live together in as great a degree of harmony, and none has succeeded so well in merging them into a single nationality.

With the passage of the Immigration Act of 1965, the gates were opened wider than they had been for generations. No longer were Northern and Western Europeans—or *any* Europeans—favored. Some five million people entered the country in the five years from 1985 to 1990. They constituted nearly 8 percent, or approximately one in twelve, of the entire population. The largest number—even if illegal immigrants are not counted—came from Mexico and the next largest number from the Philippines. A majority of all the newcomers, 60 percent of them, had not yet become citizens.[18]

It remains to be seen how many of these people will eventually look upon themselves as Americans rather than Hispanic Americans, Asian Americans, and so on. Multiculturalists would expect to see—and would prefer to see—that very few ever do so.

But there is persuasive evidence that self-appointed spokespersons sometimes exaggerate and misrepresent the ethnic consciousness of their respective groups. A survey shows, for example, that a majority of the Hispanics in this country do not consider themselves members of a single Hispanic community with shared cultural, political, and economic interests. Instead, they think of themselves as Mexican, Cuban, or Puerto Rican in heritage, and the three groups have little interaction with one another. Most members speak English as their main or only language. Most do not favor increased immigration (their attitude is a sure sign of assimilation). "We have a population here," the survey concludes, "that is in fact very American, very pro-American and wanting to make it in the mainstream."[19]

To make it in the mainstream would be much more difficult, if not impossible, in most other countries. For example, a German is a German by virtue of German blood. A foreigner—even a foreigner's child born in Germany—must go through a long, expensive, and discouraging process to become a citizen. Hence nearly two million Turks, along with more than four million other foreigners, remain noncitizens despite their eagerness to be naturalized. As it is, they have the burdens but not the benefits of citizenship; they must pay taxes but they cannot vote.[20]

The prime minister of Turkey has called upon the German government to agree to dual citizenship for the Turks living in Germany. For them, this might be an improvement, though it would seem to mean that they would be only half-German and half-Turkish, with divided loyalties. The president of the Gabon Republic has proposed that his own country and other countries in Africa do much the same thing for blacks in the United States. "We should offer dual citizenship to our African-American brothers and sisters," the Gabon president has said. This would, no doubt, give new significance to the term "African American," which would come to mean African *and* American.[21]

Africa remains divided by tribal loyalties and enmities. Japan has never welcomed immigrants, and the Koreans residing there constitute an extremely disadvantaged minority. China, traditionally xenophobic and the scene of the Tiananmen Square massacre, is hardly a haven for the oppressed. Communists used to brag that the Soviet Union was a model of multiculturalism, a country where a great variety of ethnic groups lived in complete harmony under communism. We all know what has happened to the Soviet Union and to the formerly multicultural states of Czechoslovakia and Yugoslavia. France has its Algerian minority and Great Britain its Scottish and its Welsh nationalists, as well as its dark-skinned minorities and its problems in Northern Ireland. Indeed, there are today few if any important nations immune to ethnic and other internal strains.

"As a nation of immigrants, Australia is becoming like the United States," Ross Terrill, an Australian, writes. "Yet so far Australia is still more self-conscious about race and immigration than America," Terrill goes on to say. "Americans take a melting-pot society for granted. Australians do not." Perhaps he should have said that Americans *used* to take a melting-pot society for granted. Terrill concludes that "it will be important to maintain a continuity of established Australian values and institutions, and a clear-eyed commitment to individual liberty—as distinct from the rights of ethnic blocs."[22] It is likewise important for the United States to maintain a continuity of established American values and institutions and a clear-eyed commitment to individual liberty—as distinct from the rights of ethnic blocs.

Canada is the country that most closely resembles the United States as a nation of immigrants. But in Quebec's demand for a separate culture and identity, if not for a separate existence, Canada faces a problem of ethnic divisiveness more threatening to national unity than any that has yet arisen in the United States, if we except secession and the Civil War.

This, of course, is not to say that the United States has no problems of ethnic divisiveness. Ethnic and racial conflict is a well-known and recognized part of our history and has been from the beginning. We have always needed to temper prejudice and mitigate conflict, as Lincoln himself tried to do.

Like a great many other Americans, Lincoln was shocked by the 1863 New York draft riot, in which Irish Americans attacked African Americans. When, several months later, he was elected an honorary member of the New York Workingmen's Association, he responded with some advice for his fellow members: "Let them beware of prejudice, working division and hostility among themselves. The most notable feature of a disturbance in your city last summer was the hanging of some working people by other working people. It should never be so. The strongest bonds of human sympathy, outside the family relation, should be one uniting all working people, of all nations, and tongues, and kindreds."[23]

The question is not whether some groups have been—and are—prejudiced and hostile toward other groups. The question is, Will an emphasis on group separateness and ethnic distinctiveness tend to moderate—or to exacerbate—such prejudice and hostility? Will it contribute to national unity or to disunity?

National unity does not require the members of any group to give up their whole ethnic heritage. In this country, families have always been allowed to show pride in their ancestral homeland, to maintain a sentimental attachment to it, to speak its language, to fly its flag, even to boast of the connection on a bumper sticker. Americans have always been free to worship in the way their forebears did. To criticize multiculturalism is not to object in the slightest to the preservation of cultural vestiges of these kinds.

A great many Americans, however, can no longer trace their roots to one particular group, but have ancestors of two or more nationalities. American culture, like the American people, is a blend of elements that come from a variety of ethnic sources—including the aboriginal, African, Hispanic, and Asian as well as the European. This does not mean that all groups have contributed equally to the prevailing mix. So far, English remains the national language, and the political system is primarily English in origin.

This is due to the fact that the English were much the most numerous among the early immigrants. It is not because their language or their institutions were, or are, necessarily any better than others. It would be hard to demonstrate, though, that English is any worse for our purposes than, say, Nahuatl or Swahili. It would also be hard to demonstrate that ethnic minorities in this country would be better off if our system of law and government had derived from Uganda or China or Japan—despite the multiculturalist complaint that all the non-European minorities have been victims of an "oppression that has characterized the culture and institutions of the United States and the European American world for centuries." It would seem, rather, that this culture and these institutions have helped to attract so many and such diverse people to this country. Certainly, this culture and these institutions make it possible for multiculturalists to denounce this very culture and these very institutions freely.[24]

Lincoln did not pretend that American democracy was perfect, or anywhere near perfect. He looked upon it as an experiment, and he invited people of all countries, cultures, and creeds to share in the great political experiment as well as the economic opportunities of the United States. Only time, he believed, would tell whether the principles of the Declaration of Independence and the Constitution would permanently work. The founders of the Republic—in declaring that "all men are created equal" and are endowed with the rights of life, liberty, and the pursuit of happiness—intended to set up a "standard maxim for free society," as he said, to be "constantly labored for" and thereby to be constantly "augmenting the happiness and value of life to all people of all colors everywhere."

Today, all people of all colors everywhere are not necessarily interested in human rights as Thomas Jefferson described them in the Declaration of Independence and Abraham Lincoln advocated them in his many references to the Declaration.

At the UN Conference on Human Rights, which met in Vienna in June 1993, some of the delegates appealed to multiculturalism in denouncing the Western democratic—that is, the Euro-American—conception of individual liberties. The Chinese delegate Liu Huaqiu declared, "One should not and cannot think of the human rights standards and models of certain countries as the only proper ones and demand all other countries comply with them." A spokesman for Singapore, Lee Kuan Yew, said that many Asian countries, whose culture is Confucian, place a higher value on group consensus than on individual freedom. Representatives of other Third World governments similarly argued that there is no universal standard of human rights—that standards must vary according to economic development and cultural inheritance.[25]

This is precisely the kind of cultural relativism that multiculturalists apply to the United States when they assert, or imply, that the inherited culture of each ethnic group is of exactly the same value as the Euro-

American for standards of life, including political life, in this country. In that view, every resident of the country derives his or her own standards from his or her ethnic background. It follows that there can be no such thing as an American except as a permanent member of one or another ethnic or tribal group.

Lincoln saw it quite differently. In his view, an American is a citizen who, regardless of ancestry, believes in the democratic principles on which the Republic was founded. Lincoln was also aware that the promise of the Declaration of Independence has not been and never will be realized completely. Still, as he once asked, "Is there any better, or equal, hope in the world?" This is a good question for those who would sit by, with indifference or even with approval, while others reject the democratic ideal, with its unifying power, and call instead for a miscellany of tribalistic values and loyalties. The more diverse the people become, the greater the need for common and cohesive principles rather than a cacophony of cultures such as the multiculturalists advocate. It is well to remember and give heed to Lincoln's warning that: "a house divided against itself cannot stand."[26]

Notes

1. An excellent discussion of the semantic and other aspects of the issue is to be found in Philip Gleason, *Speaking of Diversity: Language and Ethnicity in Twentieth-Century America* (Baltimore: Johns Hopkins University Press, 1992), which contains essays on such topics as "The Melting Pot," "Pluralism and Assimilation," "Minorities (Almost) All," "Identifying Identity," and "Americans All."

Before "multiculturalism," the catchword was "cultural pluralism." I have discussed Lincoln's position on cultural pluralism in *Unity, Ethnicity, and Abraham Lincoln* (Fort Wayne: Warren Lincoln Library and Museum, 1978), which is reprinted in my *Speaking of Abraham Lincoln: The Man and His Meaning for Our Times* (Urbana: University of Illinois Press, 1983), 105–25. I have also criticized the idea in "The 'New Ethnicity' and American History," *The History Teacher* 15 (Nov. 1981): 43–53, which is reprinted in my *Arguing with Historians: Essays on the Historical and the Unhistorical* (Middletown: Wesleyan University Press, 1987), 162–73.

2. Diane Ravitch, "Multiculturalism: E Pluribus Plures," *The Key Reporter* 56 (Autumn 1990): 2, draws a distinction between "pluralistic" and "particularistic" multiculturalism. "The pluralists seek a richer common culture; the particularists insist that no common culture is possible or desirable," Ravitch writes. "Advocates of particularism propose an ethnocentric curriculum to raise the self-esteem and academic achievement of children from racial and ethnic minority backgrounds." (Ravitch's essay appeared at somewhat greater length in the *American Scholar*, Summer 1990.)

Many people use the term *multiculturalism* indiscriminately, with no apparent awareness of the difference in connotations that Ravitch points out. In criticizing the idea, I have in mind the particularist version of it.

3. "Executive Summary," in *Report of the New York State Social Studies Review and Development Committee* (Albany: The State Education Department, June 13, 1991), n.p.

4. "Preamble," *Report of the New York State Social Studies Review and Development Committee*, 1.

5. Ali A. Mazrui, "Annex," ibid., 86. Two members of the committee dissented from the report. Arthur Schlesinger, Jr., pointed out that "a basic question is involved: should public education seek to make our young boys and girls contributors to a common American culture? or should it strengthen and perpetuate separate eth[n]ic and social subcultures?" (91). Kenneth T. Jackson argued that "it is politically and intellectually unwise for us to attack the traditions, customs, and values which attracted immigrants to these shores in the first place" (80).

6. After bomb threats and explosive rhetoric, the Dade County, Florida, commissioners repealed a law making English the county's official language. "There are those for whom the language issue provides opportunity to act out their prejudices in ways that are both mean-spirited and destructive of the whole notion of living in harmony in a multicultural community," commented Arthur N. Teitelbaum, southern director of the Anti-Defamation League of B'Nai B'Rith. *Boston Globe*, May 19, 1993, 5.

In Massachusetts, State Representative Nelson Merced proposed a "multicultural state" in opposition to a movement to declare English the official state language. Yale Newman, a spokesman for US English, objected: "We see efforts being made to demand parallel language rights, and we feel that that would convert the US into a tower of Babel." *Boston Globe*, Nov. 22, 1989.

7. The Tufts University faculty, for example, approved a year course in world civilizations, to be taught by professors from several departments and required of all freshmen. The Association of American Colleges has encouraged its members to introduce similar "required survey courses with a strong multicultural content." *Boston Globe*, Sept. 16, 1991, 1.

8. See the article on Takaki and his book in the *Chronicle of Higher Education*, May 26, 1993, A9, from which the quotation is taken. Takaki sees the book as describing a "multicultural America" that celebrates "our wholeness as members of humanity as well as one nation." But he provides no unifying theme—such as the progressive realization of the Declaration of Independence—which would contribute to such national wholeness. The reviewer in the *Boston Globe*, June 7, 1993, 31, saw the book as "especially valuable in the effort to develop multicultural curricula." The book does seem interesting as the text for a course in ethnic conflict and adjustment in American history, but hardly suitable for a comprehensive survey course.

9. Wong was one of more than two hundred educators who gathered in Boston to discuss diversity in America. At the conference, according to a reporter, "Multiculturalism was discovered, rediscovered and passionately embraced . . . [as] the antidote for racism, sexism, classism, [and] homophobia," but was "as yet ill-defined." *Boston Globe*, June 30, 1991, 25.

10. Gettysburg Address, Nov. 19, 1863, in *The Collected Works of Abraham Lincoln*, ed. Roy P. Basler, Marion Dolores Pratt and Lloyd P. Dunlap, asst. eds., 9 vols. (New Brunswick: Rutgers University Press, 1953–55), 7:93 (hereafter cited as *Collected Works*).

11. *Collected Works*, 2:499–500 (speech at Chicago, Ill., July 10, 1858).

12. Ibid., 1:337–38 (resolutions on Anti-Catholic Riots, June 21, 1844).

13. Ibid., 2:323 (letter to Joshua Speed, Aug. 24, 1855).

14. Ibid., 3:301 (seventh debate with Douglas, Alton, Ill., Oct. 15, 1858).

15. Ibid., 1:108 (address before the Springfield Young Men's Lyceum, Jan. 27, 1838).

16. Ibid., 1:8 (appeal to the Voters of Sangamo County, March 9, 1832).

17. These words, from the report of a New York task force on minorities that preceded the 1991 curriculum report, are quoted in *Time*, July 8, 1991, 13.

18. U.S. Census Bureau report summarized in the *Boston Globe*, April 20, 1993, 70. The long census form, which went to one household in six in 1990, asked people about their ancestry. One family in four replied "German"; one in six, "Irish"; one in eight, "English"; one in ten, "African"; and one in seventeen, "Italian." But the largest number described their ancestry simply as "American." *Boston Globe*, Dec. 17, 1992.

19. The findings of the Latino National Political Survey are summarized in an Associated Press dispatch in the *Boston Globe*, Dec. 16, 1992. A much fuller account is given by the principal investigator for the survey, Rodolfo O. de la Garza, in the *Chronicle of Higher Education*, June 2, 1993, B1–3.

Other investigations have arrived at similar conclusions. "A 1988 study by the Educational Testing Service found that the overwhelming majority of Hispanic parents—78% of Mexican-Americans and 82% of Cubans, for example—are opposed to teaching in Spanish if it meant less English instruction, and most said that the family was primarily responsible for teaching about the native culture," Linda Chavez reported in the *Wall Street Journal* on Oct. 22, 1991. She added, "A Houston Chronicle poll last year revealed that 87% of Hispanics—native-born and immigrant—believe it 'their duty to learn English,' and a majority favored making English the official language of the country."

20. *Boston Globe*, May 31, 1993, 1, 8. Ethnic Germans who come to Germany are entitled to automatic citizenship.

21. *Boston Globe*, May 27, 1993.

22. Ross Terrill, "The Asianization of Australia," *Boston Globe*, Jan. 1, 1989, 75. "Multiculturalism is at its best a principle of tolerance," Terrill observes, and he favors that kind of multiculturalism for Australia.

But multiculturalism at its worst seems to be gaining ground. In 1992 the UN Commission on Human Rights reported that "the source of racism at the present time lies in a new ideology" that "emphasizes allegedly insurmountable differences between cultures. . . . By asserting a radical cultural pluralism, the new racism based on cultural differences tries, paradoxically, to look like genuine antiracism and to show respect for all group identities."

According to a monograph issued by the University of Virginia's Center for the Study of the Mind and Human Interaction, an "ideological commitment to the

virtues of difference" can lead to the "dark side of enlightened multiculturalism."
This happens when the encouragement of minorities to "take pride in their distinct
heritage and culture" implies that "different cultures are, in the end, profoundly
incapable of assimilating or even communicating with one another."

The preceding two paragraphs are derived from H. D. S. Greenway, "Racism
That Wears a Multicultural Cloak," *Boston Globe*, June 10, 1993, 19.

23. Collected Works, 7:259 (reply to a committee of the New York Workingmen's
Democratic Republican Association, March 21, 1864).

24. This point is well put by Everett Carll Ladd in a perceptive article originally
published in the *Christian Science Monitor* and republished in the *Boston Globe*,
Jan. 18, 1993, 15. Ladd quotes G. K. Chesterton's observation that "America is the
only nation in the world that is founded on a creed," and he cites Lincoln's view of
the Declaration of Independence as the basis of the creed. "Whatever my ethnic
roots and culture, my political culture must be American," Ladd wisely affirms.

25. On the UN conference, see the articles by Ellen Goodman, Jonathan Kauf-
man, and Curt Goering and Joshua Rubenstein in the *Boston Globe:* June 17, 1993,
23; June 20, 1993, 2; and June 22, 1993, 15.

26. The quotations are from the First Inaugural Address, March 4, 1861, and
the speech accepting the Republican senatorial nomination, June 16, 1858, *Collected
Works*, 2:461 and 4:270.

Chapter Eight

&

Abraham Lincoln—
Our Ever-Present Contemporary

FRANK J. WILLIAMS

Americans are ambivalent about authority figures and heroes. Our Revolutionary past makes us skeptics, and our typical experience with political leaders tends to confirm our suspicions. Nonetheless, modern political science suggests the public's close identification with presidents.[1] Assassination and death in office undermine our skepticism and after losing presidents we tend to overcompensate and turn them into saints. Over time, however, we fall back on traditional doubts and wear presidents down while in office then turn them into saints in death, only to tear them down again later. In part this sinner-saint cycle is a way for citizens to identify with the American political tradition that is reflected in the chief executive. Garry Wills has aptly caught the saintly side of this process in the death of George Washington, and I will explore the fuller cycle in the life and death of our first assassinated president, Abraham Lincoln, whom scholars unanimously and consistently select as America's greatest president.[2]

Lincoln in Power: Sinner to Sainthood

The names and labels given Abraham Lincoln in his lifetime reflect how he was treated as politician. Abuse was hurled freely from the North during his first year as president. His inadequacy and vacillation were condemned widely, along with his intellect: "You cannot . . . fill his . . . empty skull with brains." He was a "political coward," "timid and ignorant," "pitiable," "too slow," "two faced," a man of "no education," "shattered, dazed, utterly foolish," "an awful, woeful ass," a "blackguard," the "craftiest and most dishonest politician that ever disgraced an office in America," a "filthy story-teller," a "halfwitted usurper," the "head ghoul at Washington," a "mold-eyed monster with a soul of leather," "Abraham Africanas I," an

"obscene clown," an "orangutan," the "present turtle at the head of government," a "slang-wanging, stump speaker," an "unmentionable disease,"
and the "wooden head at Washington."[3] At the very least the press saw
Lincoln as ambiguous, some newspapers supported him for being a liberal
and some for being a conservative. Thus he was criticized regardless of his
position.

The attacks continued during the Civil War and were hardly kinder in
the South. Even his cabinet consisted of fellow politicians who initially
shared many of these views. In a sense, the general public caught on to the
Lincoln message before much elite opinion did. As David Long argues in
his exhaustive analysis of the 1864 election, the public's reaction to his
leadership even surprised the president, who was certain of his electoral
defeat although equally convinced of his policies.[4]

Lincoln became part of the national myth before the assassination, when
most people think the myth began. The letters to the president that are
part of the Robert Todd Lincoln Collection in the Library of Congress
show a clear progression in how Lincoln was viewed before and after he
signed the preliminary Emancipation Proclamation in September 1862.
After issuing the preliminary proclamation, he was regarded as something
more than a mere statesman. Of course, his assassination instantly transformed the reelected president from a finally unsuccessful politician into a
saint who would certainly challenge, if not surpass, George Washington's
apotheosis.

Lincoln knew how to write poetic prose. At his First Inaugural, he said,
"We are not enemies but friends. . . . Though passion may have strained, it
must not break our bonds of affection. The mystic chords of memory,
stretching from every battlefield and patriot grave to every living heart
and hearthstone all over this broad land, will yet swell the chorus of the
Union when again touched, as surely they will be, by the better angels of
our nature."[5]

The Second Inaugural is "probably the most famous of all inaugural
addresses. . . . The power of its sentiment is deepened even further when
it is read as a counterpoint to the first Inaugural Address, perhaps as Lincoln meant it to be. . . . On both occasions, he cited the responsibilities of
the opposing sections, North and South, as well as his own as Chief Magistrate. . . . Lincoln . . . both times appealed to the basic humanity of the
nation's citizenry, hoping that 'the mystic chords of memory' would 'swell
the chorus of the Union' and lead to that transcendent moment when all
could say, 'With malice toward none, with charity for all.' "[6]

When peace was assured, Lincoln devoted fully half of his Second Inaugural Address to a fire-and-brimstone defense of the war as punishment
sent from Heaven for the sin of slavery. He called it "strange" that both

Lincoln's greatness was not universally recognized by his contemporaries. (The Frank and Virginia Williams Collection of Lincolniana)

"The Apotheosis — George Washington Receiving Lincoln in Heaven" (The Frank and Virginia Williams Collection of Lincolniana)

sides invoked God's "aid against the other," with "the prayers . . . of neither
. . . answered fully." Although convinced that the speech would "wear as
well as—perhaps better than—anything" he had ever written, he was also
aware that it was "not immediately popular," explaining, "Men are not
flattered by being shown that there has been a difference of purpose between the almighty and them."[7]

Most people argue that the Gettysburg Address is not only his best
work but also the most eloquent statement of the American political dream.
The historian James Stevenson has suggested that Lincoln's life might have
inspired the character of Huck Finn.[8] The parallels to Lincoln's life found
in this greatest of American novels are striking.

Presidential Usage: Hero and Justification

If writers were inspired and influenced by Abraham Lincoln, subsequent
presidents have been too. Unfortunately, too often few subsequent presidents have truly understood Lincoln's leadership, although nearly all have
tried to "get right with Lincoln," as David Donald has aptly described the
process. According to Donald, Lincoln's "ambiguity" has satisfied every
conceivable national and political need, even for those who hold diametri-
cally opposed views.[9]

Theodore Roosevelt, for example, was inspired by Lincoln and identified with his life. Roosevelt's "stewardship theory" of presidential power
was an extreme version of Lincoln's wartime presidency. "Great Presidents
are products not just of their own talents and ambitions, but of the circumstances they inherit. Theodore Roosevelt complained frequently that his
times had denied him greatness. 'A man has to take advantage of his
opportunities', he said after leaving office, 'but the opportunities have to
come. If there is not the war, you don't get the great general; if there is not
the great occasion, you don't get the great statesman; if Lincoln had lived
in times of peace, no one would know his name now.' " Despite his successful activist presidency, Roosevelt was greatly disappointed that World War
I came after he had left office, and he believed that Woodrow Wilson and
not he had been given the opportunity for greatness.[10]

C. Northcote Parkinson observed that "work expands so as to fill the
time available for its completion."[11] Efforts of other presidents to wear
Lincoln's mantle expanded, like Parkinson's law, to fill the time available
for its use. Mired in the Great Depression, Herbert Hoover took solace
in remembering that Lincoln had survived much abuse and still won
reelection.[12]

Franklin Delano Roosevelt, not satisfied to claim Jefferson and Jackson,
wanted to expropriate Abraham Lincoln for the Democratic party in an ef-

Lincoln offered the nation an adaptable vision. Statue by Leonard
Volk. (The Frank and Virginia Williams Collection of Lincolniana)

fort to win votes, particularly those of blacks.[13] Roosevelt invoked Lincoln's name at every possible opportunity, placing himself in a direct line of political descent from the martyred railsplitter, and during the presidential campaign of 1948 Harry S. Truman asserted that a twentieth-century Lincoln would clearly have been a regular Democrat.[14]

In delivering his farewell to the people of Massachusetts, President-elect John F. Kennedy consciously imitated Lincoln's Farewell Address to his friends in Springfield and did not object when his civil rights bill was termed the Second Emancipation Proclamation. Lyndon B. Johnson compared his Vietnam War ordeal to that of Abraham Lincoln, as did Richard M. Nixon, who visited the Lincoln Memorial late at night during Watergate to commune with his predecessor.[15]

During the 1992 presidential race, Lincoln seemed to belong to both Bill Clinton and George Bush. Clinton, at the time of the Gennifer Flowers revelation, was seen leafing through the books *Lincoln on Democracy* and *Lincoln on Leadership*, and Bush compared himself to Lincoln, "a lonely White House occupant."[16] Perhaps because the president is a symbol of national unity and stability, Lincoln is used shamelessly for political ends: Clinton has quoted Lincoln to justify activist government; many encouraged Bush to dump Dan Quayle as his vice-presidential running-mate, citing Lincoln's replacement of Hannibal Hamlin; and William F. Buckley, Jr., advised American voters not to ignore George Bush just "because he is not Abraham Lincoln."[17]

And then there was the case of former President Ronald Reagan, who brought a hushed and reverential silence to the 1992 Republican National Convention by invoking "Lincoln's words": " 'You cannot strengthen the weak by weakening the strong, you cannot help the wage-earner by pulling down the wage-payer. You cannot help the poor by destroying the rich. You cannot help men permanently by doing for them what they could and should do for themselves.' " The problem was, however, that these words were written not by Lincoln but by a former clergyman from Erie, Pennsylvania, in 1916. They were used from time to time during the 1930s by anti-New Deal businessmen and in 1942 by the right-wing Committee for Constitutional Government. Then, in 1950, Representative Frances Bolton of Ohio read them into the *Congressional Record* as Lincoln's maxims, and *Look* magazine gave them a full-page spread. "There seems to be no way," a Library of Congress report observed in May 1950, of stopping the proliferation of the mistaken attribution.[18]

To Robert Hughes, an Australian, "if the collective work that is America . . . is broken, the possibilities of Americanness begin to unravel. If they are fraying now, it is because the politics of ideology has, for the last twenty years, weakened, and, in some areas, broken the traditional American genius for consensus." Hughes maintains that "Reagan educated America down to his level. He left his country a little stupider in 1988 than it had been in 1980, and a lot more tolerant of lies." It did not matter, argues Hughes that Reagan misquoted Lincoln because, "who was counting? For Reagan's fans, the idea that there ought to be, . . . some . . . relationship between utterance and source seemed impertinent to the memory of his presidency. . . . This was not . . . Presidential character that . . . Lincoln . . . [could] . . . imagine— or . . . respect."[19] Reagan was drawn to the Lincoln he envisioned and, as a result, did not portray him accurately. The press, with its own picture of Lincoln, was quick to expose the misrepresentation.[20]

Thirty years after John F. Kennedy's farewell remarks were compared to Lincoln's, Bill Clinton left for Washington with yet another Lincolnesque (or at least Lincoln-inspired) farewell. Lincoln said on leaving Springfield: "My friends—No one, not in my situation, can appreciate my feeling of sadness at this parting. To this place, and the kindness of these people, I owe every thing. . . . I now leave, not knowing when, or whether ever, I may return, with a task before me greater than that which rested upon Washington. Without the assistance of the Divine Being, . . . I cannot succeed. With that assistance, I cannot fail. . . . let us confidently hope that all will yet be well. To His care commending you, as I hope in your prayers you will commend me, I bid you an affectionate farewell." Clinton said on leaving Little Rock: "I'll miss my whole network of friends and what I can do. I'll miss going down to the Y in the morning, my blue-collar gym, where there's nobody in bright Spandex outfits. I have a lot of friends in Washington. I think I'll enjoy it a lot."[21] Of course, Lincoln sounds better than Clinton, but Harold Holzer has observed that much of Lincoln's reputation as an orator—especially in the Lincoln-Douglas Debates—was a myth.

Has the nation's view of leadership and the presidency changed? George Bush was never able to overcome the reversal of his no-new-taxes pledge. When he did support additional taxes, he "invoked" the words of Lincoln, explaining, "I'm doing like Lincoln did, 'think anew,'" quoting from the president's annual message to Congress on December 1, 1862 in which Lincoln not only called for restoration of the Union but also for freeing the slaves. During his 1860 campaign, Lincoln had vowed that the federal government should not interfere with slavery where it existed.[22]

Americans reelected Lincoln; they were less charitable to George Bush. Still, Lincoln's contemporaries did not universally recognize his greatness. As time passes, citizens perceive and evaluate presidents in terms of their stands on issues, party connections, leadership qualities, including record and experience, and personal qualities.[23] Time and reflection have been better to Abraham Lincoln than to most presidents, despite their real and Machiavellian identification with him.

Today, some view Lincoln as far from perfect for using less than noble methods to achieve his goals. Portrait by Adalbert and Johann Volck, "Writing the Emanicipation Proclamation." Volck was a Copperhead from Baltimore. (The Frank and Virginia Williams Collection of Lincolniana)

Perhaps we should not be too harsh on presidential use of Lincoln, for his successors merely try to come to terms with the person who has set the standard for presidential leadership and perhaps democratic leadership in general. Lincoln satisfies every international need: Lincoln the nationalist (for the early-nineteenth-century Italians trying to form a nation), Lincoln the democrat (for the early-nineteenth-century French), and Lincoln the libertarian (for his few English admirers at the time of his presidency). From this worldview it is possible to understand how a young Chinese boy learned about Abraham Lincoln at a school in Honolulu and then remembered the Gettysburg Address when he returned home. Sun Yat Sen went on to become the first president of modern China and turned to the declaration when formulating his political creed, "San min chu-yi" (three people's principles), which correspond with "of the people [Min you], by the people [Min chih], and for the people [Min hsiang]." [24]

Richard N. Current has reported that when he was in India in 1959 on the occasion of the Lincoln sesquicentennial people made constant comparison between Lincoln and Gandhi, almost always to Gandhi's advantage, although a Lion's Club member in Patna assured Current that there would have been no partition of Pakistan from India had Lincoln been in charge. There is plenty of Lincoln to go around. He is in Poland, too, thanks to Mario M. Cuomo.[25] When the Baltic states seceded from the Soviet Union, some thought that doing so was contrary to the principals of the Union Lincoln espoused. Eric Foner, a Fulbright professor at Moscow University in 1990, has observed that Lincoln, like Gorbachev, would have opposed the independence of the Baltic states, the implication being that the United States was inconsistent in opposing Confederate independence 1861 and favoring Baltic independence in 1990. However, there is a great difference between the United States in 1861 and the Soviet Union in 1991. "If the Union means the willing consent of people to forge a common destiny, the Soviet Union died long ago. Its government no longer represented a majority anywhere." To put it in terms of the United States in 1861, it would have been as if "*all* of the states had sought to secede." This is no contradiction, because Gorbachev's role was to preside over dissolving a Union, whereas Lincoln is rightly honored for saving one.[26]

Pop Culture and Lincoln

If subsequent presidents have found it difficult to meet Lincoln's performance standard, the general public must contend with the Lincoln standard enshrined in the Lincoln Memorial and on Mount Rushmore. Like ordinary presidents, ordinary mortals find it difficult to grapple with a saintly stature and so reduce it to their level. Even if doing so diminishes the heroic, it at least shows the struggle that later generations have in coming to terms with quality.

The contrast is found, for example, in Gutzon Borglum's statue of Lincoln in Newark, New Jersey; Lincoln is shown seated on a bench, which allows the public to share space and thoughts with him. The work is clearly a tribute to Lincoln, and it captures his spirit. In contrast, the J. Seward Johnson, Jr., statute unveiled in Gettysburg in November 1991 portrays Lincoln with an anonymous figure. The public is excluded from interacting with the piece. Its intent is commercial, an effort to sell Gettysburg tourism. This is not a tribute to Lincoln, but an appropriation of his good name.

The emphasis on Lincoln's rise from poverty, the journey from log cabin to White House, has been superseded by a fragmented view of a sick man who suffered from depression and Marfan's Syndrome. The National Museum of Health and Science has recommended testing a sample of Lincoln's blood to determine his DNA, prompting one commentator to ask, "Can Abraham Lincoln's DNA be cloned? . . . not to diagnose his diseases, but

Every generation makes its own Lincoln.
Carte de visite issued by Salisbury, Bro.
& Co., Providence, R.I. (The Frank and
Virginia Williams Collection of Lincoln-
iana)

to fill today's leadership gap."[27] The museum tabled the issue until, it said, testing is perfected, but perhaps it also feared being made the butt of jokes. Too late. The *Weekly World News*, a tabloid, reported on October 5, 1993 that doctors at Walter Reed Army Medical Hospital had exhumed Lincoln's body, immersed it in a "special solution," and then injected a "resurrection drug." Lincoln was said to have been revived for ninety-five seconds, time enough to ask, "Gentlemen, where am I?"[28]

Yet, Philip B. Kunhardt, Jr., and Philip B. Kunhardt III's ABC miniseries *Lincoln* and Ken Burns's PBS series *The Civil War* are part of television's "latest programming twist: the history lesson. Documentary-makers and their corporate patrons are simultaneously feeding and exploiting a burgeoning appetite for the stuff of America's past."[29] Traditionally, history draws big audiences on a regular basis.

The television view of Lincoln reaches millions. But what view? Documents aside, with all of the great Lincoln plays available for production and televising, all the viewing audience saw on April 21, 1991 was "A Perfect Tribute," which centered more on the story of a young boy who leaves home to find his Confederate brother than on President Lincoln.[30]

The avoidance of Lincoln's racial views in the Kunhardts' production of "Lincoln" in December 1992 also contributes to this reworking and, perhaps, represents a social statement about the nation's reluctance to face racism.[31] Forty percent of the documentary was devoted to the assassination, demonstrating the enormous fascination people have with Lincoln's death, an interest to which the authors and producers evidently felt compelled to pander. Consider, for example, the popularity and large membership of the Surratt Society, a group dedicated to remembering fondly the woman who, at the very least, housed the assassination conspirators. For some, there is really no rational or academic reason for such a group. Some argue this similar to those who hallucinate over the Kennedy assassination or discover Elvis at the laundromat.

How we think about Lincoln tells us much about our culture. Anyone impersonating Napoleon is assumed to be slightly mad. Yet the Association of Lincoln Impersonators has more than eighty-six card-carrying Lincoln portrayers and a newsletter, *Lincarnations*. To support the impersonators, the Friends of the Presidential Entourage of Abraham Lincoln has been formed, complete with its own quarterly newsletter, *The Reviewing Stand*. People want to be entertained if they cannot understand; in either case, Lincoln makes people feel good. With so much culture shock from Lincoln being recast in the modern image, can we do no better than a Lincoln impersonator rolling down the highway in a Winnebago that looks like a log home? Each generation makes its own Lincoln, and he may not be the Lincoln known before.

The 1960s brought Disney's animated Lincoln. "Fantasy has been entirely abandoned," said Disney of his then immensely popular life-size, automated Lincoln, which first performed in the Illinois pavilion at the 1964 New York World's Fair. For Disney, the homage was no gimmick but a new art form, "audio-animatronics," which, he believed, would "combine the best of traditional media to capture the real countenance, the warm sincerity, and the contagious dedication of Abraham Lincoln." Yet even Disney's Lincoln suffered from revision.[32] In 1990, Disneyland's officials planned to close "Great Moments with Mr. Lincoln" and replace him with Kermit the Frog until tourist and park employees rebelled. As one boy said, "Lincoln was President. Kermit is a frog."[33] As with historians, Lincoln remains at the top of the popular culture polls; Disneyland held an "election" and he defeated Kermit.[34]

Nor is Lincoln ignored in literary and dramatic humor. In his one-act play *The Query*, Woody Allen presents a Lincoln who uses his press secretary as a straight man, getting him to ask at a press conference, "Mr. President, how long do you think a man's legs should be?" "Long enough to reach the ground," Lincoln responds. Caught up in the laughter, he ignores a distraught father waiting to see him to seek a pardon for his son.[35] And the bane of academicians is that people everywhere wonder what Lincoln would do if he were alive today. In 1984 James M. McPherson appeared on a radio station in Wilmington after speaking to the Lincoln

Group of Delaware. The first question he was asked was, "If Lincoln were alive today, what position would he take on abortion and the budget deficit?"[36]

Minority Groups: Emancipator, Oppressor, and Equal

In some ways the most interesting use of Lincoln has been by emerging social and political groups, African Americans, the women's movement, the men's movement, and the gay pride movement, for example. The full circle of the saint-sinner cycle is clearest in the long African-American struggle to achieve equality. For example, the records of the Federal Writers Project in Washington, D.C., contain a recollection by a former slave, Fanny Burdock of Valdosta, Georgia, who was born in the 1840s:

> We been picking in the field when my brother he point to the road and then we seen Marse Abe coming all dusty on foot. We run right to the fence and had the oak bucket and dipper. When he draw up to us, he so tall, black eyes so sad. Didn't say not one word, just looked hard at all us, every one us crying. We give him nice cool water from the dipper. Then he nodded and set off and we just stood there till he get to being dust then nothing. After, didn't our owner or nobody credit it, but me and all my kin, we knowed. I still got the dipper to prove it.

Allan Gurganus's novel *The Oldest Living Confederate Widow Tells All* begins with that very recollection and then points out, "In reality, Lincoln's foot tour of Georgia could not have happened. In this book, it can. Such scenes were told by hundreds of slaves. Such visitations remain, for me, truer than fact. History is my starting point."[37]

The African-American perception of Lincoln is varied and ambiguous. Joseph Fowlkes, past president of the Providence Chapter of the NAACP, has said that the Emancipation Proclamation "was almost bogus, a lot of sound and fury, but there was no real enforcement power behind it."[38] He obviously had not read the results of Mark Neely's research in the National Archives that reveals that Union commanders in the field dealt harshly with slave owners, including sentences of death for those who failed to obey or recognize the proclamation. And John Hope Franklin believes that "It [the proclamation] was momentous. . . . There was no chance slavery could survive after that." Barbara Fields contends the slaves emancipated themselves, further contributing to the reworking of Lincoln's image as the Great Emancipator. Another attempt to answer the question of who freed the slaves comes from James M. McPherson, who credits Lincoln, primarily because he would have war rather than allow secession.

African-Americans' perception of Lincoln has gone through many revisions over the years. "Lincoln and the Contrabands" by J. L. G. Ferris. (The Frank and Virginia Williams Collection of Lincolniana)

By E. Nash, 1908. The Frank and Virginia Williams Collection of Lincolniana)

And without Civil War there would have been "no confiscation act, no Emancipation Proclamation, no Thirteenth Amendment, certainly no self-emancipation and almost certainly no end of slavery for several more decades."[39]

Lincoln's contemporary ups and downs with the black community began in the 1960s when *Ebony* published "Was Abe Lincoln a White Supremacist?" The reply was in the affirmative, citing doubtful evidence and using selectivity and more than some misrepresentation.[40] Conceding that historians can judge the past, one can still doubt the fairness of a verdict based entirely on ex post facto standards.[41]

The ultimate irony may be that in the African-American struggle to achieve equality Lincoln has been democratized to the point that his presidency has been reduced to Warren Harding's, with the recent advent of Presidents' Day replacing the observation of the birthdays of George Washington and Abraham Lincoln.

American Heritage Magazine, in the October 1992 issue, explored whether any historical novel may be true history. In a continuation of his thrust against Lincoln "scholar squirrels," Gore Vidal also argues that the past cannot be left to "hagiographers" too narrow to grasp the mind of Lincoln fully. He contends that his *Lincoln: A Novel* (1984) is grounded in historical sources. Yet historians have accused Vidal of gross distortions and inaccuracies in his depiction of Lincoln as "coarse-grained and devious, ignorant of economics, disregardful of the Constitution, fiercely ambitious, and a racist until the end." Vidal also has been said to have relied on outdated and discredited bits of scholarship and oversimplified complex issues. Although agreeing that he "embellished here and there," Vidal has insisted that he used primary sources.[42] He has pointed out that Americans prefer films based upon romanticized episodes from the lives of such European royalty as Henry VIII, Elizabeth I, or Napoleon but have no interest in Lincoln's presidency.[43]

The gay issue is not to be ignored, either. Consider Robert Bly's discussion of whether gays should be allowed in the military. Among the highland Mayans in Guatemala, Bly has found, knowledge is presented in four stages for men: the boy, the warrior, the community man, and the "echo" man. The step from boy to warrior is fundamental, and although he is admired, the young warrior is still not considered a finished male. The community man lives for the community, taking care of widows and orphans and using his earlier developed warrior disciplines to protect them. The last stage, the "echo" man is a person who hears; he is all ears, all grief, all intuition, and all responsive to sound. The Gettysburg Address is the speech of a true "echo" person. In speaking of a debt to forefathers and to

From a daguerreotype by N. H.
Shepherd, Springfield, Illinois, 1846,
the earliest known photograph of
Lincoln. (The Frank and Virginia
Williams Collection of Lincolniana)

the living and to the soldiers who have just died, he hears grief. Bly attempts to mitigate the military's fears of gays: "We justly admire and value the warrior, but we need not act on all of his fears. Having a wider vision, we can bless the warriors and keep the sad and echoing face of Lincoln before us."[44]

Bruce Miroff prefers the more open, nurturing style of democratic leaders like Abraham Lincoln and FDR, who emphasized "mutuality in place of superiority, education in place of dominance." To him, such democratic leaders rejected the swaggering macho style of Kennedy or Teddy Roosevelt in favor of a softer, more feminine style. To Miroff, Lincoln belongs to the leadership that "should have the strength of purpose and tenacity of will that American culture has generally designated as masculine, but also the sensitivity, openness, and willingness to nurture others, that American culture has typically disparaged as women's ways."[45]

Conclusions

A review of the sinner-saint cycle suggests why Abraham Lincoln remains an ever-lasting contemporary. His performance in the White House set the standard of presidential—and democratic—leadership. If subsequent presidents, pop culture, and minority groups have a difficult time grappling

Lincoln offers compatibility to everyone: laborers, business people, racists, and antiracists. "The Rail Splitter, 1830" by J. L. G. Ferris. (The Frank and Virginia Williams Collection of Lincolniana)

with a saint, their abuse and misuse of the Lincoln standard should not be judged too harshly. After all, historians have also created idealized versions of Lincoln in prose and poetry as well as revisionist accounts.[46] Of course, Abraham Lincoln began the cycle himself. He was a common person who became uncommon, a Machiavellian politician who became a statesman. His leadership style is one of America's greatest gifts to democracy. Preservation of the Union grew into a democratic justification for self-government's emphasis on dignity and equality as necessary for self-realization. He matured as a political leader, fulfilling himself in the public eye and extending the democratic burden to everyone, a contemporary and the personification of "the last best hope of Earth."

Notes

This chapter is a revised version of a talk presented at the Huntington conference with the use of 140 slide illustrations. I am indebted to William D. Pederson of Louisiana State University-Shreveport for his indispensable editorial help in preparing the talk for publication.

1. Fred I. Greenstein, "What the President Means to Americans," in *Choosing the President*, ed. James David Barber (Englewood Cliffs: Prentice-Hall, 1974), 121.

2. Garry Wills, *Cincinnatus: George Washington and the Enlightenment* (Garden City: Doubleday, 1984); William D. Pederson and Ann McLaurin, eds., *The Rating Game in American Politics* (New York: Irvington Publishers, 1978).

3. J. G. Randall, "Vindictives and Vindication," in *Mr. Lincoln*, ed. Richard N. Current (New York: Dodd, Mead, 1957), 317–40.

4. David E. Long, *The Jewel of Liberty: Abraham Lincoln's Reelection and the End of Slavery* (Harrisburg: Stackpole Books, 1994).

5. Roy P. Basler, ed., Marion Dolores Pratt and Lloyd A. Dunlap, asst. eds., *The Collected Works of Abraham Lincoln*, 9 vols. (New Brunswick: Rutgers University Press, 1953–55), 4:271 (hereafter cited as *Collected Works*).

6. Gary Lamolinard, "I Do Solemnly Swear . . . : L.C. Exhibition Chronicles an American Tradition," *Library of Congress Information Bulletin*, Jan. 25, 1993, 33.

7. Mario M. Cuomo and Harold Holzer, "Lincoln's Second Inaugural Address," presented at The New York Historical Society, June 11–July 19, 1992.

8. James A. Stevenson, "American Voyages of Lincoln and Huck Finn," *Lincoln Herald* 90, no. 4 (Winter 1988): 130–33.

9. David Donald, "Getting Right with Lincoln," *Lincoln Reconsidered: Essays on the Civil War Era*, 2d ed. enlarged (New York: Vantage Books, 1989), 3–18; 18.

10. Alan Brinkley, "The 43 Percent President," *The New York Times Magazine*, July 4, 1993, 23.

11. Richard W. Stevenson, "C. Northcote Parkinson, Eighty-three, Dies; Writer with a Wry View of Labor," *The New York Times*, March 12, 1993.

12. D. E. Fehrenbacher, *The Changing Image of Lincoln in American Historiography* (Oxford: Clarendon Press, 1968), 3–4.

13. Michael Kammen, "Changing Presidential Perspectives on the American Past," *Prologue Quarterly of the National Archives* 25 (Spring 1993): 48; Philip Abbott, "Prudent Archery: FDR's Lincoln," in *Abraham Lincoln: Contemporary*, ed. Frank J. Williams and William D. Pederson (Campbell: Savas Woodbury, 1994).

14. Fehrenbacher, *The Changing Image*, 3.

15. Ibid.

16. Eleanor Clift, "Testing Ground: The Inside Story of How Clinton Survived the Campaign's Worst Moments," *Newsweek*, March 30, 1992, 35.

17. Richard Willing, "Clinton Leans on 'Honest Abe,'" *Detroit News*, Sept. 27, 1992, 1B; Martin D. Tullai, "The Precedent for Dumping a V.P.," *The Evening Sun* [Baltimore], Jan. 7, 1992; William F. Buckley, Jr., "By George, Spare Us the Presumption of This Scatter-Minded Southern Statest," *The Providence Sunday Journal*, Nov. 1, 1992.

18. Arthur Schlesinger, Jr., "The History of Those Words Lincoln Never Said," *The Washington Post*, Aug. 28, 1992, A23.

19. Robert Hughes, *Culture of Complaint: The Fraying of America* (New York: Oxford University Press, 1993), 43.

20. Herbert Mitgang, "Reagan's 'Lincoln' Quotation Disputed," "Erratum," *The New York Times*, Aug. 19, 1992, A13.

21. *Illinois Times*, Jan. 21, 1993.

22. Martin Tullai, "Commentary: Mr. Bush Tries Out Abe-speak," *San Jose Mercury News*, Feb. 12, 1992.

23. Greenstein, "What the President Means to Americans," 141.

24. Herbert Mitgang, "Abraham Lincoln: Friend of a Free Press," *Sino-American Relations: An International Quarterly* 18 (Spring 1992): 106.

25. Mario M. Cuomo and Harold Holzer, eds., *Lincoln on Democracy* (New York: HarperCollins, 1990).

26. Jonathan Schell, "Union Divides Lincoln and Gorbachev," "Viewpoints," *Newsday*, 114.

27. Jerald M. Lowenstein in Frank J. Williams, "Lincolniana in 1992," *Journal of the Abraham Lincoln Association* 14 (Summer 1993): 96–97.

28. Beatrice Dexter, "Abraham Lincoln's Corpse Revived," *Weekly World News*, Oct. 5, 1993, 4–5.

29. Harry F. Waters, "Lincoln Reconstructed," *Newsweek*, Dec. 28, 1992, 61.

30. Dennis Brown (adapted from Mary Raymond Shipman Andrews), "The Perfect Tribute," ABC Television Network, April 21, 1992.

31. Philip B. Kunhardt III and Philip B. Kunhardt, Jr., *Lincoln*, Capital Cities/ABC Inc. Television Network Group, Dec. 26 and 27, 1992.

32. Harold Henderson, "Lincoln's Death and Transfiguration," *Illinois Times*, Feb. 10–16, 1983, 6.

33. Greenstein, "What the President Means to Americans," 129.

34. Frank J. Williams "Lincolniana in 1991," *Journal of the Abraham Lincoln Association* 13 (Summer 1992): 94.

35. Woody Allen, "The Query," *Side Effects* (New York: Random House, 1980), 113–21.

36. James M. McPherson, "Preface," *Abraham Lincoln and the Second American Revolution* (New York: Oxford University Press, 1990), ix.

37. Allan Gurganus, *The Oldest Living Confederate Widow Tells All* (New York: Ballentine, 1988), xvi.

38. Quoted in "Emancipation Proclamation Draws Large Crowds in D.C.," *Providence Journal-Bulletin*, Jan. 5, 1993.

39. Mark E. Neely, Jr., "Lincoln and the Theory of Self-Emancipation," in *The Continuing Civil War: Essays in Honor of the Civil War Round Table of Chicago*, ed. John Y. Simon and Barbara Hughett (Dayton: Morningside Press, 1992), 45–59; John Hope Franklin, "The Emancipation Proclamation: An Act of Justice," *Prologue Quarterly of the National Archives* 5 (Summer 1993): 151–53; Barbara J. Fields, "Who Freed the Slaves?" in *The Civil War: An Illustrated History*, ed. Geoffrey C. Ward, Ric Burns, and Ken Burns (New York: Alfred A. Knopf, 1990), 178–81; James M. McPherson, *Who Freed the Slaves? Lincoln and Emancipation* (Redlands: Lincoln Memorial Shrine, 1993), 3.

40. Lerone Bennett, Jr., "Was Abe Lincoln a White Supremacist?" *Ebony*, Feb. 1968, 35–42.

41. Fehrenbacher, *The Changing Image*, 23.

42. Daniel Aaron, "What Can You Learn from a Historical Novel?" *American Heritage Magazine*, Oct. 1992, 56.

43. Gore Vidal, *Screening History* (Cambridge, Mass.: Harvard University Press, 1992).

44. Robert Bly, "What the Mayans Could Teach the Joint Chiefs," *The New York Times*, July 23, 1993; also see William V. Davis, *Robert Bly: The Poet and His Critics* (Columbia: Camden House, 1994).

45. Bruce Miroff, *Icons of Democracy, American Leaders as Heroes: Aristocrats, Dissenters and Democrats* (New York: Basic Books, 1993), 83–124.

46. Ida M. Tarbell, *The Early Life of Abraham Lincoln* (New York: S. S. McClure, 1896); Carl Sandburg, *Abraham Lincoln: The Prairie Years*, vols. 1 and 2 (New York: Harcourt, Brace, 1926).

Chapter Nine

&

The International Lincoln

MERRILL D. PETERSON

One of the highest tributes ever paid to Abraham Lincoln came in the midst of the centennial commemoration of his birth in 1909. Leo Tolstoy, arguably the most famous man in the world, interviewed at his estate, Yasnaya Polyana, said, "Of all the great national heroes and statesmen of history, Lincoln is the only true giant." The author was amazed by the reach of the American's fame. Once, traveling in the Caucuses, he met a Muslim chief who said of Lincoln, "He was a hero. He spoke with the voice of thunder; he laughed like the sunrise and his deeds were strong as the rock and sweet as the fragrance of roses." Having himself become a saint, Tolstoy naturally thought Lincoln was one. He was "a Christ in miniature, a saint of humanity." His greatness consisted in his moral power. "He was one who wanted to be great through his smallness. . . . He wanted to see himself in the world, not the world in himself." Love was the foundation of his life, said the Russian, and he prayed that the centennial would light the flame of righteousness among nations.[1]

Americans, too, in the centennial year, showed increasing recognition of what I will call "the international Lincoln." An so, in Percy MacKaye's "Centenary Ode,"

> He stands forth
> 'Mongst nations old—a new world Abraham,
> The patriarch of peoples still to be,
> Blending all the visions of the promised land
> In one Apocalypse.[2]

Of course, there were intimations of Lincoln's fame as a prophetic world figure from the time of his assassination or even before. That heads of state should offer condolences on the death of a foreign leader was to be expected, but the outpouring of grief upon Lincoln's death among all ranks and conditions the world over was utterly unprecedented, as if to say that in homage to him all men were brothers. The image of Lincoln as the Great Emancipator, so prominent in his apotheosis, could readily enough be transformed into the image of the Great Humanitarian—the emancipator of all struggling humanity—and this was happening by 1909. In American race relations it was the era of Jim Crow; the emancipator image had faded except among blacks, and it was being generalized into the image of the secular savior of humanity.

But it was the identification of American ideals with the Allied cause in World War I that consummated Lincoln's international fame. This is my theme, although a detour here and there is necessary to develop it.

*   *   *

In one of his finest poems, "Abraham Lincoln Walks at Midnight" (1915), Vachel Lindsay conjured up the ghostly apparition of Lincoln in Springfield, pacing up and down the streets, carrying on his shawl-draped shoulders the bitterness, folly, and pain of the world:

> He cannot rest until a spirit-dawn
> Shall come;—the shining hope of Europe free:
> A league of sober folk, the workers' earth,
> Bringing long peace to Cornland, Alp and Sea.[3]

Woodrow Wilson shared "the shining hope"; increasingly, he experienced what he called "the holy and very terrible isolation" Lincoln had known in the wartime White House. Parallels between the Civil War and the World War were frequently drawn, both at home and abroad. On the fiftieth anniversary of Lincoln's death, even the *Times* of London sang his praises and maintained that his cause and that of the Allies was the same. In the leading paragraphs of the *London Spectator,* Lincoln's advocacy of the draft was urged in behalf of compulsory service, finally legislated in Britain in 1916. The *Spectator* actually printed a long and previously unpublished presidential defense of the draft in 1863. Lincoln's rejection of a negotiated peace at the Hampton Roads Conference was offered in partial justification of the Allied rebuff of the German overture in December 1916. The Vallandigham case became a leading precedent for Wilson's crackdown on dissenters and obstructionists. His proclamation of "a peace without victory" was compared to Lincoln's "charity for all" in 1865. The veteran Republican leader Joseph Choate believed it was the spirit of Abraham Lincoln that led the United States into the war. "If Lincoln were here today," Choate said in 1917, "his prayer [in the Gettysburg Address] would be verified and glorified into the prayer that all civilized nations shall have a new birth of freedom, and that government of the people, and for the people shall not perish from the earth."[4]

Allied leaders recognized the propaganda value of the Lincoln symbol. French Field Marshal Joffre, chair of the Allied War Council, led a delegation to Springfield to render his country's homage to Lincoln just after the American declaration of war. For David Lloyd George, the British prime minister, Lincoln had been a personal hero long before he became a vehicle for propaganda. Lloyd George often told how his father, a Welsh shoemaker, acquired a portrait of Lincoln after his death and accorded it the place of honor in the family's humble home. Young David read and reread the story of Lincoln's life; at every turn in his career he took guidance from it. When the war came, he studied Lincoln's leadership in the American conflict. Rejecting the peace overture in 1916, the prime minister quoted Lincoln: "We accepted the war for an object, a worthy object. The war will end when the object is attained. Under God, I hope it will never end till that time." In February 1917, Lloyd George sent a special Lincoln Day message to the American people. Here he maintained that the issue at stake in the European war was basically the same as divided the Union some fifty years before. "Has there not grown up in this continent a new form of slavery, a militarist slavery, which has not only been crushing out the freedom of the people under its control, but which in recent years has also been moving toward crushing out freedom and fraternity in Europe as well?" Regrettably, Britain's leaders had been blind to the issue during the Civil War. Now, inspired by Lincoln's example, the Allies fought to secure his democratic principles in Europe.[5]

Around the conference table at Versailles in 1919, Lincoln was a favorite topic of conversation among the Big Three: Wilson, Lloyd George, and Georges Clemenceau. Both European leaders later made pilgrimages to Lincoln's tomb. Clemenceau, in a moving tribute, recalled his grief as a student in Paris upon hearing of Lincoln's death and said the world followed Lincoln in the path he had so gloriously opened. No sooner did Lloyd George step off the boat in New York in October 1923 than he struck out for Springfield. Much as he wanted to see the country, he explained, Lincoln's home was the one spot he desired to see above all others. He had long been under Lincoln's spell, and having come through a great war he felt an even stronger bond with him. Lincoln was, Lloyd George said, "The tenderest soul who ever ruled men, and the democracy for which he stood was now the hope of mankind."[6]

Lincoln's fame in England, consolidated during the World War, had been growing for a decade or longer. What the English thought of him was important to educated Americans, many of whom imported their opinions, like their china, from England. And so when a gentleman-historian, Sir

Spencer Walpole, declared that Lincoln deserved the highest place among nineteenth-century statesmen, Henry Cabot Lodge, an American of the same stripe, was impressed. *Lincoln's Speeches and Letters*, with an introduction by James Bryce, the British ambassador to the United States, appeared in the Everyman's Library in 1907. The same year saw the publication in London of Henry B. Binns's biography of Lincoln (an Everyman's edition appeared in 1927). Lincoln's life and writings became readily accessible in England for the first time. The Binns biography, otherwise insignificant, contained a critical assessment of the British government's sympathy for the Confederacy. Such books were harbingers of Lord Charnwood's *Abraham Lincoln,* published in London in 1916. It proved a milestone in Anglo-American relations as well as in Lincoln biography.[7]

Godfrey Rathbone Benson, Lord Charnwood, was born a commoner in 1864 and educated at Baliol College, Oxford. He grew up in Litchfield, Dr. Johnson's hometown, and later served as its mayor for a time. As a boy at school he had contracted an enthusiasm for Lincoln for which, in retrospect, he found hard to account, but he supposed it had something to do with the ideal of manhood—honesty, humility, generosity, and "the Christian graces"—Lincoln represented. At any rate, he later read John T. Morse's biography, and when the war came, although he had never undertaken a literary work before, agreed to write a life of Lincoln for the series "Makers of the Nineteenth Century" published by Constable and Company. According to Lady Charnwood, who presided over stately Stowe House in Litchfield, it was "conceived as a war service" and "written in the midst of a world's agony."[8]

The author acknowledged that his book added nothing previously unknown to the Lincoln story, and he apologized to American readers for the large amount of general historical information he had included for the benefit of his English audience. He did not disguise his admiration for Lincoln, indeed, he called the biography a "tribute" to him. Nor, on the other hand, did he gloss over his hero's faults and foibles. He believed that great men are more dignified off their pedestals than on. He accepted William H. Herndon, the former law partner turned biographer, as Lincoln's Boswell and credited his veracity. Whatever may have been the faults of Lincoln's character, Charnwood philosophized, thanks to Herndon the world would soon learn the worst of it. He was eccentric in viewing Lincoln's character as essentially English—a village type—rather than peculiarly American. For him, Lincoln illustrated the paradox that genius is simple rather than complex and that the highest truths inhere in the commonplace.

Charnwood was deeply impressed with the bravery, clarity, and power of Lincoln's utterance in the debates with Douglas and the Cooper Union Address. "How rare it is," he marveled, "for statesmen in times of crisis to grasp essential truth so simply." In 1861 Lincoln saw clearly that secession not only broke the Union but also threatened the American experiment in democratic government, which was, said the author, "the most hopeful agency for uplifting man everywhere." And this, of course, was Lincoln's strongest claim to the interest of mankind. Charnwood imbibed the skepticism current in English opinion on Lincoln's military administration, yet concluded, on balance, that it was a brilliant achievement. The president sacked General McClellan after Antietam, Charnwood observed, less because he let Lee escape, which was forgivable, than because he had no regrets, which was not. On the matter of slavery and emancipation, Lincoln's course was marked by both candor and consistency. With many of his countrymen, Charnwood ranked Lincoln with Shakespeare in mastery of the English language. Of the Second Inaugural he wrote, "Here is one of the few speeches ever delivered by a great man at the crisis of his fate on the sort of occasion which a tragedian telling his story would have devised for him." In other words, it might have been written by Shakespeare.[9]

Charnwood's biography of 479 pages was the most readable ever written on the subject. It was informative, thoughtful, and discerning; above all, it had literary grace and flair. In the *American Historical Review*, where its errors and thinness might have been expected to command attention, the book was hailed as an instant classic. Reviewers were amazed that an English lord should understand Lincoln so well. William Dean Howells, who appraised the work in *Harper's* fifty-eight years after writing his campaign biography of Lincoln, thought that this must be because Charnwood, only recently titled, came from the people rather than the aristocracy. Howells, John T. Morse, and others underscored the pathbreaking significance of the book both in carrying American history beyond the nation's borders and in the belated English recognition of the achievement of American democracy and its destiny in the world. Charnwood visited the United States in the fall of 1918—the first visit since his youth. He was genuinely astonished by the book's success in this country. His principal public appearance was in Springfield, where he delivered an address at the dedication of a statue of Lincoln on the State House grounds. After returning home the noble lord wrote some desultory notes on Lincoln but never followed up on his literary success. The book went through countless editions before it was finally superseded as the most read biography by Benjamin P. Thomas's *Abraham Lincoln* in 1952.[10]

Charnwood's work inspired John Drinkwater's play *Abraham Lincoln* in 1918, which was gratefully dedicated to him. This was the first successful dramatization of Lincoln's life for the stage. He had appeared incidentally in such plays as Thomas Dixon's *The Clansman*. Benjamin Chapin, six feet four inches tall and strikingly Lincolnesque in makeup, had been impersonating Lincoln in dramatic monologues written by himself for more than thirty years. Although welcomed as a wholesome antidote to *The Clansman*, Chapin's one-man show *Lincoln at the White House* seemed never to get under the surface of the makeup and struck at least one avid Lincolnian as "akin to sacrilege." Paramount Pictures, in 1917, released a series of ten "photodramas," *The Son of Democracy*, featuring Chapin.[11]

After its opening at the Birmingham Repertory Theatre, *Abraham Lincoln* was brought not to London, which spurned it, but to a dingy playhouse in the suburb of Hammersmith. It was a spectacular success. "All Mayfair went to see it. Hammersmith became a nightly pilgrimage for the West End," it was said. Written as a chronicle play in six episodic scenes, it was far from great dramatic literature, but it was carefully wrought and stirred the audience. Drinkwater, the thirty-six-year-old author, sought to portray Lincoln under the duress of war. He employed a classic chorus that spoke in irregular rhymed verse to enhance the tragic dimension of the drama. In the first scene, at home in Springfield in 1860, a deputation calls on Lincoln to urge him to seek the Republican nomination for the presidency. (This was one of many liberties Drinkwater took with the historical record; Lincoln aspired to the presidency and needed no encouragement to run.) Mary Lincoln greets them and scolds her husband when he enters in a disheveled state. The talk is of burgeoning sectional crisis. Recalling what he supposedly said about slavery when he first observed it in New Orleans ("If ever I get a chance to hit that thing, I'll hit it hard") Lincoln is at once placed on the side of emancipation. Scene Two focuses on the Sumter crisis and the showdown with Secretary of State William H. Seward. Drinkwater could not resist the temptation to introduce into the dialogue the elevated language of Lincoln's public speech. Thus the close of the First Inaugural is spoken in conversation with Seward, which must have sounded doubly strange in the mouth of an actor, John Rea, with an Irish brogue. Between the scenes the chorus intones:

> Two years of darkness, and this man but grows
> Greater in resolution, more constant in compassion.
> He goes
> The way of dominion in pitiful, high-hearted fashion.

In Scene Three, which occurs at the nadir of the Union cause, Lincoln bares his heartbreak to a group of female callers. In Scene Four he presents the Emancipation Proclamation to the cabinet after reading from Artemus Ward. Scene Five suddenly places the president in a farmhouse near Appomattox, where "Bob Lee" is about to surrender. While there he pardons a soldier sentenced to die for sleeping on duty. The last scene occurs in Ford's Theater. After delivering to that audience the immortal passage of the Second Inaugural Address, the president is shot; and Secretary of War Edwin M. Stanton, who is in the box with him, utters the last words: "Now he belongs to the ages."[12]

Such a hasty summary does the drama a disservice. It played well. Had Lincoln been thus exposed to an English audience before the war, one critic said, he would more likely have met with ridicule than with understanding. But in 1918 and 1919 his tragedy was theirs. "He hit us in our historical Puritan's wind. He seemed to incarnate our purpose, our usefulness, our sacrifice. . . . This nobility—was it not ours? This man of government of the people for the people by the people—was this not the 'new order' promised by our politicians, nay actually being made in Paris by the peoples' representatives? And so Lincoln became the stuff our dreams are made of. . . . Lincoln caught the castigated soul of London at the hour of its release." The play had the effect of a confessional. It was a national triumph and a national purification.[13]

Drinkwater's *Lincoln* opened at the Cort Theater on Broadway on December 15, 1919. (Simultaneously, lest there be any doubt about the play's message, the author published *Lincoln World Emancipator,* which portrayed the statesman as the ideal of the English-speaking race and appealed for Anglo-American union to extend his influence around the world.) The English triumph was repeated. Burns Mantle said that the play *Abraham Lincoln* was "easily the most inspiring dramatic success of our time." Playing Lincoln, Frank McGlynn, heretofore unknown, had the role of a lifetime and made the most of it. He was awed by the responsibility. In his recollections, he said that all the actors approached the play with "profound reverence," as though they were in a church instead of a theater. McGlynn became something of a student of Lincoln, pondering such questions as the authentic enunciation of the "of, by, and for the people" line of the Gettysburg Address. The only criticism he received on the accuracy of his portrayal, he said, was that he mistakenly "scarfed the shawl." Both Robert Todd Lincoln and William E. Barton, the biographer, made the point. Later, at the Chicago Historical Society, where the shawl was, Barton took pains to show McGlynn how it was worn.[14]

Everybody—ambassadors, senators, professors, writers and artists—saw *Abraham Lincoln,* and many were led to reflect more deeply than before upon the mystery of the man's character. Columbia University President Nicolas Murray Butler, recalling the playwright's line "lonely is the man who understands," wondered whether that was not the key to Lincoln's character. He had the gift of looking deeply into the hearts and minds of his fellows. "Abraham Lincoln was lonely because he understood. Here is the secret to the pathos of the man." Herbert Croly, editor of the *New Republic,* took as his point of departure Lincoln's chastisement, in the play, of a character named Mrs. Blow for speaking vengefully of rebels and pacifists. Paradoxically, Lincoln could fight and prevail without hatred and fanaticism. Contemporary statesmen had been unable to accomplish that. Clearly, the editor continued, it was not because Lincoln was simple or common. He was neither as these words were generally understood. His simplicity was an art, "an integrity of feeling, mind, and character which he himself elaborately achieved, and which he naturalized so completely that it wears the appearance of being simple and inevitable." Crusaders and ideologues who thought to find the truth of Lincoln in some particular cause or idea missed the point. He broke out of all the political breastworks. He was a spiritual and intellectual force. He was the hero of democracy, not from commonness, said Croly, but because he embodied "consummate personal nobility."[15]

The World War sparked renewed interest on both sides of the Atlantic in Lincoln as commander-in-chief. Whether or not he had burned the midnight oil studying Clausewitz's *On War*, it was often said that he had, and this led him to view warfare as an extreme form of political action, thereby requiring close collaboration of civil and military authorities. John G. Nicolay and John Hay, in their great biography, had stressed the dominance of political considerations in Lincoln's strategic thinking, and, although unversed in military matters, they agreed with him. "War and politics, campaign and statecraft, are Siamese twins," they observed, "inseparable and interdependent; to talk of military operations without the direction and interference of an Administration is as absurd as to plan a campaign without recruits, pay, or rations." This was not the opinion of the Comte de Paris, who had said Lincoln's interference brought "frightful disasters" on his armies. The same opinion entered British military thinking through the influence of George F. R. Henderson's *Life of Stonewall Jackson* in 1898, powerfully reenforced by British General Lord Wolseley's introduction to the second edition of that work. One of the great lessons of the American Civil War, they maintained, was that civil authorities should keep hands off commanders in the field. Lincoln was offered as a bad example. Thus McClellan would have captured Richmond in 1862 had he been left alone. As for the picture of the president becoming a brilliant strategist by poring over the pages of Clausewitz and Jomini in the White House, Henderson sighed, "If it were not pathetic, it would be ludicrous." While Lincoln presumed to command, the Confederacy was victorious; when he abdicated to Grant, the Confederacy was defeated.[16]

This verdict was upset in the rethinking brought on by the war. In 1917 Captain Arthur L. Conger, an expert in military science, delivered an address, "President Lincoln as War Statesman," before the Wisconsin Historical Society, which was deemed "revolutionary" in its estimate of Lincoln as well as in the place accorded to civil authorities in grand strategy. Conger saw Lincoln's hand everywhere, even in Grant's final campaign; it was, moreover, a brilliant hand. He predicted that Lincoln's fame as a warrior would, in time, match his fame as a statesman. The prediction seemed fulfilled in 1926 by the simultaneous publication of two books in England. In *The Military Genius of Abraham Lincoln*, Brig. Gen. Colin R. Ballard made a sweeping case. The blockade of the Confederacy in 1861 showed "true strategical foresight"; the president's decisions in the advance on Bull Run, in the Peninsular Campaign, in the West were unfailingly right. In fact, Ballard thought, he abdicated too much responsibility to Grant in 1864. Even the Emancipation Proclamation was a stroke of military genius. It illustrated the "Higher Command," which Lincoln practically invented and which Britain and the Allies were slow to emulate partly because of the unfortunate influence of Henderson and Wolseley. Sir Frederick Maurice, who had been director of military operations on the Imperial General Staff, made much the same point in his book *Statesmen and Soldiers of the Civil War*. Lincoln the civilian appeared as a model war executive, whereas Jefferson Davis the soldier was a failure. Lincoln showed how a democratic nation could conduct a great war. Holding the nation to its purpose was as great a victory as any on the battlefield.[17]

In 1926 the World Federation of Education Associations polled students of high-school age in the United States and Europe on the world's greatest heroes. Lincoln finished second behind Louis Pasteur. But Lincoln's international fame reached beyond the Western world. Sun Yat-sen, the Chinese revolutionary, was an ardent admirer of the famous American, and he made "government of the people, by the people, and for the people" the cardinal principles of his creed. His first rendering of these words in Chinese (Min yu, Min chih, Min hsiang), turned back into English, was "the people are to have, the people are to control, the people are to enjoy." After further consideration he came up with the formula of the "three people's principles: nationalism, democracy, livelihood." A five-cent stamp issued in 1941 to commemorate the fifth year of Chinese resistance to Japan coupled the portraits of Lincoln and Sun Yat-sen and incorporated the three principles. In Japan, the first book on Lincoln in the Japanese language appeared as early as 1890. In 1926, and for several years, the American-Japan Society sponsored a Lincoln essay contest for pupils at two levels fJapanese education. The judging was done by the Abraham Lincoln Association in Springfield. Lincoln's birthday seldom passed unnoticed in Japan. His story was taught in the schools. To the Japanese it was, quite simply, "the greatest story" in American history. Even the emperor, it was said, worshipped Lincoln.[18]

* * *

Just before war erupted in Europe, the United States embarked, at long last, on a great monument to Lincoln in the nation's capital. This is another story, but the decisions made by the Lincoln Memorial Commission between 1911, when it was created, and 1916, when it had approved both Henry Bacon's classic design of the building and the model of the gigantic sculpture submitted by Daniel Chester French that so brilliantly complemented it, had bearings for the international Lincoln. That the Bacon design should meet with criticism was hardly surprising in view of prevalent conceptions of Lincoln as a commoner and democrat and quintessential American. "How Lincoln Would Have Laughed" ran the title of a story in the *Independent*. The planned memorial was both "a public confession of architectural insolvency" and "a bare-faced contradiction" to the life, character, and purposes of Abraham Lincoln. "Our national capital has Washington as a Roman general. Let us not add the more atrocious anachronism of Lincoln as Apollo." Instead of this course in compulsory Greek, a truly creative architect would design a monument both fitting and indigenous. "He would take the log cabin and rail fence of Lincoln's birthplace and transmute them into an edifice so glorious and beautiful that generations afterward men would admire and imitate it." Lincoln, the nation's tenderest memory, deserved better than an academic pile of marble. "In heaven's name," exclaimed Gutzon Borglum, the sculptor, "in Abraham Lincoln's name, don't ask the American people to associate a Greek temple with the first great American." Grant LaFarge undertook to answer the critics. Greek *was* compulsory because nothing else remotely equaled it in memorializing immortals. What would you have? Perhaps "an experiment station for the uncultured commemoration of Lincoln's mere personal attributes." It was not for these—his poverty and pioneering and Rabelaisian humor—that he lived resplendent in people's minds. He was a hero beyond time and place. Did Lincoln not embody tradition in his literary style? LaFarge asked. The Gettysburg Address is Doric. Bacon's design might recall a Greek temple, but only by implication and because no other style possesses such dignity, gravity, universality, and beauty. And what if it did recall a temple? Could any place be more fitting to revere a great soul? The answer would never be known because the committee barred the door to competition. The controversy passed quickly, but it touched an emerging issue in Lincoln iconography.[19]

As work went forward on the Lincoln Memorial in Washington—slowed by the war—a great fight raged over a statue to be erected in London's Parliament Square. The source of contention was George Grey Barnard's larger-than-life bronze dedicated in Cincinnati on March 31, 1917. A

$100,000 gift to the city from Charles P. Taft, it was formally presented by
former President William Howard Taft, the donor's half-brother. The poet
of the occasion hailed the statue as "a symbol of democracy." Barnard,
who worked in New York, had heretofore been acclaimed for his visionary
and allegorical sculptures. Lincoln—a realistic Lincoln—was quite a departure for him. Writing about his conception, he said his child's mind had
been impressed with one image of Lincoln: "the mighty man who grew
from our soil and the hardships of the earth." Beginning with that, he
went on to study and restudy Leonard Volk's life mask and casts of Lincoln's
hands. From these he imagined the bearing and features of the figure. "He
must have stood as the republic should stand, strong, simple, carrying its
weight unconsciously without pride in rank and culture." Riveted to this
Whitmanesque conception—"Lincoln is our song of democracy," Barnard
said—he then searched two years for a model. Finally, in Louisville, he
found a man forty years of age, six feet four and a half inches tall, who had
been born only fifteen miles from Lincoln's birthplace and on his own
testimony had split rails all his life. The model even brought to the sittings
his father's old broadcloth suit, shirt, and tie. The finished sculpture was
both original and arresting. Standing naturally, and rising more than twelve
feet straight up, one gnarly hand clasped above the wrist of the other, and
in rumpled homely attire, Barnard's Lincoln seems about to speak. His
face is beardless, thin, and wrinkled; his eyes gaze forward with quiet
earnestness. The aim, clearly, was to create a plain and earthy Lincoln.
Alas, many people felt that Barnard had only succeeded in creating a course
and vulgar effigy.[20]

The statue might have received little attention but for the fact that ar-
rangements were set in motion to place its replica in London. With that the
matter became an international scandal comparable to the earlier one over
Rodin's monumental Balzac. Just before the war, the International Commission to Celebrate the Hundred Years Peace Between Great Britain and
the United States had been formed. The Americans had proposed presentation of a replica of the Saint-Gaudens Lincoln, the quarter-century-old
icon in Chicago. The British accepted and offered a splendid site in Parliament Square for it, but the war intervened and the commemorative effort
collapsed. It was next heard of in 1917, when Charles Taft and his wife
offered a replica of the Barnard Lincoln for London. Without funds or
prospects, the American committee of the Centenary Commission gratefully accepted the gift, as did its British counterpart.[21]

Robert Todd Lincoln learned of this plan at the time of the Cincinnati
dedication. Exercising his claim to guardianship of his father's memory, he
penned an indignant protest to President Taft, begging his good offices to
put a stop to what he considered an abomination. The statue, he said, "is a

monstrous figure . . . grotesque as a likeness of President Lincoln . . . defamatory as an effigy," and to erect it in London would be a terrible insult to man and nation. He enlisted the support of Joseph Choate, who was a former ambassador like himself, Nicholas Murray Butler, and other influential friends. Barnard attempted to reason with him. "Your father belongs to future ages, and all sculptors of this generation and those to come, must have as their birthright, as children of Democracy and Art, full liberty to express their interpretations of the life of Lincoln." He emphasized his reliance on the Volk hands and face, deducing the *real* Lincoln from these artifacts; and he suggested that the seventy-four-year-old son simply did not remember the young, rough, beardless man who was his father. Robert's response to this was to elicit the testimony of Springfield relics like Clinton L. Conkling, who had known his father in Illinois, on the accuracy of Barnard's portrait. In June, *Art World,* under the editorship of F. Wellington Ruckstuhl, a voice of the arts' establishment, took up the cudgels against Barnard. The statue that was supposed to symbolize democracy , in fact, symbolized "hobo-cracy." Some younger and more independent artists, like Borglum, approved of Barnard's work, and the conservative sculptor Frederick MacMonnies, seeing it as a question of artistic integrity, also defended him. But the attack snowballed. In the end, the whole establishment—the American Academy of Design, the American Institute of Architects, even the United States Fine Arts Commission—was aligned against poor Barnard.[22]

Why were tempers so hot on this issue? In part because it went to the heart of which Lincoln, the plain western politician or the grave and dignified statesman, should be the nation's—and the world's—icon. In sculpture, certainly, Barnard's Lincoln was a radical departure. As far as it was anticipated by anyone, it was by the youthful work of Borglum. He, too, had become a deep student of Lincoln's features and had been impressed by his compelling western presence. He, too, thought that Lincoln was divined through Volk's mask and casts. Both artists, with Truman Bartlett, the foremost authority on Lincoln's physiognomy, inferred much from the hands. In 1908 Borglum had exhibited a gigantic marble head of Lincoln—four times life-size—which, although intended as a study, was sold, presented to Congress, and afterward placed in the Rotunda of the Capitol. Three years later the artist witnessed the unveiling of his seated Lincoln before the courthouse in Newark, New Jersey. The president sits wearily on a park bench, his hat resting next to his extended right hand, his left arm thrown over his knee, his face that of someone pensive, tired, and alone. The conception was utterly original. Perhaps no sculpture of Lincoln, as F. Lauriston Bullard has said, better captured the man whom the people loved.[23]

Regardless of the larger issue of interpretation, some argued that Barnard's Lincoln failed on its own terms, as the portrait of a homespun democrat. Rather, it was "a colossal clodhopper," one said. It was easy enough to see what Barnard intended, Kenyon Cox wrote, but the result was a caricature of the democratic Lincoln. People laughed at Barnard's model, the railsplitter, with his old clothes, as if that mattered. Lincoln's face was wrinkled and ugly, like the clothes. The elongated neck and prominent Adam's apple contributed to the ungainly impression. The hands and feet were too big. Moreover, for all his efforts at authenticity, the sculptor erred in the choice of footwear. He showed Lincoln in shoes when, in fact, he wore boots and, according to his son, never even owned a pair of shoes. Nothing caused as much comment as the crossed hands below the waist. It suggested Lincoln was suffering an attack of indigestion. "The Tramp with the Colic" and "The Stomach Ache Statue" were two of the ribald names given to the work. A Massachusetts congressman, John Rogers, regaled colleagues on the last day of the session in October by reciting these scathing criticisms. Ostensibly, he spoke in support of a resolution requesting the president to halt shipment of the Barnard replica to England.[24]

This proved unnecessary. After the abuse heaped upon Barnard's Lincoln in the United States, British authorities could hardly be expected to take it even as a gift; besides, it was said, ship tonnage could not be spared to any statue during the war. The choice of a proper monument for Britain ceased to be a trifling matter, the London *Times* observed, once it became apparent that American pride and self-respect were involved. A Philadelphia daily conducted a referendum on the statue of Lincoln preferred by Americans. The Saint-Gaudens was overwhelmingly favored over Barnard's or any other. In January 1918, the American Centennial Committee polled its membership: of sixty replies, forty-one favored Saint-Gaudens, none favored Barnard, and seventeen expressed no preference. Eleven months later, the committee formally endorsed the Saint-Gaudens Lincoln, thus returning to the original proposal. Robert Lincoln offered to pay for the replica, but this was avoided by the action of the Carnegie Endowment for International Peace, which made it a gift on behalf of the American people. The Tafts offered their gift to Manchester. No statue of Lincoln could be more appropriate for a working-class city, the *Guardian* observed. It was truthful to a man rough-hewn in every limb and lineament. The sculptor seemed to be saying, "Here is a man who needs no sentimental treatment." Manchester gratefully accepted. The Saint-Gaudens replica was unveiled with fitting ceremony in the Channing Enclosure of Westminster on July 28, 1920. Prime Minister Lloyd George, accepting it for the British people, underscored the international significance of the dedication when he said of Lincoln: "In his life he was a great American. He is no longer so. He is

one of those giant figures, of whom there are very few in history, who lose
their nationality in death. They are no longer Greek or Hebrew, English or
American; they belong to mankind."[25]

*   *   *

The Lincoln Memorial in Washington was dedicated on Memorial Day,
1922. Henry Bacon's white marble temple—a work of pure Hellenic beauty
—magnificently completed a great vista and enshrined an American immortal who had become one of the world's gods. French's noble statue was
an instantaneous success. The contrast with the response to the Barnard
statue could hardly have been greater. Of course, there were some, such as
Borglum, who didn't like anything about the Lincoln Memorial, but seldom were artistic opinion and public opinion in such complete accord.
The statue quickly became the nation's foremost sculptured icon. The reverence millions upon millions of viewers have felt before it is a function
partly of the templed space, partly of its elevation as if upon an altar, and
partly of the compelling figure itself. As Lincoln was consecrated in the
hearts of the people, so was his grand memorial. Before long, a million
people a year were coming to visit it. Some came out of no more than
curiosity. Some came in search of peace and strength. Some came with
questions.

> O Father Abraham;
> O Liberator,
> What message for us now?

Some, like Langston Hughes, came with mingled feelings of gratitude and
hope.

> Let's go see old Abe
> Sitting in the marble and the moonlight
> Sitting lonely in the marble and the moonlight
> Quiet for ten thousand centuries, old Abe.
> Quiet for a million, million centuries.
> Quiet,—and yet a voice forever
> Against the timeless wall of time,
> Old Abe.

And some, like the foreign tourist of Charles Olson's verse, came to worship.

> Reverse of
> sic transit gloria, the
> Latin American whom the cab driver told me
> he picked up at Union Station had
> one word of english—link-

cone. And drove him
straight to the monument, the man
went up the stairs and fell down on his knees
where he could see the statue and stayed there
in the attitude of prayer.[26]

With such a memorial Lincoln's international fame could only increase,
and in time French's sculptured portrait would eclipse Saint-Gaudens' in
the world's imagination. Tolstoy's centennial tribute to Lincoln proved prophetic for his international fame. Seventeen years later, an English historian,
David Knowles, in his brief history of the Civil War, epitomized the international recognition of Lincoln that occurred during the World War I era.
"Alone of modern statesmen," wrote Knowles, "he realizes in some measure the dim familiar ideal of all modern peoples. . . . Alone he approaches
nearly to the ruler for whom the nations of the earth have yearned, as for a
Messiah, since the days of the French Revolution; one who should govern
not in virtue of his differences from others or of his origin in a class born to
rule, with a hundred gifts of education and influence and blood, nor
because, with none of these gifts, he should wish to shatter the whole
existing order of the world, but in virtue of his sympathy for all men, his
belief in them, and his unwillingness to treat any man as his inferior."[27]

Notes

This chapter is drawn substantially from a section of my book *Lincoln in the American Memory*.

1. *New York World*, Feb. 7, 1909.
2. Percy MacKaye, *Ode on the Centenary of Abraham Lincoln* (New York: Macmillan, 1909).
3. Vachel Lindsay, *The Poetry of Vachel Lindsay*, ed. Dennis Camp (Peoria: Spoon
River Poetry Press, 1984), 1:169.
4. On Wilson, see *New York Times* editorial, Sept. 5, 1916, and Ida Tarbell's
interview in *Collier's*, included in *The Papers of Woodrow Wilson*, ed. Arthur Link
(Princeton: Princeton University Press, 1966), 38:326; *London Spectator*, Sept. 26,
1914, Oct. 21, 1916, March 9, 1918; *New York Times*, Aug. 19–20, 1917; Choate's
speech, New York City, April 23, 1917, is included in *Modern Eloquence* (New
York: Modern Eloquence, 1928), 1:243–44.
5. J. Hugh Edwards, *David Lloyd George* (New York: Sears, 1929), 1:48–49;
New York Times, May 28, 1917, Dec. 21, 1916, Feb. 11–12, 1917, Dec. 1, 1922.
6. Ibid., Oct. 7, 19, 22, 1923; Lloyd George speech in *Journal of Illinois State
Historical Society* 17 (1924): 241–45.
7. Henry Cabot Lodge, *The Democracy of Abraham Lincoln* (Malden: Dunbar-
Kerr, 1913), 3.
8. See Charnwood's address in Springfield in *Journal of Illinois State Historical*

Society 12 (1920): 498–502; "Some Further Notes on Abraham Lincoln," reprinted from *Anglo-French Review* in *Living Age* 305–7 (1920): 403–13, 100–108, 532–42; Lady Charnwood, *An Autograph Collection and the Making of It* (New York: Holt, 1930), 314.

9. Charnwood to William Roscoe Thayer, Feb. 28, 1918, Houghton Mifflin Collection, Houghton Library, Harvard University; the quotations are from *Abraham Lincoln* (New York, 1916), 155, 181; 438.

10. Carl Russell Fish, in *American Historical Review* 22 (1918): 413–15; John T. Morse, in *Massachusetts Historical Society Proceedings* 51 (1918): 90–105; Howells, in "Easy Chair," *Harper's* 138 (1918): 134–36.

11. On Chapin, see *New York Times*, April 1, 1906; "Lincoln in the Hearts of the People," *The Independent*, Feb. 11, 1909; Daniel Fish, "Lincoln Collections and Lincoln Biography," in *Papers of the Bibliographical Society of America* 3 (1908): 51; Jay Monaghan, ed., *Lincoln Bibliography* (Springfield: Illinois State Historical Library, 1945), 1:336, 2:69–70.

12. John Drinkwater, *Abraham Lincoln: A Play* (London, 1918) was followed by an American edition (Boston, 1919), with an introduction by Arnold Bennett; "An English View of the Success of Abraham Lincoln," reprinted from *English Review* in *Living Age* 304 (1920): 791.

13. "An English View of Abraham Lincoln."

14. Burns Mantle, *The Best Plays of 1919–1920* (New York: Small, Maynard, 1937), v; Frank McGlynn, *Sidelights on Lincoln* (Los Angeles: Wetzel, 1947), especially chs. 8 and 9.

15. Nicholas Murray Butler, *Looking Forward* (New York: Scribner's 1932), 354; Herbert Croly, "The Paradox of Lincoln," *New Republic* 21 (1920): 350–53.

16. For a general discussion, see John M. Palmer, "President Lincoln's War Problem," *Journal of Illinois State Historical Society* 21 (1928): 200–217; John G. Nicolay and John Hay, *Abraham Lincoln: A History* (New York: Century, 1890), 4:59; Comte de Paris, *History of the Civil War* (Philadelphia: Porte & Coates, 1: 1875), 1:573–74, G. F. R. Henderson, *Stonewall Jackson and the American Civil Wars* (London: Longmans, Green, 1900), 1:xii–xv, II, 334.

17. *Wisconsin Historical Society Proceedings, 1917,* 106–40; M. M. Quaife's comment in *Mississippi Valley Historical Review* 14 (1927): 412. The books by Ballard and Maurice were both published in London in 1926; chapters from the latter's work appeared in *Atlantic Monthly,* 138 (1926): 224–36, and *Forum* 75 (1926): 161–69.

18. *New York Times*, Nov. 16, 1926; Lyon Sharman, *Sun Yat-sen: His Life and Its Meaning* (New York: John Day, 1934), 92; Randle Bond Truett, *Lincoln in Philately* (Washington: 1959), 10; *Lincoln Lore*, no. 1149 (1951).

19. See, in general, Charles Moore, "The Memorial to Abraham Lincoln," *Art and Archaeology,* 13 (1922): 247–52; *The Independent* 72 (1912): 320–22, 74 (1913): 280–92, 993–94.

20. *Barnard's Lincoln* (Cincinnati: Stewart and Kidd, 1917), 21–30; Milton Bronner, "A Sculptor of Democracy," *Independent* 89 (1917): 355.

21. The controversy may be followed in the pages of the *New York Times* from Aug. 26, 1917, the *Times of London* from Aug. 27, 1917, and the magazine *Art World* 2 (1917).

22. The Robert Todd Lincoln Papers, Illinois State Historical Library, beginning with his letter to William Howard Taft, March 22, 1917, contain much information and include Barnard to Lincoln, April 14, 1917, and Conkling to Lincoln, April 27, 1917. For MacMonnies, see *North American Review* 206 (1917): 837–40.

23. Gutzon Borglum, "The Beauty of Lincoln," *Everybody's Magazine* 22 (1910): 217–20; F. Lauriston Bullard, *Lincoln in Marble and Bronze* (New Brunswick: Rutgers University Press, 1952), 209–16; Truman Bartlett, "The Portraits of Lincoln," in Carl Schurz, *Life of Lincoln* (Boston: Houghton, Mifflin, 1907), 5–39.

24. Kenyon Cox, "Barnard's Lincoln as a Noted Painter Sees It," *New York Times Magazine*, Oct. 28, 1917; see editorials in *New York Times*, Aug. 26, Oct. 3, 21, Nov. 15, 1917, and Jan. 2, 1918; *Congressional Record*, 26 Cong., 2d sess., 7919.

25. *London Times*, Sept. 24, 1917, July 29, 1920; *Philadelphia Evening Telegraph* cited in Bullard, *Lincoln*, 230, 84–86; *New York Times*, Jan. 1, Dec. 21, 1918, and, quoting *Manchester Guardian*, Jan. 3, 1919; American Association for International Conciliation, *Presentation of the Saint-Gaudens Statue of Lincoln* (New York, 1920).

26. See, in general, *The Lincoln Memorial* (Washington, 1927); Margaret Cresson French, *Journey into Fame: The Life of Daniel Chester French* (Cambridge: Harvard University Press, 1947), ch. 17; Ralph Adams Cram, "The Lincoln Memorial," *Architectural Record* 53 (1923): 475–508. The poets quoted are R. L. Duffus, "Lincoln Memorial," *New York Times Magazine*, Feb. 9, 1941; Langston Hughes, "Lincoln Monument," *Opportunity*, 4 (1927): 85; and Charles Olson, in *Lincoln and the Poets: An Anthology*, ed. William W. Betts, Jr., (Pittsburgh: Pittsburgh University Press, 1965), 139.

27. David Knowles, *The American Civil War: A Brief History* (London: Clarendon Press, 1926), 204.

Contributors

JEAN H. BAKER is professor of history at Goucher College in Baltimore. Among her books are *Affairs of Party: The Political Culture of Northern Democrats in the Mid-Nineteenth Century* and *Mary Todd Lincoln: A Biography.*

RICHARD N. CURRENT is emeritus professor of history at the University of North Carolina at Greensboro. He has written many books on Lincoln and the Civil War era, including *The Lincoln Nobody Knows; Lincoln's Loyalists: Union Soldiers from the Confederacy;* and (with James G. Randall) *Lincoln the President: Last Full Measure.*

WILLIAM E. GIENAPP is professor of history at Harvard University and author of *The Origins of the Republican Party, 1852–1856.* He is completing a biography of Lincoln.

HAROLD HOLZER is chief communications officer for the Metropolitan Museum of Art in New York City. He has written and edited several books on Lincoln and on the Civil War, including a new edition of *The Lincoln-Douglas Debates* and, with Mark E. Neely, Jr., *Mine Eyes Have Seen the Glory: The Civil War in Art.*

JAMES M. MCPHERSON is professor of history at Princeton University and author of several books on the Civil War era, including *Abraham Lincoln and the Second American Revolution* and *Battle Cry of Freedom*, which won a Pulitzer Prize in History.

MARK E. NEELY, JR., is professor of history at Saint Louis University and the author of several books, including *The Last Best Hope of Earth: Abraham Lincoln and the Promise of America* and *The Fate of Liberty: Abraham Lincoln and Civil Liberties*, which won a Pulitzer Prize in History.

PHILLIP S. PALUDAN is professor of history at the University of Kansas and author of several books, including "A People's Contest": The Union and Civil War and The Presidency of Abraham Lincoln, which won the Lincoln Prize in 1995.

MERRILL D. PETERSON is emeritus professor of history at the University of Virginia. After writing several distinguished books about Thomas Jefferson, he turned his attention to the image of Lincoln in American culture with his book Lincoln in American Memory.

KENNETH M. STAMPP is emeritus professor of history at the University of California at Berkeley. The author of numerous books on slavery and the Civil War era, including America in 1857: A Nation on the Brink, he won the Lincoln Prize in 1993 for his classic work on slavery, The Peculiar Institution.

FRANK J. WILLIAMS is a lawyer in Providence, Rhode Island, and past president of the Abraham Lincoln Association. He has written numerous articles on Lincoln, and he has compiled an annual summary of symposia, books, papers, articles, and other activities related to Lincoln for the Journal of the Abraham Lincoln Association.